Grit, The Secret to Advancement

STORIES OF SUCCESSFUL WOMEN LAWYERS

Prepared and Written for the Commission by Milana L. Hogan, Ed.D.

AMERICAN BAR ASSOCIATION
Defending Liberty
Pursuing Justice

Commission on Women
in the Profession
American Bar Association

The materials contained herein represent the opinions of the authors and/or the editors, and should not be construed to be the views or opinions of the law firms or companies with whom such persons are in partnership with, associated with, or employed by, nor of the American Bar Association or the Commission on Women in the Profession unless adopted pursuant to the bylaws of the Association.

Nothing contained in this book is to be considered as the rendering of legal advice for specific cases, and readers are responsible for obtaining such advice from their own legal counsel. This book is intended for educational and informational purposes only.

Library of Congress Cataloging-in-Publication Data

Names: Hogan, Milana L., author.
Title: Grit, the secret to advancement : stories of successful women lawyers / Milana L. Hogan.
Description: Chicago : American Bar Association, 2017. | Includes index.
Identifiers: LCCN 2017027231 (print) | LCCN 2017027282 (ebook) | ISBN 9781634259040 (diskette) | ISBN 9781634259033 (pbk.)
Subjects: LCSH: Women lawyers—United States.
Classification: LCC KF299.W6 (ebook) | LCC KF299.W6 H64 2017 (print) | DDC 340.092/520973—dc23
LC record available at https://lccn.loc.gov/2017027231

Printed in the United States of America.

21 20 19 18 17 5 4 3 2 1

ISBN: 978-1-63425-903-3
e-ISBN: 978-1-63425-904-0

Discounts are available for books ordered in bulk. Special consideration is given to state bars, CLE programs, and other bar-related organizations. Inquire at Book Publishing, ABA Publishing, American Bar Association, 321 N. Clark Street, Chicago, Illinois 60654-7598.

www.shopABA.org

THE COMMISSION ON WOMEN IN THE PROFESSION
2016–2017

Chair
Michele Coleman Mayes

Members
Richard N. Bien
Michelle Gallardo
Samantha C. Grant
Juanita C. Hernández
Elaine Johnson James
Nancy Laben
Wendi S. Lazar
Sandra R. McCandless
Maureen Mulligan
Wendy C. Shiba
Melvin Williams, Jr.

Special Advisors
Roula Allouch
Laurel G. Bellows

Board of Governors Liaison
Ruthe Catolico Ashley

Staff
Melissa Wood, Director
Lynnea Karlic
Barbara Leff
Bre'Anna Moore-Gordon

American Bar Association Commission on Women in the Profession
321 N. Clark Street, Chicago, Illinois 60654
Phone: 312-988-5715
Email: abacwp1@americanbar.org
Website: www.americanbar.org/women

Any proceeds from this publication will go toward the projects of the ABA Commission on Women in the Profession.

Contents

From the Chair of the ABA Commission on Women in the Profession

How many times have you asked yourself the question, what separates successful individuals from those who are not? Research on the intangible concept now known as "grit" has shed light on this vexing question. The Grit Project has been one of the ABA Commission on Women in the Profession's key initiatives since 2013. Based on a study two years earlier that revealed that grit and a growth mindset were two traits shared by highly successful women lawyers, the Grit Project has provided the legal profession with tools to teach and understand these traits in order to increase the advancement of women lawyers and to help them achieve success, however that is defined for each individual.

It was obvious from the start that women beyond those in large law firms were keenly interested in learning more about grit and growth mindset. Thus, the Commission decided to expand the initial research to all legal work environments. You will read the findings from this latest research in the chapters that follow.

But we wanted to dig deeper and go beyond these findings to hear from women for whom grit and growth mindset were important to their careers and their success. The result is the collection of 47 letters contained in this volume.

As you see in these letters, everyone's path is unique—professionally and personally. Some of these women were born with grit or a growth mindset, and being gritty came naturally. Others developed their grit later in life and/or less easily. Not everyone necessarily could put a name to these traits, but they can now, thanks to this research. Regardless of their work environments, however, they all recognized that grit played a critical role in how they were able to handle difficult situations and ultimately be productive, rather than have their frustrations lead to inertia.

Grit gives you permission to fight, to stand up for yourself, and provides you with an approach for handling those tough situations. There is a wide range in *how* you do that, but in the end, grit teaches you that you can say and believe that no one has more power over you than you do. No matter where you are on the grit continuum, it is never too late to learn or to increase your grittiness. Another very important message to take away from this research is that grit can be taught; you can learn and practice these skills. This is truly an invigorating thought. The Commission will continue to enhance the Grit Project to assist you in your effort. Be sure to visit our grit resources online at www.ambar.org/grit.

We owe a huge debt of gratitude to Dr. Milana Hogan for working with the Commission to establish and launch the Grit Project, developing and spearheading our expanded research into work environments in addition to BigLaw, and then writing this manuscript. Her dedication, commitment, and enthusiasm helped turn the idea for this publication into a reality. She had to call on her own grit to complete this research and book.

Special thanks also go to Natasha Galvez, Juanita Hernández, Elaine Johnson James, and Deborah Rhode, who reviewed the manuscript and provided valuable feedback. In addition, we appreciate and acknowledge the staff of the Commission and particularly our executive director, Melissa Wood, and the Commission's communications and publications manager, Barbara Leff, who shepherded the book through production.

Last, and most important, we thank the authors of the letters that you will read in this book. You are the heart of this work. Thank you for taking the time to tell your stories and share your life experiences. Your honesty and words of wisdom will undoubtedly inspire other women lawyers as they blaze their own trails to success.

Michele Coleman Mayes, Chair, 2014–2017
ABA Commission on Women in the Profession

Introduction

WHY GRIT AND GROWTH MINDSET

In August 2013, the American Bar Association Commission on Women in the Profession ("Commission") launched the Grit Project. The Grit Project was created under the leadership of then-Commission Chair Roberta "Bobbi" Liebenberg to educate women lawyers about the science behind grit and growth mindset—two important traits that many successful women lawyers have in common and that have shaped their success. Grit is defined as "perseverance and passion for long-term goals,"[1] whereas a growth mindset is defined as the belief that talent can be developed through dedication and hard work and that perseverance, persistence, and effort eventually pay off.[2] Grit and growth mindset are known as noncognitive traits—that is, traits that are not based purely on measures of intelligence. Both of these traits have been shown to predict achievement above and beyond traditional measures or predictors of success—such as grade point average (GPA) or class rank—that are heavily relied upon by employers, including legal employers.

The Grit Project provides individual women, bar associations, law firms, law schools, corporate legal departments, government agencies, and other organizations with tools to assess, teach, learn, and understand these traits, ultimately improving the retention and promotion of women lawyers in the profession and enabling women to succeed on their terms. Liebenberg describes in the letter she contributed to this book (included in its entirety in chapter 3):

> [M]y vision was to create a comprehensive training program that would teach women lawyers to master these traits, empowering them to navigate everyday challenges

and barriers. The Commission's grit toolkit allows women lawyers to take charge of their careers and dispel the inner voices of doubt everyone has heard, making you think you won't or can't succeed.

Information about the Grit Project and the Grit Project Toolkit and other resources are available online at www.ambar.org/grit and in appendix B of this book.

When it launched, the Grit Project relied on earlier, ground-breaking work. Dr. Angela Duckworth developed the grit construct in 2007 and has continued to study its impact in a number of academic and professional settings. Dr. Carol Dweck has spent her career studying achievement and, along the way, developed, and then extensively explored, the concept of growth mindset. The Grit Project also relied on the work of Dr. Milana Hogan, who researched the specific ways in which grit and a growth mindset impact the success of women in BigLaw (defined for research purposes as the law firms that appear on *The American Lawyer's* annual "Am Law 200" list). In many of these 200 BigLaw firms, one could walk into a room with the senior-most decision makers and find only one woman seated at the table—in some firms, there would be no women at the table at all. This state of affairs is discouraging for the many employers who recognize the significant and convincingly demonstrated benefits—financial and otherwise—associated with having women lawyers in leadership positions.[3]

The representation of women in BigLaw leadership has led members of the legal profession and academics to study the progression of women's careers to determine why they seem to evolve so differently than the careers of their male counterparts. Some of these studies focus on the obstacles or barriers that prevent women from reaching the most senior positions. Other studies attempt to identify the root causes of this year-over-year failure to reduce the gender gap at the leadership level. Finally, there is a body of literature that looks at women who have achieved a high level of success and seeks to ascertain common characteristics that these successful women share.

This book contributes to the latter collection of research and, in particular, expands on Dr. Hogan's 2013 study. Since the focus of her 2013 research was limited to the impact of grit and growth mindset on women in BigLaw, a group that represents only a small subset of practicing women lawyers, it seemed critically important to explore the ways in which these traits impact the many women working as solo practitioners, in small and mid-size firms, in corporations of all sizes, and in government and nonprofit positions. In other words, the Commission wanted to understand more broadly, and also very specifically, whether and how grit and a growth mindset are, or are not, characteristics common to successful women lawyers everywhere. In 2015, under the leadership of then-Commission Chair Michele Coleman Mayes, the Commission embarked on a second round of research to discover the answers to some of these important questions.

> The Grit Project was an immediate success. We realized that the concepts of grit and a growth mindset struck a nerve among women lawyers. Bar associations, law firms, and law schools throughout the country presented programs based upon the materials provided in the Grit Project Toolkit. It was clear that women in environments beyond BigLaw were interested in these principles. We wanted to know more—we needed to know more.

It should be noted that BigLaw is not the only area where gender disparity in leadership is at play. Indeed, this is a much larger and deeper issue: for roughly 30 years, 50 percent of law school graduates have been women (and in 2017 women represented more than half of the incoming law school class), yet only 18 percent of law firm equity partners and 24 percent of general counsel are women.[4] Although women and men have entered law school in roughly equal numbers, there has been very little movement at the top levels of leadership. It is clear, then, that the significant number of women entering the profession alone has not translated into parity at the top of the organizational chart. Instead, as lawyers ascend the leadership ranks, there is a steady decline in the number of women occupying positions of authority. By the time women arrive at the most senior leadership levels—those lawyers who hold an ownership interest in their firms or occupy the most prestigious, powerful, and best-paid positions in-house or in government—they represent a mere 18 to 24 percent of the overall population.[5]

As we will share in detail in the coming pages, our latest round of research suggests that grit and a growth mindset are not only traits that many highly successful women lawyers practicing in many different capacities possess, but also that they are valuable tools for women to draw upon when building successful careers in the law. Grit and growth mindset have the potential to help women navigate their way through the (sometimes overwhelming) obstacles—both personal and professional—that may present themselves along the way. Furthermore, this research provides legal employers, bar associations, law schools, and other entities with additional tools to support women in the workplace and to begin to chip away at the gender gap at the leadership level. In other words, our research suggests that there is a path to reach a different, more positive outcome.

HOW THE BOOK IS ORGANIZED

Chapter 1 dives into the Commission's expanded research involving solo practitioners, law firms of all sizes, in-house legal departments, government, and nonprofits. It defines key terms: grit, perseverance, passion, deliberate practice, the grit scale, mindset, and the mindset quiz. The chapter next describes the research process—the survey used to collect data (the quantitative research), as well as interviews and other feedback (the qualitative research)—and concludes with a summary of the key findings of this research effort.

The four chapters that follow focus on specific work environments: solo practitioners (chapter 2), law firm lawyers (chapter 3), in-house lawyers (chapter 4), and government and nonprofit lawyers (chapter 5). Each of these chapters begins with a detailed summary of the demographics of the women in that group, including the number of women surveyed, practice areas, length of practice, academic performance, family history, ambition levels, and grit and mindset scores. Each chapter also includes a description of the relevant measures of success for those lawyers. The key findings for that group are discussed next, and, last, the chapter contains letters from women lawyers representing that work environment.

In presenting the findings, we draw upon the results of the survey in addition to interviews and quotes from the letters themselves. For the women who have practiced in more than one group (for example, a participant may have started in a BigLaw firm, moved in-house, and then ultimately started her own practice), we have included their letters in the section where they are now, where they spent the greatest amount of time, or where they devoted the greatest amount of real estate in their respective letters.

Following a brief conclusion, appendix A discusses what employers can do to nurture and evaluate grit and to reward and encourage grit in their employees. Appendix B lists grit resources available through the Commission's Grit Project, and for those interested in learning more about the science of grit and growth mindset, appendix C offers a summary of the research on these important traits. This research is not limited to lawyers but instead examines research outside the legal sphere and includes a summary of some of the factors that have been known to impact female professionals across industries.

SUCCESSFUL WOMEN LAWYERS TELL THEIR STORIES

This book goes beyond the quantitative research to offer letters from 47 successful women lawyers. The reader will find real-life examples of the critical role that grit and a growth mindset have played in these women's advancement in the legal profession and in achieving success on their own terms. These letters will inspire, reaffirm, and provide much food for thought.

Notes:

1. Duckworth, A., Peterson, C., Matthews, M., and Kelly, D. 2007. "Grit: Perseverance and passion for long-term goals." *Journal of Personality and Social Psychology* 92(6): 1087–1101.
2. Dweck, C. 2006. *Mindset: The new psychology of success.* New York: Random House.
3. Cohen, R., and Kornfeld, L. 2006. "Women leaders and the bottom line." *Bloomberg Corporate Law Journal* 1: 55–61.
4. ABA Commission on Women in the Profession. A Current Glance at Women in the Law . . . https://www.americanbar.org/content/dam/aba/marketing/women/current_glance_statistics_january2017.pdf. Accessed January 2017.
5. *Id.*

1

Important Definitions, Methodology, and Key Findings

DEFINITIONS AND KEY CONCEPTS

It is common knowledge outside of academic journals, including in many examples of children's literature, that noncognitive traits—such as motivation, tenacity, and perseverance—are essential traits for success in life.[1] For example, the classic children's story *The Little Engine That Could*, first published in the *New-York Tribune* on April 8, 1906, teaches the value of persistence and a positive outlook. For those who are not familiar with this story, it goes like this: a stranded train carrying presents for children is unable to find an engine willing to take it over a steep mountain to its destination. For various reasons, several larger trains refuse to assist and only a little blue train is willing to give it a try. Although the odds are stacked against the tiny train, by repeating the mantra "I think I can, I think I can," the little engine is ultimately able to climb the mountain and deliver the presents to the children. The story is often used to teach children the value of optimism and hard work (it was a favorite in the household of this researcher), because the message is clear: the protagonist is able to succeed only by demonstrating grit and a strong growth mindset.

Given the prevalence of these kinds of stories in the American cultural narrative, it is surprising that so much of the academic literature on success focuses on cognitive abilities—such as memory, attention, and other measures of intelligence—and tends to overlook the importance of noncognitive skills in general.[2] Indeed, we often tend to overemphasize the importance of intelligence and romanticize intellectual genius in a way that can be inadvertently discouraging for those to whom things don't come easily the first time around or to those who choose to pursue careers that are universally demanding, such as a career in law. Certainly, the practice of law is a challenging one. As one of the women who participated in the research for this book shared with us, her motto, which she posts on her website for all to see, is: "If it's easy, then you don't need me." Not only is the practice of law challenging, and this may in and of itself be a significant understatement, but it is also a profession in which a baseline intelligence is a necessary, but nevertheless insufficient, condition for success. Indeed, a good lawyer not only needs to be smart and intellectually curious but also must possess a strong will to succeed and, more importantly, the belief in her ability to do so. She must possess the grit that it takes to persevere and to continue to pursue her goals, even, and especially, when the going gets tough. So, if grit and a growth mindset are so important, what are these traits and how do we define them?

Grit

The dictionary defines grit as "firmness of mind or spirit: unyielding courage in the face of hardship or danger."[3] This definition provides us with a basic understanding of grit and begins to suggest how we might recognize gritty behavior. Of particular importance is the notion that a gritty individual may be less likely than a nongritty individual to suffer setbacks, because she possesses a strong will (firmness of mind) and an unrelenting bravery (courage). Duckworth and Peterson build upon this basic understanding of grit by describing it as a lasting and unwavering dedication to a specific objective, and they refine the concept further by suggesting that grit also includes a certain degree of passion, zeal, or fervor. Their official definition of grit is "perseverance and passion for long-term goals."[4] In their groundbreaking work on grit, Duckworth and Peterson suggest that grit entails "working strenuously toward challenges, maintaining effort and interest over years despite failure, adversity, and plateaus in progress."[5] For the gritty individual, success is a marathon and requires great endurance and stamina. In fact, it is this emphasis on long-term stamina, rather than short bursts of effort, that distinguishes grit from achievement and self-discipline.[6] For a further discussion of the differences between grit, achievement, and self-discipline, see appendix C. Whereas some individuals may change trajectories or abandon their goals at the first sign of boredom or disappointment, the gritty individual will persevere and stay the course.

For purposes of this study, we've relied primarily on Duckworth and Peterson's definition of grit but also have considered additional research on the key elements of grit—namely perseverance, passion, and deliberate practice—that appear throughout the literature and help to shed light on some of the nuances of the trait. A more comprehensive review of the literature on grit, growth mindset, and the way in which these traits have been shown to impact success can be found in appendix C.

Perseverance

The single most common element of grit—and the most commonly used synonym—is perseverance. While much of the literature on perseverance has focused on the persistence of beliefs, thoughts, and attitudes, there has been a recent focus on behavioral persistence, such as specific actions or performance at work. The subset of the literature that focuses primarily on how perseverance plays out in the workplace is most relevant to the present analysis, as it seeks to explore how perseverance may be used as a predictor of workplace success. Eisenberger defines perseverance as one's tendency to persist and endure in the face of adversity. He suggests that perseverance influences individuals' courses of action, the level of effort that they exhibit, and the endurance and resilience exhibited toward setbacks and failures that they may encounter along the way.[7] Similarly, Stolz defines perseverance as the perceived ability to overcome adverse circumstances and suggests that success is determined by the extent to which individuals persevere despite potentially insurmountable obstacles or adversities.[8] To persevere, an individual cannot be easily subdued or overcome and must relentlessly pursue her desired objectives.

Passion

Passion is another key element of grit. Indeed, the definition of grit includes not only a tenacious pursuit of goals but also a passionate pursuit. When giving talks about the importance of grit, one of the questions often raised is, "How can anyone in her right mind possibly suggest that what women need to do in order to succeed is simply to work harder?" This is, of course, a valid concern, but it is not, in fact, what we are suggesting. Instead, we are suggesting that women need to be able to tap into a "well" of passion for their practice in order to be able to sustain the kind of effort that it takes to have a long-term career as a successful practicing lawyer. As one of the women who participated in this research effort explained, "Grit is not about keeping my head down and just working super long hours. Grit is not about paper-pushing to keep all partners and clients happy. Instead, grit is being a team player, but also being tenacious about my own priorities and living consistent with my values." The women we know who do manage to succeed, and who defy the statistical odds, have all been—almost to a person—incredibly passionate about their work and very aware of the importance that passion has played in helping them stay in the game. As leadership expert Simon Sinek explains, "Working hard for something we don't care about is called stress; working hard for something we love is called passion."[9] Of course, it must be said that almost no one is capable of sustaining high levels of passion for their work every second of every day. Passion ebbs and flows sometimes, and we all have moments when we feel a sense of dread rather than great passion toward the task at hand. The key is to know how to tap into the passion well when you need to and to remember that demonstrations of grit happen over years and across decades rather than in single moments in time.

While passion is not the only element of grit, it has been referred to as "the lynchpin of grit."[10] As modern organizations develop more nuanced understandings of what predicts success within their walls, they are increasingly looking for employees who will bring both commitment (perseverance) and passion to the job. Unlike in decades past when employees were encouraged to leave their passions and emotions at home—and many of the women in these pages describe situations in which they were expected to do this— there has been increasing attention paid to employees' emotions and emotional intelligence.[11] Emotional intelligence is defined as "the ability to monitor one's own and others' feelings and emotions, to discriminate among them, and to use this information to guide one's thinking and actions."[12] Indeed, an employee's emotional intelligence (sometimes expressed as passion and enthusiasm) can have a greater impact on individual and group performance than traditional measures like IQ. There are countless examples of high-IQ individuals who failed to achieve success in life because they lacked self-discipline and individuals with low IQs who achieved great success by virtue of sheer persistence.[13] While the study of emotional intelligence is still a relatively nascent field, the research clearly suggests that there is an important connection between emotional intelligence and a variety of life outcomes, including those at work.[14] While the theory of emotional intelligence is outside the scope of what we explored in this study, it warrants mention because it underscores the fact that certain elements of grit, such as passion in particular, and how one manifests that at work, have much to offer to our understanding of professional success.

Truly gritty individuals demonstrate not only a rare single-mindedness in pursuit of their goals but also a healthy passion for the goals they pursue. Oftentimes, passion fuels perseverance. However, it is important to note that while passion and perseverance are often intimately connected, it is not always the case that passion precedes grit. In some cases, passion for a particular subject can develop over time, as a result of persistent dedication to the subject matter. Often the most satisfying and rewarding aspects of a complex discipline—such as chess, engineering, or the practice of law—become apparent only after deep immersion.[15] In other cases, passion for challenges or a desire to test one's limits may fuel an individual's drive to doggedly pursue a long-term objective, in spite of the difficulty of the task. Endurance athletes provide a good example of this as some of them spend months or even years training for a marathon or a triathlon, not so much because they love the act of running, swimming, and biking long distances but rather because they want the personal satisfaction and sense of accomplishment that accompany such undertakings.[16] An admired colleague of the author regularly participates in the New York City Marathon not because she particularly enjoys running (or the inevitable blisters and 5 a.m. wake-up calls) but rather because she craves the feeling she gets when she successfully completes her training and crosses the finish line.

Importantly, as Duckworth explained in her 2016 book *Grit: The Power of Passion and Perseverance*, when she considers the perseverance portion of a grit score vis-à-vis the passion portion of the score, it is most often the case that gritty individuals are more persistent than they are passionate. This finding is an important one because it suggests that there may be many women currently practicing law who are very persistent and yet do not score as highly on the grit scale as one might suspect. Furthermore, it suggests that for women who want to increase their grit scores and to develop and nurture grit, focusing on the passion elements of the trait might be an effective way to do so. This perhaps presents the single greatest opportunity for women in the law, many of whom have learned, and then relearned the importance of persistence and yet have still not managed to achieve all of their personal or professional goals.[17]

Deliberate Practice

Hard work alone does not always lead to success. Indeed, while hard work is likely a key ingredient for success, there must be other ingredients at play beyond just the sum of time that one devotes to the pursuit of a singular objective. Ericsson and Charness suggest that it is not only how hard you work but also the way in which you work that ultimately impacts your ability to excel. Specifically, they suggest that deliberate practice—defined as "those training activities that were most closely associated with consistent improvements in performance"—is what sets expert performers apart from their less-proficient peers.[18] Importantly, the amount of time an individual must spend engaging in deliberate practice in order to achieve professional expertise requires, in most cases, roughly ten years. As Ericsson points out, "this ten-year rule of required engagement in domain-related activities is the most compelling evidence for the necessity of experience to attain high levels of performance."[19] Indeed, the amount of time a protégé engaged in deliberate practice was a more reliable predictor of world-class performance than innate talent or inborn ability. Ericsson goes on to explain that deliberate efforts to increase one's performance beyond its current level involve problem solving and finding better methods of performing the task at hand. Engaging in practice activities with the explicit goal of improving some aspect of the performance is an essential part of deliberate practice.[20] Along these same lines, Ericsson notes that "more plausible loci of individual differences are factors that predispose individuals towards engaging in deliberate practice and enable them to sustain high levels of practice for many years."[21]

Duckworth connects deliberate practice to grit by suggesting that grittier individuals are more likely to engage in deliberate practice. Indeed, it seems to be the case that having high levels of grit is one of the things that helps to enable individuals to actively engage in deliberate practice.[22] Whereas individuals who are only moderately gritty may choose to engage in easier, more immediately rewarding forms of practice—such as those that warrant regular, positive reinforcement—a gritty individual tends to persevere in spite of the fact that deliberate practice is rated as more effortful and less pleasing than other, less-effective kinds of preparation. When gritty individuals engage in deliberate practice, they reap the myriad benefits associated with it and tend to be more successful as a result. Sometimes women lawyers can fall into the trap of volunteering to perform tasks that they are naturally good at and are likely to be recognized for instead of raising their hand for the tasks that are more strategic, harder, and therefore less likely to result in a positive outcome. While the immediate thrill of praise can be very compelling, ultimately it does less to further a woman's professional development and to improve her lawyering skills. If something like case or project management comes easily, she may be best served professionally by stepping outside of her comfort zone and offering to take a stab at the first draft of the summary judgment motion—even, and especially, when the risk for failure is high.

The Grit Scale

In building the case for grit as a legitimate, scientific construct worthy of further exploration and study, Duckworth and colleagues developed a self-report questionnaire called the Grit Scale, designed to be a stand-alone measure of grit. When Duckworth first introduced the construct, she argued that grit differs from existing constructs in its emphasis on both sustained effort and focused interest over time.[23] Once they had developed and validated the Grit Scale, Duckworth and her colleagues used it in a series of studies designed to test the hypothesis that grit may be as essential to high achievement as IQ, and furthermore that it might be more important than similar traits, like self-control and conscientiousness—both discussed in greater detail in appendix C—in setting exceptional individuals apart from their less exceptional counterparts.[24] The results of these studies suggest that the presence of grit does indeed predict a variety of success measurements over and beyond IQ and other cognitive traits and measures of pure intelligence. Duckworth and Peterson argue that "collectively, these findings suggest that the achievement of difficult goals entails not only talent but also the sustained and focused application of talent over time."[25] We will discuss how we incorporated the Grit Scale into our research later in this chapter.

Mindset

Like grit, having a growth mindset has been shown to be predictive of success, often above and beyond other seemingly critical measures, such as IQ and GPA. The dictionary defines mindset as "a particular way of thinking: a person's attitude or set of opinions about something."[26] The social science concept of mindset comes from the work of renowned psychologist Carol Dweck. Dweck suggests that individuals can be categorized according to their implicit beliefs regarding the origin of ability. Individuals who believe that ability is innate are said to have what Dweck refers to as a "fixed" mindset or an entity theory of intelligence.[27] Dweck argues that these individuals are "stubbornly wedded to the idea that accomplishment, especially outstanding accomplishment, is about endowment. [They] ignore the fact that Mozart, Darwin, Michael Jordan, and Tiger Woods all practiced feverishly and single-mindedly for years and instead believe that they were born with one-in-a-million ability."[28] Collectively, individuals with a fixed mindset have a tendency to overlook the years of commitment and training that led these individuals to such momentous and significant achievements.

Conversely, individuals who believe that ability is developed and enhanced through hard work and learning are said to have a "growth" mindset or an incremental theory of intelligence.[29] Individuals may not necessarily fall neatly into one of these categories, and many people have different mindsets in different domains of their lives. For example, an individual may have a fixed mindset when it comes to academics but a growth mindset when it comes to professional achievements. Such an individual may believe that her ability to succeed in math is dependent on her genetic disposition, whereas her ability to successfully climb the corporate ladder is a direct result of how much effort she is willing to put into it.

The Mindset Quiz

Dweck argues that while individuals may not be consciously aware of their own mindset orientations, they can be easily discerned based on their behaviors. In order to determine an individual's dominant mindset, Dweck has developed a 16-question mindset quiz in which participants use a traditional Likert scale, a format that asks them to agree or disagree with a series of predetermined fixed and growth mindset statements. An individual's dominant theory of intelligence can be determined based on the extent and number of fixed or growth mindset statements that she agrees with. We will discuss our use of the mindset quiz in the coming pages.[30]

METHODOLOGY

In this research effort, we used a mixed-methods approach and relied on both quantitative (i.e., a survey) and qualitative (i.e., interviews and written feedback) methods of data collection and analysis. As Creswell and other researchers have pointed out, "to include only quantitative or qualitative methods falls short of the major approaches being used today in the social and human sciences."[31] Because it was important to us to produce a comprehensive and rigorous analysis of the nature of the relationship between grit, growth mindset, and success, we felt that a holistic approach to the research was both appropriate and necessary.

The quantitative portion of the research—our survey—was designed to test the hypothesis that both grit and a growth mindset contribute to success for women in the law. Quantitative research is deductive,[32] so this was a good method to use because it allowed for thorough exploration of the nature of the relationship—the cause and effect—between all of the variables. Furthermore, it produced statistically significant results and hard "evidence" that allow us to present our findings with a high degree of confidence in their validity and accuracy. As we all know, nothing makes a lawyer quite as happy as sound evidence. We also knew that our audience would be very smart and very discerning, so we wanted the findings, no matter what they might look like, to carry some scientific weight and to hold up to some good old-fashioned (and healthy) scrutiny.

The Survey

The survey we used to collect the data for the quantitative portion of this study ultimately contained roughly 70 questions (although the exact length was dependent upon certain branching that happened as a result of participants' responses—e.g., if a participant answered yes to a certain question that might lead to more follow-up questions, whereas if they answered no, they would move on to the next section). The survey was divided into several sections, as shown and described in Table 1.1.

Table 1.1   Grit and Growth Mindset Survey Summary

Section	Description
Practice Overview	This section included questions about current position, length of time in practice, practice area, long-term career plans, etc.
Measures of Success	This section included questions related to the success measures we defined for each group of lawyers (e.g., solo practitioners, in-house lawyers, etc.) and is discussed in further detail below.
Family History	This section included questions related to family history, including whether participants were married, had children, the number of children, etc.
Academic History	This section included questions related to academic performance measures, including law school and college GPA, rank of academic institutions attended, etc.
The Grit Test	This section included the grit test, as discussed in further detail earlier in this chapter.
The Mindset Quiz	This question included the mindset quiz, as discussed in further detail in this chapter.
Ambition	This section included questions related to ambition, such as the extent to which promotion and advancement mattered.
Interest in Further Research	This section included questions about the extent to which participants were interested in participating in further research and/or writing a letter about their personal experiences with grit and growth mindset.

Practice Overview

The Practice Overview section was included so that we could properly identify the demographics of our participants. We wanted to confirm that we had participants from all industries and practice areas and at all stages of their careers—from new lawyers to seasoned veterans. We also wanted to confirm that the participants identified as female and that they were currently practicing law. This was an important, albeit fairly straightforward section that would allow for appropriate "slicing and dicing" of the data as needed once all of the responses had been collected.

Measures of Success

The Measures of Success section was a far more nuanced and challenging section to draft, and we had to do quite a bit of research and analysis before we felt comfortable that we had asked the right questions therein. We had to begin by acknowledging that success means many different things to many different people, and that it would be impossible to come up with a single definition of success that could reasonably be applied to all women lawyers. For example, a junior associate at a large law firm may measure the success of her first year as a practicing lawyer according, in part, to the feedback she received in connection with an annual performance evaluation process. Of course, this measure of success would be meaningless to a solo practitioner in her 35th year of practice who had not received a performance review—at least from anyone other than herself—in several decades. A lawyer working in-house for a large corporation might measure her success according to how quickly she was promoted within the organization, while someone working in a government position during a hiring freeze would likely not be able to relate to or rely on that same measure as an indicator of progress (or lack thereof). It became readily apparent that we would need to understand what success looked like for women lawyers in all areas of practice and at each stage of their careers. Developing such an understanding was a significant undertaking and a mission-critical first step.

In order to arrive at measures of success for each of the groups of practicing women lawyers we wanted to study (solo practitioners, law firm lawyers, in-house lawyers, etc.), we started by asking them to share their own, personal definitions of success with us. We asked all of them one very simple question: *How do you define success, both for yourself and for your peers?* We were mindful to consider the views of women at all stages of their careers, as well as women from a range of diverse backgrounds, geographies, and ethnicities. We wanted to benefit from as many perspectives as we could reasonably seek to collect.

As you can imagine, the answers we received provided tremendous insight into how women weigh their own achievements. Some of the answers we heard were very narrow and specific to individuals, but several consistent measures for each group quickly began to emerge. As those measures began to take shape, we shared them with more lawyers in similar practices. We asked those new lawyers to react to them and let us know if those measures resonated and what, if anything, might be missing from the list. This exercise produced more helpful feedback and additional suggestions that we used to further refine each set of measures. The refined measures were then shared again with yet more lawyers and the process was repeated. At the end of this highly iterative process, we felt confident that while not every measure of success would resonate with every participant, we had enough options that all participants could relate to at least one of the measures. So, for example, while not all law firm lawyers considered their performance evaluations to be a measure of success, there were other measures (e.g., whether they were on partnership track) that they may relate to and that may fit into their personal definitions of success. All told, we spoke to more than 40 lawyers before arriving at our final measures of success.

Family History

The Family History section included questions about participants' immediate family situations, including whether they were married or in a domestic partnership and whether they had children (and if so, when). It also included a question about the level of education that their mothers had obtained, as this has been shown elsewhere to be a predictor of both academic and professional success. Including these types of measures allowed us to be able to consider the implications of the results for those in long-term relationships vs. those who chose to remain single, parents vs. those without children, and parents who had children while they were practicing law vs. those who had children either before or after (or both). It also allowed us to consider the impact of having highly educated mothers at the analysis stage, so we could see a more unadulterated picture of the impact of grit. To be clear, the family structure comparisons were not the focus of this research effort, but we wanted the option to explore these connections if there was ever a compelling reason to do so down the line.

Academic History

The Academic History questions were included because these measures of academic success, perhaps over and above other identifiable measures, have the most influence over the job opportunities available to junior lawyers. Putting aside the question of whether these are accurate and reliable predictors of success, it is demonstrably the case that those who perform well in law school have more job options than those who do not perform well. Again, the relationship between academic performance and success was not the main focus of this research effort, but it did come into play, and we found connections between grit, growth mindset, and GPA, among other things, which will be discussed further below.

Grit Test and Mindset Quiz

The grit test and the mindset quiz were discussed in detail above and were included here so that we would have an accurate measure of these traits for each of the women who participated in the study.

Ambition

The Ambition section was included so that we could account for those who had not achieved success according to our measures but were, by their own accounts, uninterested in these types of success (we should note here, again, that our research efforts did not capture all definitions of success, and there will be plenty of people who rightfully consider themselves successful and yet do not track against our criteria). It was important to be able to identify ambition levels at the outset, so we did not mistakenly categorize those who were not particularly ambitious as women who wanted to succeed and did not or could not. Instead, they were correctly categorized as women who were simply content in their current roles and about whom the success measures did not communicate all that much (if you are someone for whom success does not matter, we cannot assume anything if/when you do not achieve it). The more important question, for these purposes, is the following: When women are ambitious and really want to succeed, do grit and growth mindset help them do so? The measure of ambition was included so that we could work toward an answer.

Interviews and Written Feedback

The second part of this study employed a qualitative approach in order to provide a more nuanced understanding of how women lawyers are thinking about and experiencing their roles in the legal industry. The qualitative results were used to draw out consistent patterns and themes and to focus on the personal experiences of a subset of the women in the study (we will discuss in more detail below how we identified participants for this portion of the research). As Hyde and other researchers have pointed out, a qualitative approach allows the researcher to study issues in depth and can produce a wealth of detailed data on a limited group of people.[33] As mentioned above, we used interview techniques in order to develop and then refine the measures of success that appeared in the written survey. We also used interview techniques throughout the research process to understand, and in some cases validate, some of the initial quantitative findings. With the exception of the roughly 40 conversations we had in order to define the success measures, most of the qualitative portion of this analysis was performed after we had a chance to do a preliminary assessment of the quantitative findings. All told, we spoke to close to 100 women in total (note that this number includes the 40 conversations and interviews mentioned above). More specifically, we spoke to roughly 15 solo practitioners, 25 in-house lawyers, 10 government lawyers, 10 nonprofit lawyers, and 40 law firm lawyers in firms of all sizes. We use the term "roughly" here as some lawyers had held multiple roles and thus were able to address their experiences within multiple environments.

The primary function of the qualitative portion of this research was to provide a more nuanced understanding of the topic and to help refine, test, and validate our emerging theories and hypotheses.[34] To that end, we used a purposeful sampling technique; that is, we deliberately selected participants who represented all levels of seniority across industries and had demonstrated—according to the survey results—varying degrees of grit, growth mindset, and success. We solicited volunteers in the initial survey, then made a judgment about who should be contacted based their individual survey responses, our personal knowledge of the domain, and the emerging data—an approach advocated by Marshall, among others.[35]

In addition to the interviews, we relied on written feedback in the form of letters—which appear in this book. We asked those who drafted the letters to reflect on the ways in which grit and growth mindset have aided their own paths to success, and their honest, humbling, and inspiring stories shed much light on what grit and growth mindset look like for women in the law. Indeed, these letters and the stories contained therein are the heart of this research and—as you will see—provide a great example of why this topic interests us so much in the first place. All told, we collected 47 letters—nine from solo practitioners, 26 from law firm lawyers, seven from in-house lawyers, and five from government or nonprofit lawyers (as noted in the introduction, many of the letters cover significant time periods—including several different positions over a lifetime of practice—and as such, we have taken the liberty of placing the letters into each chapter as we deemed appropriate based on their contents).

Why We Used a Mixed-Methods Approach

There are a number of compelling reasons to have used a mixed-methods approach in this analysis. First, a mixed-methods approach allows for a more comprehensive, nuanced understanding of the interplay between the variables (in this case: grit, growth mindset, and success). As Kaplan and Maxwell point out, a mixed-methods approach allows the researcher to consider both regularities that are assessed through empirical observation, as well as the mechanisms or complex processes that are identified through qualitative analysis.[36] Second, a mixed-methods approach allows for stronger conclusions, as the strengths of the qualitative approach will compensate, at least in part, for some of the weaknesses of the quantitative approach.[37]

Data Collection and Timing

The data for this analysis, then, was drawn from three sources: (1) the confidential online survey, interviews with select participants, and the letters themselves. The survey was emailed to lawyers by the American Bar Association Commission on Women in the Profession beginning in September 2015. Several follow-up emails were sent, and outreach was made to women's bar associations across the country.

Participants

All told, we heard from close to 4,300 women lawyers, all of whom took time out of their undoubtedly busy schedules to respond to our survey and/or to speak to us in formal interviews or informal information-gathering conversations. In addition, as women often do, they then went on to exceed our expectations by volunteering to participate in our research efforts in other ways—more than 50 percent of the women we surveyed agreed to speak to us on the phone about their experiences, and another 20 percent volunteered to write letters about their personal experiences with grit and growth mindset and the ways in which these traits have played an important role in their lives. For some, these generous offers were in and of themselves demonstrations of their grit. As one letter writer aptly quipped, "What is grit? Taking the time to write this letter when I have a trial to prepare for and one million other things to do!" Fair enough and yes—gritty.

We will discuss the specific demographics of each of the subsets of women we looked at in each of the relevant chapters, but we had a terrifically diverse group of women in all respects—from age to seniority to size and scope of practice to geographic, ethnic, and socioeconomic background and every other measure we could think of. It was important for us—from the outset—to ensure that we heard from as many people as possible and that all voices were heard. We all recognized that in order to be able to generalize and to draw broad and sound conclusions about the importance of grit and growth mindset to the success of women lawyers, we needed to hear as many stories as we could, and we needed to be able to back that up with some good old-fashioned hard science.

We also want to point out that although we did ensure that we had a diverse group of women in all respects, we did not look at the extent to which diversity itself impacts an individual's grit or growth mindset score or any of the success measures. In other words, we did not look at whether one ethnic group was more or less gritty or growth mindset–oriented than another or whether the successes of one group were more or less influenced by these traits than the successes of another group. It would be very interesting to explore the interplay between diversity, grit, and growth mindset, and there could very well be important learnings to be gleaned from this exploration, but that falls outside of the scope of the current research effort. For an in-depth look at the issues relevant to women attorneys of color, the Commission offers numerous resources through its Women of Color Research Initiative, which are available online at www.ambar.org/womenofcolor.

A summary of the key demographics of our participants can be found in Tables 1.2 to 1.7.

Table 1.2   How Long Have You Practiced Law?

1–2 years	7%
3–5 years	8%
6–9 years	10%
10–14 years	12%
15–20 years	16%
21 years or more	47%

Table 1.3   Current Practice Area

Banking and Finance	3%
Bankruptcy	1%
Benefits	1%
Children and Family	7%
Civil Rights	1%
Corporate	7%
Criminal	3%
Education	1%
Environmental	2%
Foreclosure	0%
Health	3%
Housing	0%
Immigration	1%
Insurance	3%
Intellectual Property	4%
International	1%
Labor and Employment	10%
Litigation	20%

(continued)

Mergers and Acquisitions	1%
Real Estate	5%
Securities	2%
Tax	3%
Torts	1%
Trusts and Estates	5%
Other	15%

Practice areas indicated as 0% are due to rounding.

Table 1.4   Length of Time at Current Employer

Less than 1 year	9%
1–2 years	13%
3–4 years	14%
5–6 years	9%
7–8 years	8%
9–10 years	7%
11–15 years	14%
16–20 years	8%
More than 20 years	18%

Table 1.5   Number of Full-Time Lawyer Positions Held

0	22%
1	24%
2	22%
3	14%
4	9%
5 or more	9%

Table 1.6   Long-Term Plans

I plan to stay where I am for the rest of my career.	46%
I plan to stay where I am for at least the next 3–5 years.	25%
I plan to stay where I am for the next 1–2 years.	15%
I am currently looking for a new job in the same environment (e.g., in-house, government, BigLaw, etc.).	4%
I am currently looking for a new job in a new environment (e.g., in-house, government, BigLaw, etc.), but I still plan to practice law.	9%
I am currently looking for a new job, and I do not plan to continue to practice law.	1%

Table 1.7   Current Role

I work for a law firm.	62%
I work in-house.	14%
I work for a government agency.	5%
I am a judge.	2%
I am a solo practitioner.	12%
I work for a nonprofit.	4%
Other	1%

Limitations of the Research

There are a few limitations of this study that ought to be noted before we delve more deeply into a summary of the findings. The first limitation—which was discussed in some detail earlier in this section—is the fact that it is impossible to come up with a universal definition of success within the practice of law. We defined success broadly for each subgroup of lawyers, relying on common themes that emerged through the interview process, but the fact remains that not everyone will agree on which elements should be the subject of our focus.

The second limitation is that all of the data collected in this research effort, in both the quantitative (i.e., online survey) and qualitative (i.e., letters and interviews) phases, was self-reported by participants. This means that we were relying on them to tell us whether they had been successful according to our measures. Some of the self-report data collected in the qualitative portion of the study can be validated through other means (e.g., a lawyer's title and the number of years she's been practicing can generally be verified through her firm's website or through other public records). This subset of the data, which can be broadly described as demographic data, generally presents the least concern from a self-report perspective, as even if the data cannot be verified, the nature of the problems posed seldom offset the convenience of collecting it through self-report methods.[38]

For other subsets of the data (e.g., the message the lawyer received at her most recent performance review and the relative measure of her compensation), no such validation is possible. As such, triangulation—defined as the process of collecting information from a variety of sources and methods in order to ensure its accuracy—is not possible here. As Podsakoff and Organ point out, when we ask people to report on past behavior or personality traits, measures that cannot be verified through other sources, the greatest risk is common method variance.[39] Common method variance occurs when measures of two or more variables are collected from the same respondents and an attempt is made to interpret correlations among them. In this case, for example, we asked respondents to report on both their grit behaviors and mindset orientations. Because the measures come from the same source, any defect (e.g., a tendency to exaggerate or inflate) will contaminate both measures.[40] In other words, if a woman believes herself to be a high performer (perhaps misinterpreting whether she is on partnership track or over-inflating the message she received at her last performance review), and then we use those inaccurate measures of success to interpret the impact of her grit and mindset orientation, it will lead to inaccurate results. Unfortunately, no simple statistical procedure can sufficiently eliminate the problems associated with same-source variance.[41] However, we have attempted to reduce some of the variance by implementing a procedural technique called separation of measurement. This technique requires that measures of grit, mindset, and the success variables are collected at different points in time and through different media.[42] We have employed this method for the respondents who participated in the qualitative portion of this study by collecting data from them over the phone, online, and through their written letter accounts of how they view and employ these important traits. The collection of this data was done through three different means and at three different points in time—some conversations occurred before the online survey was distributed, some during, and some after. As Podsakoff and Organ suggest, this approach helps to mitigate some of the problems associated with common method variance. While this is not a perfect solution to the problem, many researchers have noted that, despite the problems inherent in the use of self-report measures, the utility of these types of measures makes them virtually indispensable.[43]

The final obvious limitation is the fact that it is very difficult to capture the results of women lawyers who are no longer practicing, so our study considers only those who are still in the game. It would perhaps be more effective to include lawyers in the study who have recently left the practice of law in order to gain a more complete, holistic picture of the ways in which grit and mindset influence success. Unfortunately, for logistical reasons, that has not been possible here, but perhaps we will have an opportunity to explore that down the line.

SUMMARY OF THE KEY FINDINGS

Not only are grit and growth mindset important, but there is substantial anecdotal evidence—both here and elsewhere—that grit is a trait many highly successful women lawyers possess, often as a direct result of having overcome challenging obstacles along the path to leadership positions. As Heckman and Rubinstein point out, grit and perseverance may be as much a consequence as a cause of success.[44] In other words, successful women lawyers may be gritty precisely because it is difficult to achieve success in the practice of law (and many of the women you will hear from in the following pages will offer strong support for this theory).

Hand and Savas provide some of the earlier anecdotal evidence of the importance of these traits. They interviewed 40 successful women from different ethnic backgrounds and geographies, all of whom were pioneers who helped pave the way for younger generations of women. The women they interviewed came from a variety of industries and included a state Supreme Court justice. Almost all of the women interviewed for the project referred to grit or a synonym of grit as an essential contributor to their overall success.[45]

In point of fact, we don't need to go very far back in history for anecdotal evidence of the importance of these traits. Indeed, it would be hard to discuss women in leadership without some mention of one of the most prominent women of 2016—also a lawyer—Hillary Rodham Clinton. In her exuberant introduction of Secretary Clinton at the Democratic National Convention (when Secretary Clinton became the first woman in U.S. history to accept a major-party presidential nomination), Meryl Streep said: "What does it take to be the first female anything? It takes grit and it takes grace."[46] Interestingly, while many women clearly have grit to begin with, others suggested that it was necessary for them to foster, develop, and nurture this trait over time in order to achieve their goals. Importantly, Hillary, and the female subjects Hand and Savas studied, came from an earlier generation of women who likely faced a path that was far more perilous than the path faced by women executives in today's workplace environment. All of these women were trying to define new territory and, in many cases, had to battle strongly held beliefs that presented continual challenges to their very presence. For these women, the road to success and especially to leadership positions was fraught with challenges that required an ability to persevere and to resist the temptation to abandon the pursuit of success in these fraught environments. On this hazardous road, these women needed to rely regularly on grit.[47]

In spite of the fact that the path to leadership is less precarious for women today than it was for earlier generations, it is clear that grit is still an important factor in a woman's ability to achieve high levels of success. For example, when asked what they feel is needed in order to achieve success, many of the women we surveyed said things like: "iron-willed perseverance," "fire in the belly and determination," "persistence," "drive and determination," and "total tenacity." The women in all of these studies, including our own, agreed that grit and a growth mindset had been the key to their success—and we'll discuss this in much more detail throughout the book.

Along those same lines, Forbes considers the careers of successful women and suggests that high-performing women possess the grit and determination to make visionary career leaps or game-changing business decisions in order to get ahead. These powerful women "display the sheer willpower and resolve to achieve success on their own terms and in their own way."[48] Success, Forbes suggests, is driven by the way in which women are able to conquer moments of profound adversity by ultimately choosing to take risks that lead to fractured egos and yet still managing "to dust themselves off and aim for even higher goals in the future."[49]

The anecdotal evidence discussed above—and more deeply in the chapters that follow—helps to establish that there is a widely held belief among females that grit and mindset are critical to success. Indeed, as Hornett and Finn point out, the repetition in these female narratives becomes a source of reassurance as career women all seem to have similar stories and perspectives on the nature of success.[50] Nevertheless, aside from the work we have done here, there is, to our knowledge, no real empirical evidence to support the claim that successful women lawyers are gritty. Rather, it is a belief that many women seem to share but one that had not been appropriately tested. The intent of this study was to do just that—to test the connections between grit, mindset, and success for women in the law. Below is a summary of what we found.

What We Learned

As you will discover in the following chapters, we learned a great deal about the connections between grit, growth mindset, and various measures of success for women lawyers practicing as solo practitioners, in law firms of all sizes, in-house, and in government and nonprofit organizations. Ultimately, what we discovered was what we had expected to discover: Grit and growth mindset are linked to several important measures of success for women lawyers in every work domain that we explored. It is important to note, however, that while we did uncover strong—and statistically significant—links between grit, growth mindset, and success, there is a difference between causation and correlation. In other words, we cannot say definitively that grit or growth mindset alone *causes* success. Indeed, there are far too many factors that contribute to success for lawyers (or any single subset of the population) for any researcher, even a very good one, to be able to identify a single, surefire formula for success. At the end of the day, success is a somewhat messy business. That being said, we are able to say, definitely, that grit and growth mindset are *highly correlated* with success, meaning that they affect and depend upon one another, at least to some extent.

The specific ways in which this plays out differ by practice area and are discussed in detail in each chapter. For example, for solo practitioners, there is a statistically significant relationship between grit and the level of satisfaction they experience with respect to the overall quality of the matters they are working on. For women in law firms, government, and the nonprofit world, grit is linked to an individual's performance rating. For women practicing in-house, grit is linked to when and how they are brought into the decision-making process and whether they are thought of as strategic contributors and business partners within their organizations. The chart below (Table 1.8) highlights the key findings specific to each group. Each of these findings will be discussed in greater detail in each chapter, and then, more interestingly, we will share, in full, the 47 deeply personal and compelling letters we received from the women who volunteered to be a part of this important undertaking. While we think the research is powerful and can be used to further our current understanding of women in the law, the letters are the heart of this book. They are all thoughtful, tremendously inspiring, and full of great advice for women at all stages of their careers.

Table 1.8 Summary of Grit and Growth Mindset Findings

Solo Practitioners (Chapter 2)	Key Finding #1	Solo practitioners believe, overwhelmingly, that grit and growth mindset are important contributors to career success.
	Key Finding #2	There is a statistically significant relationship between grit and the level of satisfaction solo practitioners experience with respect to the overall quality of the matters they are working on.
	Key Finding #3	Solo practitioners with a growth mindset orientation are more likely to have had academic success in law school.
Law Firm Lawyers (Chapter 3)	Key Finding #1	Grit is highly correlated to a number of measures of success in law firms of all sizes, including billable hours.
	Key Finding #2	Grit is closely related to the overall quality of the work that a woman receives when practicing in firms of all sizes.

(continued)

	Key Finding #3	Both grit and growth mindset are very closely related to ambition.
	Key Finding #4	Grit is strongly related to how well women in law firms perform on formal performance evaluations.
	Key Finding #5	Mindset is strongly related to compensation.
	Key Finding #6	Law firm lawyers believe that grit and growth mindset are important contributors to success.
In-House Lawyers (Chapter 4)	Key Finding #1	In-house practitioners believe— almost to a person—that grit and growth mindset are important contributors to success.
	Key Finding #2	Grit is strongly related to the message that in-house lawyers receive in their performance evaluations.
	Key Finding #3	Grit influences the point at which women lawyers are brought into the decision-making process, as well as how long they will stay in the game.
	Key Finding #4	Mindset predicts seniority within the organization.
Government and Nonprofit Lawyers (Chapter 5)	Key Finding #1	Grit is a reliable indicator of how well a woman performs in a government or nonprofit role.
	Key Finding #2	Both grit and growth mindset are closely related to how far a woman has advanced within her organization.
	Key Finding #3	Ambition is closely tied to both the grit and growth mindset scores of women practicing in government and nonprofit organizations.

Notes:

1. Heckman, J., and Rubinstein, Y. 2001. "The importance of non-cognitive skills: Lessons from the GED testing program." *The American Economic Review* 91(2):145–149.
2. Heckman, J., and Rubinstein, Y. 2001. "The importance of non-cognitive skills: Lessons from the GED testing program." *The American Economic Review* 91(2):145–149.
3. Merriam-Webster, 2016.
4. Duckworth, A., Peterson, C., Matthews, M., and Kelly, D. 2007. "Grit: Perseverance and passion for long-term goals." *Journal of Personality and Social Psychology* 92(6):1087–1101.
5. *Id.*
6. Duckworth, A. 2016. *Grit: The power of passion and perseverance.* Simon and Schuster, New York.
7. Eisenberger, R., Kuhlman, M.D., and Cotterell, N. "Effects of social values, effort training, and goal structure on task persistence." *Journal of Research in Personality* 26.3(1992):258–272.
8. Stolz, P. 1997. "Adversity Quotient." HarperCollins e-books; Van Gelderen, M. "Perseverance strategies of enterprising individuals." *International Journal of Entrepreneurial Behavior & Research* 18.6 (2012):630–648.
9. Sinek, S. 2009. *Start with why: How great leaders inspire everyone to take action.* Penguin, New York.
10. Doskoch, P. 2005. "The winning edge." *Psychology Today.* Retrieved from https://www.psychologytoday.com/articles/200511/the-winning-edge.
11. Barsade, S., and Gibson, D. 2007. "Why does affect matter in organizations?" *Academy of Management Perspectives* 21.1 (2007): 36–59.
12. Salovey, P., and Mayer, J. 1990. "Emotional intelligence." *Imagination, Cognition and Personality* 9:185–211.
13. Heckman, J., and Rubinstein, Y. 2001. "The importance of non-cognitive skills: Lessons from the GED testing program." *The American Economic Review* 91(2):145–149.
14. Barsade, S., and Gibson, D. 2007. "Why does affect matter in organizations?" *Academy of Management Perspectives* 21.1 (2007): 36–59.
15. Doskoch, P. 2005. "The winning edge." *Psychology Today.* Retrieved from https://www.psychologytoday.com/articles/200511/the-winning-edge.
16. *Id.*

17. Duckworth, A. 2016. *Grit: The power of passion and perseverance.* Simon and Schuster, New York.
18. Ericsson, K.A., and Charness, N. 1994. "Expert performance: Its structure and acquisition." *American Psychologist* 49(8): 725.
19. Ericsson, K.A. 2004. "Deliberate practice and the acquisition and maintenance of expert performance in medicine and related domains." *Academic Medicine* 79(10): S70–S81.
20. *Id.*
21. Ericsson, K.A., and Charness, N. 1994. "Expert performance: Its structure and acquisition." *American Psychologist* 49(8): 725.
22. Duckworth, A. 2016. *Grit: The Power of Passion and Perseverance.* Simon and Schuster, New York.
23. *Id.*
24. Duckworth, A., et al. 2007. "Grit: perseverance and passion for long-term goals." *Journal of Personality and Social Psychology* 92(6):1087.
25. *Id.*
26. Merriam-Webster. 2016.
27. Dweck, C.S. 2008. *Mindset: The new psychology of success.* Random House Digital, Inc., New York.
28. *Id.*
29. *Id.*
30. *Id.*
31. Creswell, J.W., and Garrett, A.L. 2008. "The movement of mixed methods research and the role of educators." *South African Journal of Education* 28(3): 321–333.
32. *Id.*
33. Hyde, K.F. 2000. "Recognising deductive processes in qualitative research." *Qualitative market research: An international journal* 3(2): 82–90.
34. Miles, M.B., and Huberman, A.M. 1994. *Qualitative data analysis: A sourcebook.* Sage Publications, Beverly Hills.
35. Marshall, D., Johnell, O., and Wedel, H. 1996. "Meta-analysis of how well measures of bone mineral density predict occurrence of osteoporotic fractures." *The BMJ* 312(7041): 1254–1259.
36. Kaplan, B., and Maxwell, J.A. 2005. "Qualitative research methods for evaluating computer information systems." *Evaluating the organizational impact of healthcare information systems.* Springer, New York: 30–55.

37. Johnson, R.B., and Onwuegbuzie, A.J. 2004. "Mixed methods research: A research paradigm whose time has come." *Educational Researcher* 33(7):14–26.
38. Gupta, N., and Beehr, T. 1986. "A test of the correspondence between self-reports and alternative data sources about work organizations." *Journal of Vocational Behavior* 20(1):1–13; Podsakoff, P.M., and Organ, D.W. 1986. "Self-reports in organizational research: Problems and prospects." *Journal of Management* 12(4):531–544.
39. Podsakoff, P.M., and Organ, D.W.1986. "Self-reports in organizational research: Problems and prospects." *Journal of Management* 12(4):531–544.
40. *Id.*
41. *Id.*
42. *Id.*
43. *Id.*; Gupta, N., and Beehr, T.A. 1982. "A Test of the Correspondence Between Self-reports and Alternative Data Sources About Work Organizations." *Journal of Vocational Behavior* 20(1):1–13; Eden, C. and Sims, D. 1979. "On the nature of problems in consulting practice." *Omega* 7(2):119–127.
44. Heckman, J., and Rubinstein, Y. 2001. "The importance of non-cognitive skills: Lessons from the GED testing program." *The American Economic Review* 91(2):145–149.
45. Hand, E., and Savas, T. 2010. *Women of true grit.* Canterbury House Publishing, Ltd., Florence, AL.
46. Democratic National Convention, Monday, July 25 to Thursday, July 28, 2016.
47. Hand, E., and Savas, T. 2010. *Women of true grit.* Canterbury House Publishing, Ltd., Florence, AL.
48. Forbes, M. 2010. What Do Highly Successful Women and 7-year-olds Have in Common? Retrieved from https://www.forbes.com/sites/moiraforbes/2010/10/12/what-do-highly-successful-women-and-7-year-olds-have-in-common-2/#41d2dd4e1bf3
49. *Id.*
50. Hornett, A., and Rinn, R. 2006. *Advancing Women in Leadership Online Journal* 20 (Spring 2006).

2

Solo Practitioners

KEY FINDINGS

➤ Solo practitioners believe, overwhelmingly, that grit and growth mindset are important contributors to career success.

➤ There is a statistically significant relationship between grit and the level of satisfaction solo practitioners experience with respect to the overall quality of the matters they are working on.

➤ Solo practitioners with a growth mindset orientation are more likely to have had academic success in law school.

THE WOMEN WE SURVEYED

We surveyed more than 400 women in our efforts to understand more about the connections between grit, growth mindset, and success for solo practitioners. The women we surveyed practiced law in almost every conceivable practice area, including children and family law, banking and finance, civil rights, criminal law, immigration, intellectual property and insurance law, labor and employment, real estate, trusts and estates, tax, torts, litigation, and corporate law. They also represent a wide range of practice experience, ranging from one to two years of experience to more than 21 years of experience—and everything in between. Some had become solo practitioners as soon as they passed the bar, effectively managing to "hang a shingle" right out of law school (while anyone can, in theory, hang a shingle, building and maintaining a practice with little to no practical experience is no easy feat). On the other end of the spectrum, there were solo practitioners who had held more than five full-time lawyer positions, including roles in private practice, government, and the nonprofit sector before ultimately starting their own practices.

The women we surveyed were graduates of law schools that ran the gamut of the *U.S. News & World Report* rankings, from the very top ranked law school, Yale Law School, all the way down to the fourth (and bottom) tier.[1] Some of the women we surveyed did extraordinarily well in law school, ranking in the top 1 percent of their graduating classes, while others fell into the bottom 50 percent, and, again, we saw everything else in between. The benefit of such a broad academic spread is that it provided us with a look at those who were academically gifted, those who found law school to be extremely challenging, and those who fell somewhere in the middle of these two extremes.

We heard from women who were married or in domestic partnerships and from women who were currently single, divorced, or never married. We heard from women with children (with as few as one and—in some cases—more than five) and women without children. For those who had children, some had their children while they were practicing law and some had them during a break from practice or before or after practicing. Finally, we heard from those whose mothers had earned advanced professional or doctoral degrees, including—in a number of cases—those who were medical doctors or lawyers themselves, as well as those whose mothers had not completed high school. Interestingly, the solo practitioners were more likely to have had a mother who had completed a higher level of education than many of the lawyers in the other groups we surveyed. Research has shown that a mother's education may predict the academic success of her children, and, indeed, some of the women we heard from shared stories about the ways in which their mothers' educational achievements had inspired and motivated them. That said, even absent a mother who had attained a high level of education, many of the women we surveyed—regardless of their roles—often cited their mothers as particularly motivating, supportive, and critical to their success. One solo shared that her mother had always told her she could be whatever she wanted to be, and that this had been very influential for her while she was coming of age. As a result of hearing this so often, she came to believe it was true. It is safe to say that the mothers of the solo practitioners we heard from often played instrumental roles in their daughters' lives and were supportive in ways that continually encouraged them along the path to career success.

In terms of an overall career outlook, the solo practitioners we surveyed generally wanted to be in a position where there were clear opportunities for advancement, and it mattered to all of them, without exception, to be in a job that they found challenging. Furthermore, they tended to make these desires known to those around them and particularly to anyone who was in a position to affect their work or their future career trajectories. We measured their ambition scores and found that the majority of these women were goal-oriented, highly motivated to achieve something of lasting importance, and driven to succeed. They expressed a desire to be the best in the world at what they did. They also tended to disagree with the statement, "ambition is overrated" and to readily agree with the statement, "I am ambitious."

MEASURING SUCCESS

As discussed in chapter 2, no survey could begin to adequately measure success for any subset of the population, no matter how specifically defined or how small. "Success" is a loaded term and tends to mean vastly different things to different people, even among groups of people who share a multitude of common characteristics. In our attempts to understand how to think about success for solo practitioners, we interviewed many women at different career stages and in different practice areas to understand how they themselves thought of success, what really mattered to them, and why. There were several common themes that emerged from these discussions.

First, while it made sense for most of the lawyers we surveyed to measure success in terms of traditional measures like annual performance evaluations or promotions and the like, for this group, those measures were largely irrelevant. In addition, compensation (if not as a fixed measure then as a measure relevant to one's similarly situated peers)—an important measure for many of the other subsets of the female lawyer population we surveyed—was also less likely to be listed among the measures of success for this group. Rather, this group was more interested in whether they had been able to maintain their livelihood as a solo practitioner for the period that they had sought to do so and whether their personal financial goals had been met. Essentially, this measure was a proxy for compensation. For some solo practitioners, this meant bringing in just enough to supplement a spouse's income or enough to be an equal contributor to the household. For others, this meant bringing in enough to support an entire family or to take lavish vacations, live extravagantly, and retire at a young age. As would be the case with any subset of the population, this group had vastly divergent financial goals and expectations for themselves.

Second, the group of solo practitioners that we interviewed were very focused on the measures of control that they had over their own schedules. For many, they had pursued this avenue of practice precisely because they knew it would be more likely to afford them the kind control over their own schedules—how much to work and when—that prior positions had not allowed for. Whether they were raising young children, enduring long commutes, taking care of elderly parents, or otherwise juggling life's many complications, control was key and was, for many of them, the most important way in which they evaluated their own success. Similarly, this group was very focused on the control that they had over the types of work that they chose to take on. For many, being a cog in a wheel, or the low (wo)man on the totem pole, either in a law firm setting or in-house, was undesirable and led them to seek out a working arrangement that allowed them to take on matters that were more interesting and professionally satisfying. Many of them openly stated that they wanted to be their own boss.

Finally, being able to identify and accomplish personal and professional goals, whatever those might be—and they varied tremendously from lawyer to lawyer—was paramount to their ability to achieve an overall sense of satisfaction and professional accomplishment. What seemed to matter most, in the end, was that their practices afforded them the opportunity to do what they wanted and, in some cases, felt called to do.

Once the individual conversations we had with solo practitioners had been distilled into measures of success that were largely common to the group, we were left with five overarching success measures, as follows:

1. How satisfied are you with the level of control you currently have over your work schedule? (very satisfied, satisfied, neutral, dissatisfied, or very dissatisfied)
2. How satisfied are you with the overall quality (e.g., interesting, challenging, and/or professionally satisfying) of the matters you are working on? (very satisfied, satisfied, neutral, dissatisfied, or very dissatisfied)
3. How satisfied are you with your current level of income relative to your personal financial goals for your practice? (very satisfied, satisfied, neutral, dissatisfied, or very dissatisfied)
4. Have you been able to maintain your livelihood as a solo practitioner for as long as you have sought to do so? (yes or no)
5. To what extent have you been able to accomplish your personal and professional goals, whatever those might be? (I have accomplished all of my goals, I have accomplished many of my goals, I have accomplished some of my goals, or I have accomplished none of my goals.)

While we knew at the outset that we could never come up with one list that would comprehensively capture and define success for all solo practitioners, we hope this list resonates with those who are practicing in this capacity. We will discuss each of the key findings for solo practitioners below.

Key Finding #1

Solo practitioners believe, overwhelmingly, that grit and growth mindset are important contributors to career success.

Putting aside the results of the grit and growth mindset tests and the extent to which these traits impact the success measures outlined above for this group, we first wanted to know whether solo practitioners themselves believed that these traits had been an important factor in their careers. We asked everyone who took the survey the following question:

> Have you personally found that being gritty (a gritty person is a person who demonstrates both passion and perseverance in pursuit of her long-term goals) or having a growth mindset (a growth mindset–oriented person believes that her success is based on hard work, learning, training, and doggedness) has been a factor in your overall career success?

Of the 400 female solo practitioners who took the survey, more than 97 percent said that these traits mattered, and fewer than 3 percent believed that they were not a factor. Many of the women we surveyed told us unequivocally that putting bread on the table requires regular demonstration of grit. One of the lawyers we surveyed, who opened her own practice at the age of 53, says that the practice of law "is not for the faint of heart, I assure you. That is especially true when you do it as a solo practitioner." Most of the solo practitioners we heard from described grit as an essential ingredient for success and went on to suggest that they would advise young women who were just embarking on their careers to do what they could to find—then nurture—their inner grit. Clearly, then, this is a group that has a strong belief in the power of effort, persistence, and passion for long-term goals, and this is the first key finding of this research.

Key Finding #2

There is a statistically significant relationship between grit and the level of satisfaction solo practitioners experience with respect to the overall quality of the matters they are working on.

When we individually consider the relationship between grit, growth mindset, and each measure of success for this group, we find several interesting takeaways. The first of these—and the second key finding of this research—is that there is a statistically significant relationship between grit and the level of satisfaction solo practitioners experience with respect to "the overall quality" of the matters they are working on. Specifically, the grittier a solo practitioner is, the more likely she is to find her work interesting, challenging, and professionally satisfying. Conversely, as her satisfaction levels increase, from neutral to satisfied and from satisfied to very satisfied, her grit levels are also likely to increase. When asked to speculate on what might account for this important relationship between grit and this particular measure of success, one solo practitioner posited that there may be a link between grit and optimism. She suggested that gritty solo practitioners may be more likely to view challenging situations in which they are taking on new matters (often in areas in which they lack significant expertise) or tackling whatever obstacles may present themselves as rewarding rather than overwhelming or crippling. She described her first 1,000 days as a solo practitioner as days that were seemingly filled with endless reading and research as she tried her best to interpret the nuances of the footnotes in appellate court decisions. While she found the work to be mentally exhausting, it did not deter her, and she even found that despite the effort she was putting into it, she was enjoying the experience of being a practicing lawyer.

Similarly, another lawyer somehow managed to take care of an ailing mother, raise two small boys, participate in local community and bar association activities, and build her practice from the ground up. Although she has a tremendous amount on her plate, she found inspiration in her work, and this prevented her from feeling completely overwhelmed. The experience of building something that was hers and hers alone was exciting to her and made it possible for her to persevere and continue to put forth the incredible effort needed to keep her practice and her family afloat. Along those same lines, another solo practitioner made the decision to enter law school—a four-year evening program—with a nine-month-old son. She "studied when [her] son napped, and

[she] had babysitters (teenagers who lived in [their] building) on the many nights when her husband [a resident physician] had to work. . . . A few years into the program [they] had [their] second baby." While she took a few months off while the baby was an infant, she soon returned to the program full-time and managed to graduate on time with her class. Once she began practicing, she found that she loved the job and, like the other solo practitioners mentioned above, felt that she was gaining important, valuable professional experience.

What is it that allows these gritty women to persevere and find joy in working beyond the point of exhaustion and, more important, to find the experience not only interesting but also professionally satisfying? Why is grit so strongly related to this measure of success? While further research is needed before we can draw definitive conclusions, I think there are three possible reasons why this connection is as strong as it is. The first possible explanation is that gritty individuals tend to be among the highest performers on the job, and therefore they tend to attract high-quality work—work that is very important to the clients and for which the clients actively seek out the most dedicated and talented lawyers. For example, one may be less inclined to spend the time seeking out a top-notch lawyer to negotiate a parking ticket than one would be for an important family matter. A second possibility is that the gritty lawyers, who tend to embrace challenges and to see them as opportunities for learning and personal development, run toward, rather than shy away from, challenging assignments. They do this even though—or perhaps precisely because—these types of assignments tend to be the most demanding in terms of the effort required to successfully complete them. They don't mind "doing the majority of . . . brief writing late into the night" or jumping wholeheartedly into the practice of law with "staggeringly burdensome student loan debt [and] . . . three babies in diapers." They don't steer clear of positions where they will be "out of [their] comfort zone most of the time . . . [and] totally unfamiliar with many of the environments [they were] immediately thrust into." A gritty solo practitioner is likely to *want* to push herself and would certainly not avoid a task that required long hours. Instead, the most interesting matters are the ones she would be likely to raise her hand for.

A third possibility is that gritty women lawyers are so focused on the work they have, and so committed to working hard and getting the most out of each engagement, that they are more likely to experience the matters they are working on as professionally satisfying, even if others working on similar matters might disagree. For example, one lawyer described her first assignment as a solo practitioner, after she had reopened her father's office following his death, as follows:

> My first client, who was a friend of my eldest brother, consulted with me about a white truck he had purchased, but he had changed his mind about the color he wanted. The client hired me to draft and send a letter to the dealer, and although I counseled the client that this effort might not achieve the result he wanted (a different colored truck), I typed up the letter and was paid my first fee in the amount of $25.00. I was ecstatic. The client was pleased.

Certainly, there are lawyers out there who would not use the word "ecstatic" to describe their reaction to this kind of work. One can imagine that there are other lawyers who might have panicked had this been their first engagement and quickly imagined themselves doomed to a lifetime full of such pedestrian assignments. The fact that she experienced joyful excitement at this moment and fully celebrated the accomplishment of her first paying client speaks to both her underlying grittiness and her strong growth mindset orientation. She saw this event, and rightfully so, as the first step in what would eventually become a very successful and personally satisfying career. One could aptly describe this solo practitioner as an optimist.

Similarly, a solo practitioner who realized the importance of grit and a growth mindset at an early age and overcame many hardships along the path to a successful legal career shares advice for young lawyers that is truly the embodiment of optimism and a strong growth mindset orientation:

> In adversity, see the cup as half full instead of half empty, and remain grateful for what you have while striving to achieve what you don't. Set your goals and achieve them,

because you can, no matter where you come from or what you've endured, because when you open your eyes each day, you have another chance, another opportunity, to make a difference for yourself and others.

If optimism is indeed a factor here, the connection can be explained by the fact that gritty lawyers are more likely to respond to a question like this one in a positive way: How satisfied are you with the overall quality (e.g., interesting, challenging, and/or professionally satisfying) of the matters you are working on? Do you love your work? Yes! Is it interesting and satisfying and all that you had hoped for? Yes! There is some support for this idea in the larger body of grit research. In a study of novice teachers, Duckworth, Quinn, and Seligman found that more optimistic teachers had higher grit and life satisfaction scores and that grit and life satisfaction, in turn, predicted greater teacher effectiveness.[2] It could very well be the case here that gritty solo practitioners are also more optimistic and thus more likely to view and experience their work positively.

Key Finding #3

Solo practitioners with a growth mindset orientation are more likely to have had academic success in law school.

The third key finding of this research is that solo practitioners who have a strong growth mindset orientation—those who believe strongly in the power of effort—are more likely to have had academic success in law school. Specifically, these women are more likely to (1) have been highly ranked in their law school classes and (2) have attended law schools that are more highly ranked by *U.S. News & World Report*.[3] We will explore each of these points separately in this section, beginning with the second point. As many law schools place tremendous value on undergraduate GPA as a criterion for admission, the latter data point may also be suggestive of superior performance as an undergraduate. Indeed, many of the women we surveyed did extraordinarily well as undergraduates—more than 30 percent of them earned GPAs of 3.8 or higher. In addition, 36 percent of the women we surveyed earned an equally impressive GPA in high school, and a few had even been the valedictorians of their high school classes.

That said, there were many women we heard from who chose which law school to attend for purely practical reasons. One chose to attend Chicago Kent College of Law because her husband found a residency program that met his needs in Illinois, and the evening program at the law school was taught by the same professors who participated in the full-time program. Similarly, another one chose Taft Law School in Santa Ana, California, so that she could continue to work while in law school. I raise these examples in order to point out that the particular rank of the law school that one attended may or may not be an indication of grit or a growth mindset orientation. While gaining admittance to a highly ranked school like Harvard or Yale may be suggestive of academic persistence, dedication, and a strong growth mindset, attendance at a less highly ranked law school does not—by any means—imply the opposite.

With respect to the first point—that women with a strong growth mindset are more likely to have achieved a higher class rank in law school—there is evidence in the larger body of grit work that suggests that grit is often a predictor of high academic achievement. Duckworth and her colleagues used the Grit Scale in a series of studies designed to test the hypothesis that grit may be as essential to high achievement as IQ in setting exceptional individuals apart from their less exceptional peers.[4]

The first of these studies collected data on more than 1,500 adult participants aged 25 years or older. Participants were asked to indicate both how old they were and what level of education they had achieved: some high school, high school graduate, some college, associate's degree, bachelor's degree, or post-college graduate degree. These data points were then compared to participants' individual grit scores, and the more highly educated adults were grittier than their less-educated peers of equal age.[5] This study does provide some evidence that gritty individuals tend to achieve more in the academic domain than those who are not gritty. Along those same lines, a second study considered the association between grit and cumulative GPA while controlling for general mental ability or intelligence—as measured by SAT scores—at an elite undergraduate university.[6] The results of this study demonstrated that gritty students outperformed their less gritty peers. In this study, success was defined as cumulative GPA, which is a clear measure of success in the academic domain.

A third study expanded the scope beyond pure academic achievement by considering whether grit was predictive of cadet retention and GPA at West Point, the United States Military Academy. More than 1,200 freshman cadets completed the Grit Scale upon arrival at West Point in 2004.[7] This data was compared to other data maintained by West Point, such as Whole Candidate Score (a weighted average of SAT scores, class rank, demonstrated leadership ability, and physical aptitude), which is used in their rigorous admissions process.[8] The results of the study revealed that grit predicted whether a candidate would survive his/her first summer as a cadet better than any other known predictor. Additionally, grit was predictive of both a cadet's first year GPA and his or her Military Performance Score, a combined measure of performance ratings and grades.[9]

Collectively, these three studies make clear that grit is often a predictor of academic success, and when we consider the stories of the women we surveyed, it is clear that both grit and growth mindset played a role in their own academic achievements. As one lawyer explained to us in an interview, instead of throwing in the towel when she got extremely negative feedback on a first draft of a paper in law school, she used it as an opportunity to improve. Although she continued to struggle with that paper, and with her writing in general at first, she eventually went on to win a writing competition. Honing her writing skill has served her extremely well in her current practice, where she writes something every single day and actually finds that she enjoys it and excels at it!

Similarly, in another classic example of a strong growth mindset orientation driving academic success, one of the solo practitioners we heard from describes her experience in law school as follows:

[W]e first-years only had two final exams in December. I got a B on each of those exams—and that became my grade for each class. (I had received maybe two Bs in my academic life at this point, and here my GPA was just 3.0 after one semester). . . . I started to work only to understand the material. I enjoyed talking in class and continued to participate actively. I read all the cases, took thorough notes, and made detailed course outlines. I formed a fun study group, but did not feel quite so pressured to "get results." Then I started to get As, and even A-plusses. At the end of my second year, I got a note from the dean in my mailbox: "Congratulations. We are pleased to inform you that you are ranked seventh in your class (of 350 students)."

Had it not been the case that these women had strong growth mindset orientations, they could easily have given up on law school and interpreted their initial setbacks as evidence that they simply lacked the ability to succeed in the law school environment. Fortunately, they chose this moment to dig deep and do whatever it took to be successful. These two stories perfectly illustrate why both grit and a growth mindset predict success in law school and underscore the third and final key finding of this chapter. The following letters offer many more stories that help to explain why and how grit and growth mindset can and do impact female success for solo practitioners.

Notes:

1. https://www.usnews.com/best-graduate-schools/top-law-schools/law-rankings
2. Duckworth, A.L., Quinn, P.D., and Seligman, M.E.P. 2009. "Positive predictors of teacher effectiveness." *The Journal of Positive Psychology* 4.6:540–547.
3. https://www.usnews.com/best-graduate-schools/top-law-schools/law-rankings
4. Duckworth, A.L., et al. 2007. "Grit: perseverance and passion for long-term goals." *Journal of Personality and Social Psychology* 92.6:1087.
5. *Id.*
6. *Id.*
7. *Id.*
8. *Id.*
9. *Id.*

Helen B. Bloch

Meet Life's Challenges with Perseverance and You Will Succeed!

I'm a 21st-century attorney of the sandwich generation. It follows the motto, "Need something done? Ask a busy person to do it." I have taken care of an ill mother, raised two small boys, and participated in bar association, charitable, and professional organizations, all while growing a law practice from ground zero. Technology and the flexibility to work in nontraditional environments have played key roles.

Let's return to 2007, at which point I had been practicing for nine years. I was an associate at Bellows and Bellows, P.C., where I learned a great deal about running a business. My clients were interesting and diverse. I could be counseling an executive in an employment matter who was about to be terminated as to how to position her/himself for a severance package to preparing for an out-of-state arbitration on a securities matter before FINRA. In between, I handled estate planning, divorce, business disputes, and whatever else came through the door.

Fortuitously, in the summer of 2007 I bumped into a colleague whom I had had cases against when I was an assistant corporation counsel. We decided to catch up at Starbucks. Our meeting reminded me of the various other areas in which I had experience from my prosecutorial and defense days at the city that I had not encountered in private practice. I say "fortuitously" because our reunion led me to open my own general practice, which enabled me to take care of my mother and raise my children without risk of losing my job. This is key because, in today's society, a family needs two revenue generators to survive. Because I had my own practice, my income never dwindled from the salary I made as an associate even when family needs required that I spend little time in the office.

When I started my firm in the fall of 2007, it was on a shoestring budget. After I mailed notices detailing my diverse practice, I was pleasantly surprised by the response. Police officers who remembered me from my city days asked for help in landlord–tenant disputes. Executives recommended me to their colleagues who were being terminated. Friends asked that I help form their companies and review their contracts. Government attorneys who recalled that I had workers' compensation experience recommended that I assist their injured buddies. Real estate folks who remembered that I was a prosecutor asked that I defend their interests against the city.

Truly I was enjoying the practice that I was building and the freedom to be my own boss. The joys of freedom hit me about six months in. While on my way to the office from the Wheaton courthouse I stopped at a mall to buy a purse. My phone rang. It was a client for whom I was in the midst of negotiating a separation package. We were on a deadline and an answer was needed ASAP. I stepped into the store dressing room and walked the client through what needed to be done. As I went up to the cashier to buy my purse I realized that this one call just paid the bill. What a great feeling to know that I could support myself even while straying from the office.

In March 2009, my first child Megill was born. I was determined to breastfeed, raise my son, and continue working. The last thing I wanted to happen was to lose my practice that was just beginning to flourish. There were times when Megill would be resting on my "breast friend" suckling, while I was on the phone with clients or responding to emails. Before Megill started daycare, I arranged for my husband to watch him while I was in court. New client meetings were scheduled around Megill's feedings and my husband's availability. Clients simply thought I was a busy person and were happy to meet at mutually agreed upon times. They were unaware that I had been pregnant and was a new mom.

Megill was three months old when the bomb hit. My mother, who had Parkinson's disease, was out of money. Her caregivers walked out on her. Shortly thereafter she sustained an infection and was hospitalized. Overnight I had to petition the court to become her guardian. This was no simple task. A guardian-ad-litem was appointed, and each decision I made was scrutinized and subject to court order.

While maintaining my law practice and keeping my pledge to breastfeed a newborn, I had to manage my mother's healthcare and finances, clean her apartments, and research facilities that were suitable for her needs. Emotionally, it was hard to keep it together. My mother needed me. It broke my heart to see her in the condition she was in, knowing that my son and children-to-be would never know the strong, brilliant woman who shaped me into who I am. I wanted to do more for her, but could not because I had to keep working, raise a son, and be a wife.

I was heartbroken over my mother's steady decline and frustrated with her institutional life. In 2010, I brought her home with a 24/7 caregiver. Emotionally, her care became easier. However, I was now responsible for two additional people: mom and caregiver. I arranged her social calendar and visits with doctors, and bought the household supplies. But I had peace of mind that she was in good hands.

I missed working from the office for days on end. I spoke with clients from waiting rooms, in the car, or at my mother's apartment while cleaning or checking on her and her caregiver. I reviewed documents and agreements from wherever I needed to be. My schedule was anything but routine. Despite the challenges, I maintained a steady stream of income—an impossible feat had I not been my own boss.

I have an amazing husband who continues to pitch in with child-rearing responsibilities. Still, it is only I who can maintain my practice. While at times I have forgone networking opportunities that could have generated significant business, I always returned calls from potential clients and never neglected a client; I just worked in nontraditional settings and at my own schedule with deadlines in mind.

My family situation has stabilized. Nevertheless, as a mother who wants to participate in school activities, having my own law practice gives me the flexibility to participate in life's occasions—whether mundane or grand. There are times when I will work late into the evening because I know that I have an upcoming hearing or deposition around the same time as my son's school assembly. I love the ability to schedule most work deadlines around my children's needs without answering to anyone as to my whereabouts.

My practice has continued to flourish. I am back to attending events and engaging in the extracurricular activities that are necessary to building and maintaining a business. Luckily, I can include office support staff, in addition to my immediate family, when I calculate my yearly financial goals.

My mother passed away March 8, 2015. I had no regrets. As we say in my mother's tongue, it was *basheret*—or meant to be—that I took the risk to work for myself. Had I not done so, I could not have maintained a job and taken care of my family.

Helen B. Bloch is the principal of the Law Offices of Helen Bloch, P.C. in Chicago, a general practice firm, which includes employment, real estate and related municipal code violations, workers' compensation, business counseling, and corporate services.
www.blochpc.com

Robin Bresky

My story of grit and perseverance started early in my childhood with a passion for long-term goals and developing my abilities with a growth mindset. But I will fast-forward to the time when the road was wide open, just prior to law school. I was 24 years old and had been married and working for two years, supporting my husband and myself while he was in medical school. We moved to upstate New York from our home in South Florida so he could begin a medical internship program. While he was in his internship, we both applied to programs around the country: he sought a residency program and I applied for law school. We both found programs that met our needs in Illinois.

We packed up the car and headed to Chicago with our nine-month-old son. I entered a four-year evening program at Chicago Kent College of Law. I chose it because the professors in the evening program were the same as those in the full-time program. I studied when my son napped, and I had babysitters (teenagers who lived in our building) on the many nights when my husband had to work. Those were the days when resident physicians worked for many days and through the nights with no time off. A few years into the program, we had our second baby. I took a few months off while she was an infant. However, I went back to the program full-time so I could graduate with my class. By the time I returned home to South Florida, I had two toddlers and a law degree! Fortunately, I was still married to a supportive husband—apparently not the norm when there are two rigorous academic programs during the first years of marriage.

I began my legal career as an assistant state's attorney. I loved the job, but sometimes I had to leave home before the kids went to school and returned after they went to bed. Although that was difficult, I was getting fantastic experience and the children were well cared for. However, there came a point where the security procedures of the office changed due to death threats made to several local judges. Assistant state's attorneys had previously been allowed to enter through the back gate, the same as the judges, but the new procedure meant that I had to stand in line to go through the security check and metal detectors with the defendants we were prosecuting. As a young mother, I was so concerned with the security that I went to the State's Attorney and made my concerns known. During that in-person meeting, my concerns were dismissed as unfounded. The State's Attorney told me that there were no serious criminals coming through the misdemeanor satellite division where I worked, so I could safely stand in line with the defendants prior to the security checkpoint.

I disagreed, as I had seen the prior record of those defendants; and although I was prosecuting them for misdemeanors, many of the defendants had very long rap sheets that included serious felonies. I decided my safety needed to come first. Many years later we were made aware that two of the 9/11 terrorists came through that very same satellite courthouse shortly after I resigned. In addition to grit, gut feelings and intuition are important. I find that I make the correct decision when I follow my instincts, and I have regrets when I don't follow them.

I had known that I wanted to do appeals ever since my last two years of law school when I was an extern in the Cook County State's Attorney's office and assisted with appeals. During the mid-1990s the appellate department I was assigned to was nicknamed "the mommy track." It was not the reason I was drawn to appeals, but I did have a great deal in common with the women who worked there as they were working mothers. I found great mentors there along with my law school mentor, Susan Meyer, who was a few years ahead of me in law school and also was a working mother. (Susan went on to establish her own law practice and became a remarkable attorney. She is now with the Chicago office of Nixon Peabody, concentrating on intellectual property and franchise law.) Susan was a great model for balancing motherhood with a law practice. She taught me that you are only as good as your reputation, and decades later she still gives me sound advice.

When I started my own firm 16 years ago, my long-term goal was to concentrate exclusively on appeals and complex litigation support. Yet, I had gained a lot of trial experience with the

State's Attorney's Office, and I decided to start with somewhat of a general practice. At first I did whatever I felt I was competent to handle, including some criminal defense, litigation support, and real estate law. Then I began doing pro bono appeals with the Legal Aid Society of Palm Beach County. I took advantage of a mentoring program with the Florida Bar where I was connected to established appellate attorneys with whom I could discuss my cases and seek guidance. I immediately got involved with my local voluntary bar association, eventually working my way up to president. I also got involved at the local and state level of the Florida Association for Women Lawyers (FAWL), ultimately becoming president of my chapter and then president of the state FAWL. Additionally, I became involved at the national level with the National Conference of Women's Bar Associations. I took on leadership roles within organizations I wanted to be a part of. I became invested in those organizations and really liked the attorneys who did the same thing. Ultimately, I became, and still am, a member of the board of directors for the legal aid society in my county. My firm continues to do pro bono work for legal aid.

When the firm first opened, I networked a good part of the day and did the majority of my brief writing late into the night. At the beginning, I worked out of my home and was thrilled to have early mornings with my children and to pick them up at the bus stop in the afternoons. As the years grew, the firm grew. Fortunately, I had successes in the appellate arena. A few years after I began, I hired an associate and found office space. We have continued to grow, and we are now a boutique appellate law firm with offices in Boca Raton, West Palm Beach, and Miami. The firm now has seven attorneys that include myself as partner, three associates, three full-time of-counsel attorneys, and four staff members. I have worked hard to build the firm. There have been the typical incidents of being erroneously perceived as a court reporter, secretary, or associate. I've experienced extraordinarily inappropriate comments by male colleagues and many other similar frustrating incidents—some of which are now laughable. Most important, however, I am proud of what I have accomplished. I believe grit is essential to achieving your goals. I would advise young women embarking on their careers to constantly be open to growth, follow your gut instinct as often as possible, and find the grit that you know is inside of you!

Robin Bresky is the principal of The Law Offices of Robin Bresky in Boca Raton, Florida, and is an appellate attorney practicing in civil, administrative, and criminal appeals and complex litigation support matters, including family law, probate/guardianship, personal injury, and commercial litigation. www.breskyappellate.com

Brenda J. Edwards

Growing up in rural Wisconsin, between Janesville and Beloit, I encountered grit and growth at a young age. I learned that law is something you have to fight for, something that tries to flee, but something you can attain.

My story begins with a young girl, sibling to four brothers, with two parents. Her father moved the family quite a bit until landing a job at a coal-powered plant and getting the family a stable home. The little girl was seven. Her mother was a full-time mom. Her father, trying to make ends meet, took overtime, worked holidays, rotated shifts, and didn't take sick days. He was the epitome of work ethic. When her father was not working, he would take the family to parks and lakes in the summer and to stores to browse in the winter. The classic rural family. Except it wasn't. It was also like *Lord of the Flies.*

The little girl was fourth in a family of five. One of her older brothers tried to help her. He made her a homemade "zapper" for self-defense. But it was not enough. The little girl was abused intermittently from ages 6 through 14 when her parents were not around. At age 9, she knew she could overcome this—with music. She wanted to play a xylophone and made one out of cardboard. She received a mini keyboard for Christmas. She began teaching herself how to play the piano. But she needed more. So, she excelled with school and exercise.

When the young girl was 11, her mother was diagnosed with ovarian cancer and endured multiple surgeries and rounds of chemotherapy in Madison, Wisconsin, before passing away when the girl was 14 years old. The young girl began cooking and cleaning for the family at age 11 to help out.

A year after her mother's death, the girl's father had to find another job because the coal-powered plant he was working at was failing emission standards. Every employee was out a job. They were moving to Washington in a week. So, that week, a large dumpster was rented and the family threw away what they had and only took what they could carry in the car. In the blink of an eye, the little girl had left what she had known in Wisconsin.

In Washington, she'd endured a brother stealing her money (so she got a checking account), some of her brothers selling her things while she worked (so they could buy pot), and getting locked out of the house after work at 10 p.m. some days when her father was working late, as well. But she was still able to complete all of her homework, though at times she would fall asleep in class. She was still able to play the piano for her church. She was still able to bake cakes for people she knew when they'd have a birthday. There was a lot she could do, so she did.

However, this young woman didn't think she was smart enough to go to college. No one in her family had ever graduated from college. Only the rich people did that. She was ready to join the Air Force and travel the world. She was ready for freedom. At a physical screening at Fairchild Air Force Base in Spokane, Washington, she hit another wall. She couldn't join. She had migraines. No one would take her. It was the end of her senior year of high school and options were limited. She had been abused, her mother died, her stuff was stolen, and now she couldn't get out. She couldn't have freedom. She was stuck.

The young woman did what no one in her family had done and applied for college. She thought it was too late to get in, but she was accepted. She was valedictorian of her high school and did okay on the SATs, so she told herself she got lucky. Got lucky this time, but she couldn't mess this up.

This young woman didn't waste any time in college. She sat up straight in the front row in class and didn't care about what other people thought. She cared about graduating. She studied the course book and took only required classes after her first trimester. She studied in the summer as well, working part-time for the university while writing music and exercising as a hobby. Her father worked extra shifts to pay for her college and was proud. She graduated in three years with the highest honors in English and special education and became a special education teacher in Oregon.

This young woman got married, had a son, and got her master's degree in education but still felt a void. She didn't think she was smart enough to be a lawyer, but she had seen so much in her life. She wanted to help others. She took the road less traveled, earning a Juris Doctor degree from Taft Law School in Santa Ana, California, so that she could continue her job while attending law school. She studied for and passed the Baby Bar in San Francisco, California. She printed sample essays from prior bar exams to improve her writing. She kept her Kaplan series for all of her classes and studied the multiple-choice questions over and over again. She studied the questions and sample essays in her *Gilbert* series. She wrote several performance exams to gain fluency in the process. She took control and was ready, passing the California bar exam her first try in July 2013.

Another wall. Her husband and her son didn't want to move. If she moved, it may cause a divorce, but if she stayed, she couldn't practice law. After a couple of trips to California by herself, this young woman, now 31, decided to open a virtual law practice in transactional law: wills, trusts, contracts, powers of attorney over financial affairs, and advance health care directives. She is now working as a virtual attorney and, as a twist, still also working as a special education teacher, serving as the area's qualified trainer for extended assessment. She has written and published on Amazon an educational book about the self-contained classroom (*The Self-Contained Classroom: What You Didn't Learn in College and Will Need to Know for Your Job*), as well as a legal how-to for wills and trusts (*California Estate Law: Wills and Trusts Made Easy*). She is planning a mobile attorney workshop in select California cities, where she will meet with clients one-on-one to get all of their estate planning needs done in one day. She is not giving up. Her story is still just beginning.

For anyone reading this, my advice to you is to be the change you want in your life. In adversity, see the cup as half full instead of half empty and remain grateful for what you have while striving to obtain what you don't. Set your goals and achieve them, because you can, no matter where you come from or what you've endured, because when you open your eyes each day you have another chance, another opportunity, to make a difference for yourself and for others.

Brenda J. Edwards is the founder and manager of CA Legal Help You Can Afford with Brenda Edwards, based out of Seaside, Oregon, where she focuses on estate law, contracts, and business formations. www.calegalhelpwithbrendaedwards.com

Leslie A. Jaluria

My first understanding about life is that work is essential. No matter the situation, work meant survival and, if lucky, prosperity.

I was raised in a predominantly blue-collar town in New Jersey. My mother was from Costa Rica, and my father was an electrician whose family emigrated from Poland to America through Ellis Island. From a young age, I witnessed what hard work meant. My parents worked more than anyone else I knew to give my brother and me a better life, including the possibility of a college education.

As a child, I told myself that one day I would go to college though it felt foreign to me. Against the odds and stereotypes, I followed my intuition and forged a fearless path that led me to graduate college as a chemist. I later became a wife, mother, and then law school graduate. Along the way, I learned the value of expressing empathy and remaining authentic. As an attorney today and mother of three young boys, I work on maintaining creativity and constantly revisiting what it means to be happy. In the following paragraphs, I further discuss the themes introduced here in two parts: Part 1. Fluidity & Negativity—Defining yourself and maintaining your internal drive while using external negativity as motivation; and Part 2. Sustaining Creativity—Cultivating your happiness today.

Part 1. Fluidity & Negativity

How you define yourself shapes the role you play in the main act, your life.

Discover what external concepts or beliefs you use to define your inner self. Think of it this way: your past does not define your future self. By learning how to find these answers, one can forge a life path to success. Constantly work to reevaluate your life plan, because no single plan is going to work. A life plan must be fluid by having an innate flexibility to incorporate lessons learned. I periodically revisit several memories that have affected my life's course to further deepen my understanding of their impact and to gain more insight into the person I was, am, and have yet to become.

I find myself reflecting upon particular moments that have been pivotal in defining my journey in life. At times, I recall a moment I experienced in my teens while preparing for the SAT exam. It was the 1990s and my SAT prep course was in a teacher's smoky basement with fellow classmates. As the teacher puffed away chain smoking and reviewing questions, he asked what I wanted to study in college. I told him I was thinking of becoming a chemist. I'll never forget how he scoffed at my response and told me I did not have enough math skills to succeed in chemistry. I thought to myself, how is that possible? Isn't college all about learning and discovery? Why can't I take the necessary courses to earn a science degree? I was determined to use the negativity to drive past all the deafening stereotypes around girls in science. It was not an easy task, but I kept my focus and worked toward transforming negative energy into deliberate acts of productive work toward my goals.

In the years since, I have used this negative smoky memory, along with other such brief exchanges, to motivate and fuel my desire in becoming a successful female chemist and licensed attorney. If I had accepted the teacher's negative comment as part of my inner dialogue, I would not have studied calculus, nor would I have experienced the incredible world of quantum mechanics while earning my undergraduate degree. This example is one of several brief exchanges that I have learned to cultivate to transform myself and stay focused on my goals, all the while reinventing the stories I tell myself to achieve the truths of my life plan.

Regardless of the lessons learned, I believe it is vital to remain flexible in your pursuit of habit building and career development. One of the hardest times I have experienced was graduating law school while pregnant with our second child, and taking the bar exam eight months pregnant. I learned that if an opportunity does not seem ideal, maintain a positive perspective and redefine your motivation to get it done for your own benefit in the end. Just like training for a race or obscure mountain trek, you must train for the life you want to live.

Part 2. Sustaining Creativity

It is necessary to be aware of your state of happiness while developing and working through your life plan. On a daily basis, recall your motivations and the truths you live by. Be present to experience the loving life you've worked so hard to build and cultivate. Practice empathy to remain humble and authentic because if you hide your true self from others, you are also hiding from yourself. Be cautious not to focus heavily on the external and become soulless, for you will deteriorate in your own self-demise. Often, I visualize the actions of women, such as Rosa Parks, who have made their mark in history to deepen my empathy and understanding of the risks involved. When empathy and authenticity are not practiced, your environment suffers and you will struggle more to reach your goals.

Don't disregard the small steps, for they are a necessary part of the process. There is no reason to waste energy over a difficult situation that you chose and are now not able to change. Over time, one can build the confidence to calculate smart risks that do not damage but allow for being creative. I learned this lesson when I started law school with a one-year-old child at home, and a nearly three-hour daily commute. I thought creatively and began to work during my daily drive by obtaining some audio case files and legal analysis.

Summary

The extraordinary is not born from the pursuit of an ordinary day. Progress is change. Immobile forces break down; they destabilize because environments will always change. One must be prepared for change to first identify and take on new challenges that, in the end, leave you in a better position than you had originally imagined. Life is about short-term struggle for long-term gain, not the pursuit of short-term gain for long-term struggle.

Some say "[i]t takes just as much work to do something mediocre as to do something legendary" (Mike Maples, Jr.). People may call you crazy, which is a typical perspective of the majority in areas of great innovation. To remain rigid is to refrain from cultivating your passion and creativity. Value is subjective in the end. Individual creativity and passion drive wonderful social change. One could say there is no creativity without the necessary grit in using rejection to fuel motivation.

Leslie A. Jaluria handles regulatory affairs within the life sciences industry in San Francisco, and also is the principal and founder of Jaluria Law LLC, where she focuses on estate planning, intellectual property, and business issues. www.jaluria.com

Barbara N. Lyons

I grew up in a violent household; there were no laws against spousal and child abuse back then, and my mom with six kids and an eighth grade education had no options.

I went to work outside the house at the age of 13 to get away from the violence, to earn money to help with the household expenses, and to save to get me through high school and then college. I made the decision early on to be financially independent so I would never have to depend on a man for financial security.

I didn't think I was very smart; being an abused kid leaves with you an internal wall of shame that for me included a belief that I may be clever and hardworking, but not smart. But I knew how to get the job done, so I did well in high school, worked my way through college, and graduated with honors. The idea of going to law school never entered my mind.

My initial career choice toward financial independence took me to a small bank in Boston. I was hired as a manager trainee making $110/week. Soon after, the bank hired a guy just out of high school who made $120/week. I asked the manager why the new guy was making more than me with only a high school degree and was told it was because he was a man and was going to have a family one day, and he will have to support his family, whereas I am a woman and would get married and have a husband to take care of me.

Around this time, I had a friend going off to law school who convinced me I was smart enough to become an attorney. So, in response to the lesson on banking hiring practices, I quit the bank and decided to go to law school.

Like the SATs, if you could flunk the LSATs, I did. According to the test, I was not going to be a success in law school. But I was determined, so I applied to the evening division of Temple Law School and following my first (successful) year, transferred into the day school.

I still felt like I had to work harder than anyone to get through law school. I felt like a fraud, and I was there by the skin of my teeth, and soon someone will figure out that I didn't belong. But I was on a mission to learn how to think like a lawyer. I graduated, passed the bar on the first try, and got a job in a small firm in Bucks County. Bucks County and the small law firm were not my first choice—the Philadelphia district attorney's office was, but they didn't offer me a job. However, this failure, if you will, provided the route to my professional success.

I became a partner in three years and had a baby. Three years later I had a second baby and then had to leave that firm when I learned that my partner was playing fast and loose with the clients' escrow accounts. I had to sue him for my financial interest in the firm. But at this point, I had a solid client base and the flexibility to choose where I would go and settled on a small firm in Doylestown, where I made partner within a year. Then I had my third child. I have been married throughout my career in law. I won't even go into the work necessary to have a successful marriage.

Women in the profession can't ignore the sometimes-stronger need for motherhood. I detest the word "balance" as it applies to women who work and prefer to see the women in the profession I know, who are also mothers, achieve excellence at both, but not necessarily at the same time. They are excellent with their clients or in front of a jury, and excellent at reading to their child or perusing the *What to Expect* series on childbirth and childrearing. Women in the profession of law are not just lawyers. They are equally and at all times mothers, volunteers, homemakers, daughters, and so many other things.

From the beginning of my law career to the birth of my third child, I was a civil trial attorney. Preparing for trials and making the billable hours were a challenge I met, but when the litigation practice came to interfere with my drive for excellence as a mother, I had to make a change. I couldn't hear my children because the bits and pieces of my clients' cases were constantly rattling around in my brain. But I couldn't and wouldn't even contemplate giving up my work.

I was teaching peer mediation at the time as a volunteer for the Bucks County Bar Association and came to realize that, if I could teach mediation to middle school students, I should be able to practice it. I had 15 years' experience with plaintiff and defense litigation, so I felt I could learn to approach both sides of an issue and be received as a neutral attorney. I decided to leave my litigation practice and spent a year taking every course and class and reading every book on the practice of neutral law. At the end of that year, I felt competent to establish a neutral practice, so I wrote to every attorney I had ever dealt with and told them of my new practice as a mediator and neutral arbitrator. It took a while, but I started booking cases, and now I am the Bucks County alternative to the large mediation and arbitration services in Philadelphia.

This change in practice afforded me the time and temperament to be the mom I wanted to be, one that could hear and attend to the needs of her children

I made a promise to myself as a child to put away all men who abuse their wives, even though at the time I had no idea how I would accomplish this. I discovered how early in my career and spent 30 years representing women in protection from abuse actions as a volunteer for legal aid. My other promise to become financially independent has been fulfilled and, for many years now, I have lectured and mentored women on how to achieve financial independence.

That secret belief that I was intellectually inferior turned into a positive love of learning not only to improve my law practice, but also to try new things. I started piano lessons in my 30s and voice lessons in my 40s. Now I sing in several choirs and special solo performances. I am always working toward something. I am always prepared, focused, and committed. I do what I say I am going to do, because I came to realize that one of the most important attributes of an attorney, or to anyone for that matter, is her reputation. I have always striven for one of integrity.

I learned vigilance by watching my abusive dad to detect his moods, which gave me the ability to read micro-expressions and hear what is not being said—both valuable tools in mediation. He also was a bigot and a racist, and because I was not going to be like him, he unwittingly taught me how to be accepting and nonjudgmental of all people, an essential character skill for the practice of neutral law.

I honestly don't know if I was born gritty or the circumstances into which I was born made me this way. I suspect it's both. All I know is that I scored high on (your) grit test.

Thank you for this opportunity.

Barbara N. Lyons is the founder of Bucks County Mediation and Arbitration Center in Doylestown, Pennsylvania, where she serves as a civil law mediator and neutral arbitrator. www.bcmac.org

Dena Silliman Nielson

When considering the impact of grit and growth mindset on the advancement of women lawyers and how this may have affected my own career, I'm reminded of just how random and accidental things happen in life.

I knew I wanted to be a lawyer since about age 12, but I never had the opportunity to go to college until I was in my 30s and married with children. After finally completing my undergrad degree at age 37, I spent the next few months trying to figure out how to pay for law school and preparing for and taking the LSAT. It was several months later before I finally got the letter that I had been accepted at the University of Oklahoma Law School. I was so relieved, happy, and filled with optimism. Entering classes that fall, the first order of business was the orientation. At that orientation, a girl gave a presentation on the *American Indian Law Review*. I was so interested in that because in undergrad I had taken Oklahoma history, which was really the history of how the Indians were displaced and how many tribes had been forced to settle in Oklahoma. It was one of my favorite classes so, of course, I immediately wanted to be a member of that organization. I was told that there might be one problem—I'm a white girl from Arkansas with absolutely no connection to any tribe. In fact, I had never really known an American Indian personally before that day. Luckily I was misinformed, because membership on the *American Indian Law Review* is open to anyone interested in working hard. I immediately signed up and thus began a journey that I would have never expected.

In my second year of law school, I was looking for a clerk or intern position and wanted it to be in Norman, Oklahoma, where the university is located. As it happened, or some would call it fate, another student on the *American Indian Law Review* mentioned to me that Browning Pipestem's office was hiring clerks and that he liked to hire students from the *American Indian Law Review*—but she warned me that I should not take it personally if he did not hire me since I am not American Indian. I recognized Mr. Pipestem's name, as he had recently been a speaker at the law school, and I had read his bio that had been posted along with his picture. He was a member of both the Otoe Tribe and the Osage Tribe and had graduated from Oklahoma University Law School in 1968. His practice exclusively represented tribes. I hesitated for about a week but finally decided he would have to tell me himself that he would not hire me because I'm non-American Indian.

I called and made the appointment for the next day to speak to Mr. Pipestem about a clerk position. I arrived at his office at the appointed time of 2 p.m., but the door was locked and the lights were off. My first thought? He must have somehow found out that I'm non-American Indian and he's not even going to bother showing up. As I was about to turn and leave, the elevator opened behind me and Mr. Pipestem came bustling out apologizing for being late as he walked to the door. He wore red athletic shorts and a white polo shirt—I thought maybe I had interrupted his golf game! But when we sat down for the interview, it was immediately apparent that he was not interested in my race, gender, or anything else; he was only interested in someone who wanted to become the best attorney she could be. And that was me! He hired me on the spot and gave me his promise that, if I was willing to put in the work, he was willing to be my mentor and help me get through law school and beyond. We both kept our promises made that day.

During my eight years with Pipestem and Associates, my learning curve was steep, and I was out of my comfort zone most of the time. Although I had worked as a paralegal before law school, I was totally unfamiliar with many of the environments I was immediately thrust into—tribal courts, CFR Courts, as well as administrative courts with the Bureau of Indian Affairs, the Veterans Administration, and other state and federal agencies. But I quickly made new friends with many of the people we represented and worked with and had experiences that enriched my life and made me a better lawyer and person. Mr. Pipestem had been an attorney for more than 20 years when we met—about as long as I've been an attorney now. He was an excellent teacher and mentor, and, truthfully, I can't imagine my practice now without him and the influence he had on me.

Unfortunately, in August 1999, Mr. Pipestem passed away. I tried to continue our work in Oklahoma, but it became apparent very quickly that the practice would not be the same without Mr. Pipestem. He really had a larger than life presence in the firm and within Indian Country in general. I decided that I needed new scenery and possibly a new purpose. Within a few months, I moved to Colorado to work with a small firm that focused on American Indian housing. I stayed with that firm about 4 years but, ultimately, knew that I needed to go out on my own.

At 53 years old, knowing only a handful of people and having never appeared in a state court in Colorado, I opened my own solo practice. This practice, for one reason or another, slowly moved away from the American Indian law roots I established early on as I found it increasingly difficult to maintain my practice as an active Indian law practitioner. I was living in a state with only two tribes, all of my connections were in Oklahoma, and maybe most importantly I found I had little desire to continue in Indian law. I wanted a change, but it scared me to think about leaving something I knew so well to start doing something totally different. Yet it had to be done or this firm would be very short-lived.

My practice now is exclusively family law. In many ways, this has not been an easy transition. I changed states and needed to be licensed in both states, I left federal court practice and started practicing in state courts with unfamiliar rules, and I had to learn an entire new area of the law. This is not an undertaking for the faint of heart, I assure you. That is especially true when you do it as a solo practitioner. However, one can make new friends and have trusted colleagues. One can work hard and learn a new area of the law. And one can appear in state courts and have just as gratifying a practice as federal court provides. But I don't think it would have happened at all without grit and determination and a growth mindset for my practice.

Dena Silliman Nielson is the owner of Dena Silliman Nielson, P.C. in Westminster, Colorado, where she focuses on family law, mediation, and appellate matters. www.linkedin.com/in/dena-nielson-5a246bb

Valerie C. Raudonis

The incessant rolling of the waves reminds me that we are but a drop of water in an ocean of humanity.

Born to second generation Lithuanian and Polish immigrants who were raised during the Depression era, and who became self-made professionals as a teacher and as a lawyer, I observed, was influenced by, and ultimately learned at a young age the benefits of traveling limitlessly in my mind. As a middle child, surrounded by three brothers, the comfort of family connectivity formed a life-long foundation from which I follow my mindful journeys.

My mother, demonstrating her own growth mindset, told me that I could be whatever I chose to be. She told me to be a teacher, like her, or a nurse. I said I wanted to be a marine biologist. She said, "No," because it would mean that I'd have to live near an ocean, but that may not be possible if my husband's work brought us elsewhere! At the time, I listened to my mother's traditional advice.

I then decided that I wanted to help people and become a lawyer, like my father, but not be my father. The plan was to work with my father, who was a true general practitioner solo lawyer. Some folks who knew him would say that he was "a country lawyer." In the 1970s, he knew a little about everything, which is different now that lawyers specialize and know everything about a few things. My father died during my second year of law school. Approximately two years later, in 1978, I "re-opened" his office. The rent was $150 a month located in the Odd Fellows Building on Main Street in our hometown of Nashua, New Hampshire. My first client, who was a friend of my eldest brother, consulted with me about a white truck he had purchased, but he had changed his mind about the color he wanted. The client hired me to draft and send a letter to the dealer, and although I counseled the client that this effort might not achieve the result he wanted—a different colored truck—I typed up the letter and was paid my first fee in the amount of $25.

I was ecstatic. The client was pleased. I telephoned my mother to excitedly explain that I had my first paying client. She responded, "Alright. Now that you have accomplished becoming a lawyer, are you ready to have children?" I was shocked and surprised with my mother's traditional viewpoint, especially because she was the one person who had planted the seed some 10 years earlier that I could be anything I chose to be. I carefully explained to her that I had not come this far just to achieve it: no, having become a lawyer, my purpose was and is to BE a lawyer. I was feeling my father's absence. Due to his death, he was not available to offer me emotional support. And maybe he wouldn't have either. After all, in the grand scheme of law practice, this first legal service that I provided to my first paying client was such a relatively small accomplishment. But for me, and maybe partially due to my father's absence, I felt an exhilaration of finally arriving at this point, solo. And having arrived, I relished plodding forward and demonstrating my own true grit and commitment to the profession despite my mother's unsupportive reaction. So this time, I did not follow my mother's traditional advice. My focus was to dedicate my energy to the practice of helping people. My passion was to explore the challenges surrounding the assistance of clients and to work with them to evolve their problems to a satisfactory resolution. The passion of motherhood had to wait. And it did wait, but gratefully eventually arrived.

Shy and sensitive to a fault, I am transfigured when working as an advocate for my client. I learned the depth of personal advocacy and grit when my son was being bullied in elementary school. We talked with the principal. We talked with the parents. Recognizing that change must come from within, we enrolled our son, as well as our daughter, in taekwondo classes. Both children continued with their practice until achieving their black belt. The taekwondo course of mental studies and physical exercises assisted their self-esteem and continues to positively influence their own current professional paths with tenacity. My son will complete law school this year and will work as a patent lawyer. My daughter is pursuing a master's degree in occupational therapy, because she desires to combine science with helping people. Family first is my creed.

After a dozen or so years of practicing law, a new lawyer asked me for advice while opening his solo law office. My reply: Show up and BE present 100 percent with each person, whether client, lawyer, or other person related to the matter, such as court clerk, mediator, witness, etc. In a geographically shrinking world, with an increasing population, and an excess of lawyers, respect and ethics become even more paramount. While a personally referred client may be the best client in some respects, the most common manner in which a client arrives to their chosen lawyer is now via the impersonal Internet.

The client wants satisfaction, and I want to satisfy their legal needs in an ethical manner. This is not easy. Not all clients understand ethics. Some folks who understand it don't want it if it interferes with accomplishing their goal. But we as lawyers know that laws reflect society's behavior. Laws define us as a civilization. The interpretation of the laws and the ethical representation of the clients affected by the laws are the essence of practicing law. At the end of each day I look in the mirror and I find peace—amidst the legal and emotional turmoil—that the job has been well done, and that means everything to me.

An introvert, who wants to help people, I naturally speak quietly, efficiently, and without excess of words or drama, so that when I do speak, it makes a difference. Listening and hearing the client's needs, stated and unstated, is most important. Then I proceed with interpreting the facts and translating the laws for each situation to explain to the client, and when appropriate, to the court, and now increasingly in mediations. It is all a process. A step-by-step journey. The going has to be good, albeit difficult; the getting there is the reward.

Being able to put "bread on the table" through the practice of a solo existence means continuity of attention to the needs of the clients and regular demonstrations of grit. With each of the two caesarean births of my children, I was medically advised to stay home for a minimum of 10 days. My assistant brought to my home the mail to review and provide responses, letters to sign, and documents to prepare, and I worked (without painkillers to avoid interfering with my thought processes). This was in the 1980s, prior to the reliance on computers and the Internet. On the 11th day post-surgery, I was driving to the office to be present with my clients. Later, in 2010, while temporarily wheel-chaired due to two broken toes and a broken wrist, I experienced the same situation. Attention to my clients did not cease due to my physical hindrances. The work of helping my clients also moved me forward with my healing. While my physical energy went to healing my broken bones, my emotional and mental energy focused on assisting my clients. Likewise, during my times of emotional distress of experiencing two divorces, the death of my mother, and the deaths of my two brothers, the dedication to "showing up and being fully present" were the keel and the rudder in the stormy winds of adversity on the ocean of humanity that is the practice of law.

When helping others, I am most alive. When I am alone, my fuel is replenished to resume. Walking in nature shows me the innate and beautiful arrangement of our world.

Valerie C. Raudonis is the founder of Raudonis Law Offices in Nashua, New Hampshire, where she focuses on family law, probate, estate planning, mediation, and collaborative law. www.raudonislawfirm.com

Karen Green Rosin

As a sole practitioner building my family law and mediation practice in Los Angeles, I very much enjoy being my own boss. I am fortunate that I was able to be supported financially (and emotionally) both while I was in law school and then more recently, while breaking into family law and mediation. I married my husband at age 21, one week after graduating from UCLA with a degree in Theater Arts, but my ability to persevere in working toward long-term goals started well before that. I was the kid who kept climbing back on the bike until she didn't fall anymore, setting my sights on the future from an early age. I knew I would need a scholarship to go to college, so whatever other teenage shenanigans I got into, I always did my homework, always studied for tests, joined clubs and the volleyball team and even the cheerleading squad in my very small NYC prep school . . . and, oh yeah, I became president of the student council, for good measure. Yet when someone once called me an overachiever, I was offended: I thought I was just "fulfilling my potential."

After a brief stint in the Master of Fine Arts program in playwriting (again at UCLA), I enrolled in UCLA's law school. My thinking at the time was that I would practice entertainment law for a while and become a producer. To my surprise, I really loved the intellectual stimulation, but the fact is that law school is not easy. There is so much material to read, analyze, remember, and apply that it is hard to imagine surviving and thriving without grit—and then, there is the California bar exam.

Here is my nightmare story: During the multistate bar exam multiple-choice-question section (day two of three), I finished the morning session and realized that I had misnumbered. I had been filling in the little circles incorrectly. I immediately concluded that I had flunked the bar exam and started berating myself for being so careless—and to make matters worse, I had another whole day of testing to get through.

At the lunch break, I called my husband to break this news and told him I did not see how I could continue on with the test.

I was devastated. He was sympathetic at first, until he realized I was on the verge of throwing in the towel. That's when he yelled at me to "snap out of it!" He said, "You didn't go through three years of law school to give up now! You are going to stop crying and pull yourself together and go finish that test already! I know you can do it—and besides, you owe it to me for being a law school spouse for the past three years."

That did the trick. I beat back my depressed state enough to force myself to finish the exam. I was in a funk for a while, but by the time I started as an associate in the entertainment department of a prestigious Los Angeles firm, I was able to put it out of my mind and start to hope for the best. I received great training from terrific mentors working with interesting clients.

As the months passed and the test results were due to be announced, I decided to try some positive thinking. I visualized myself receiving a congratulatory letter saying, "We are pleased to inform you. . .," growing more relaxed and confident with each passing day. I noticed some of my peers, however, were now barely managing to keep food down, they were so anxious about their own results.

The end of the story is that I did pass that monster bar exam despite whatever I did wrong. From this experience, I learned that I really could benefit from more positive self-talking and recognized that anticipatory anxiety is (a) not based on reality and (b) causes suffering. I have had to re-learn this lesson hundreds of times since then.

Another law school experience illustrates that I had a "growth mindset." After the first semester, we first-years only had two final exams in December. I got Bs on each of those exams—and that became my grade for each class. (I had received maybe two Bs in my academic life at this point.) I did some on-campus recruiting interviews but saw that only the A students were getting offers for the summer following our first year. So I went out for law review instead—where I learned proofreading skills that have served me to this day and wrote an article that helped me land a terrific summer clerkship after my second year. I took my two Bs as meaning that I should relax about my grades and accept that maybe I just wasn't going to be an A student in law school, and I started to work only to understand the material. I enjoyed talking in class and continued to participate actively. I read all the cases, took thorough notes, and made detailed course outlines. I formed a fun study group but did not feel quite so pressured to "get results." Then I started to get As, and even A-plusses. At the end of my second year, I got a note from the dean in my mailbox: "Congratulations. We are pleased to inform you that you ranked seventh in your class" (of 350 students).

I also did something few students did: In addition to being on the law review, I took part in the moot court competition, and I won the Distinguished Advocate Award. I just kept pursuing opportunities, and most of the time, they turned out pretty darn well. I ended up being invited to the Order of the Coif, which was almost as much of a surprise as making Phi Beta Kappa in college. Time and again, my hard work was directly connected to mastery, as well as the accompanying rewards and praise, but most importantly to me, to increased confidence, which allowed me to venture into each new phase and challenge, however daunting they may have seemed at the outset.

After the birth of my first child in 1985, I tried to return to the 24/7, "always on call" schedule of an associate at a big firm, but it didn't work so well while nursing an infant. A senior associate after four years, I took a break from law practice after only a few months back on the job. I then raised three kids while returning to my earlier pursuits of acting and writing, which I found more child-friendly careers at the time. But I had always noticed that the Harriett Buhai Center for Family Law offered a free training in return for volunteer hours and decided to give it a try. My "legal" brain was rusty, and gears started turning that had been dormant for a number of years. It was daunting to learn new legal skills, to revisit "brief writing" and research and—gasp—to go into court myself and talk to the judge. But it was also exciting and stimulating and incredibly rewarding.

In my "second" law career, I have become a litigator specializing in family law matters. I have dealt with some vicious opposing counsel, some with very questionable ethics, and have been able to stick to my guns. I have seen judges being persnickety and insulting to counsel in court. But I am no longer a young woman who might have quaked with fear at such treatment, because I know their behavior is more about their own needs and flaws than a reflection of my worth, and I don't seek their approval to feel good about myself.

I have met and worked beside (and opposite) some excellent attorneys and rely on them for mentoring, advice, and general comradery; it is always comforting to know we are not alone. This leads me to state what I feel is an important life lesson: No one can go it alone, and a support network is a most vital asset. The support I received from my family, my husband, and his wonderful parents, as well as encouraging teachers, gave me the basis to go confidently out into the world and try to do good work. My mentors who became friends, my friends who became fans and boosters, my colleagues who have worked with me in the trenches, they are all people I can call upon when life deals me or my clients a bad hand—as it will for everyone at one time or another. That support is what everyone needs to succeed, and it is why one must never give up on building a support network, whether for a long life, or a long career. This is why I mentor others, and facilitate study groups, and give of my time. I am just paying it forward, with gratitude.

Karen Green Rosin is the founder of the Law and Mediation Offices of Karen Rosin in Los Angeles, where she focuses on family law. www.krosinlaw.com

Anne Thomas Sulton

I retired from the practice of law in 2015, after 30 years in solo practice as a trial lawyer. I litigated civil rights and social justice cases in state and federal trial and appellate courts across the United States.

In 2007, I was awarded the William Robert Ming Advocacy Award by the NAACP at its national convention in Detroit. This is considered the most coveted award an American civil rights attorney can receive. The NAACP began giving this award in 1973. I am the third woman to receive this award. When I began practicing law in 1985, I never dreamed I would even be considered for such a prestigious award.

In 1985, my goal was clear—at the end of my career as an attorney I wanted to be listed among those considered a "social engineer" as defined by Howard University Law School Dean Charles Hamilton Houston. In the 1930s, Houston said: "A lawyer's either a social engineer or . . . a parasite on society . . . A social engineer [is] a highly skilled, perceptive, sensitive lawyer who [understands] the Constitution of the United States and [knows] how to explore its uses in the solving of problems of local communities and in bettering conditions of the underprivileged citizens."

I was uncertain whether I would reach this lofty goal. The obstacles were daunting. Like many graduating from law school, I was saddled with what then felt like a staggeringly burdensome student loan debt. Unlike most of my classmates, I was married with three babies, all in diapers.

These challenges were offset by my distinct advantages. I already had a Ph.D. I had a husband with a steady job and the flexibility to take our children to school and coach their sporting teams. And, I am an African American female. That's right, my race and gender were an advantage because I usually was the only one appearing on behalf of plaintiffs in complex civil cases. Court clerks and judges remembered me; the all-white juries were fascinated to see a real live black lady trying a case.

In 1985, with the help of two white male attorneys, Ralph Kalal and Alan Habermehl in Madison, Wisconsin, I opened my law office. My first 1,000 days were filled with seemingly endless nights reading the exceedingly small print footnotes in appellate court decisions discussing the nuances of state and federal civil and criminal procedure and constitutional law, searching though the legislative history on substantive law, drafting complaints and motions, writing briefs, and preparing jury instructions.

My days often were spent sitting in courtrooms watching the best and brightest lawyers arguing their cases—I learned a great deal by just observing them. I also obtained valuable information by reading articles contained in the *ABA Journal* and taking ABA-sponsored CLE courses.

The work was mentally exhausting. On more than one occasion, I shed a tear while studying the facts presented by my clients' cases. During these quiet moments alone, it was then I that I fully understood the depth and reach and truly odious nature of racism and bigotry. Most of the challenged conduct was illegal—but all of it should have been. It was sad, frightening, and frustrating. It was frustrating because, too often, there was no legal cause of action or a woefully inadequate remedy at law.

However, this did not deter me. I decided to argue for an extension or modification of existing law based upon public policy considerations. For example, using my own money I filed a lawsuit in the U.S. District Court for the District of Colorado, essentially alleging that the city of Denver, State of Colorado, and halfway houses had an obligation to contact the Veterans Administration and try to get needed medical assistance for mentally disabled veterans before jailing them, revoking their parole, or kicking them out of the halfway house for minor infractions. The defendants' responses to this lawsuit included "failure to state a claim upon which relief can be granted." However, the defendants did modify their policies to include procedures facilitating mentally ill veterans' connections with the Veterans Administration to help ensure they had access to needed medications and counseling services.

Despite the challenges encountered, I enjoyed practicing law. Perhaps among my most fun moments was dealing with judges refusing to accommodate my child care schedule. I would ask judges to schedule hearings when my children were in school or at day care. When judges refused to so do, then I would bring my three small children to court with me, sit them in the front row behind my counsel's table, and give them toys with which they could play. Yes, my small children were very noisy and this distracted the judges and opposing lawyers—which gave me a huge advantage during these hearings. It took only a few months for judges and opposing counsel to get the message—schedule hearings when it makes sense for female lawyers having small kids. My children spent quite a bit of time in those courtrooms—perhaps this is why two of the three became lawyers.

My advice to other female trial lawyers is: (1) Dream big—set your goal beyond your current reach; (2) Work until you are almost completely exhausted—you know then that you have given your very best effort; (3) Remove the phrase "it can't be done" from your reality—do not be afraid to argue for the extension or modification of existing law; (4) Schedule time each month to increase your knowledge of the law and techniques used by successful trial lawyers; and (5) No matter how busy your law practice might be, find time to take your children and grandchildren out for ice cream.

Anne Thomas Sulton, Ph.D., is from Racine, Wisconsin, and is the founder of Sulton Law Offices, where she focused on civil rights litigation.

3

Law Firm Lawyers

KEY FINDINGS

➤ Grit is highly correlated to a number of measures of success in law firms of all sizes, including billable hours.

➤ Grit is closely related to the overall quality of the work that a woman receives when practicing in firms of all sizes.

➤ Both grit and growth mindset are very closely related to ambition.

➤ Grit is strongly related to how well women in law firms perform on formal performance evaluations.

➤ Mindset is strongly related to compensation.

➤ Law firm lawyers believe that grit and growth mindset are important contributors to success.

THE WOMEN WE SURVEYED

Close to 2,000 women who are currently practicing in law firms participated in our research efforts. This group was by far the largest of the groups that we looked at. We heard from women in law firms of all sizes, ranging from small firms with as few as two or three practicing lawyers to the largest firms in the United States, some of which had more than 1,000 practicing lawyers. Although our initial plan was to write separate chapters about small, medium, and large law firms, we ultimately grouped firms of all sizes together because many of the findings about law firm practice were quite similar and we found that it made the most sense to discuss them collectively. In addition to coming from firms of all sizes, this group of women lawyers came from single-office firms, as well as firms with more than 15 offices in locations around the world. We also heard from roughly an equal number of firms both inside and outside of the *American Lawyer* 200.

In addition to the diversity of the firms represented by our sample, the women themselves were equally diverse across a number of spectrums, including their level of seniority within their firms. We heard from roughly an equal number of partners and associates. The partners we heard from were both equity and nonequity partners and partners who both had and had not served in leadership/management roles at their respective firms. The associates we heard from were both those who were on partnership track and those were not—some by choice and some not by choice.

As was the case with the solo practitioners in our study, the law firm lawyers we heard from practiced many different kinds of law, with the greatest concentrations in corporate, labor and employment, litigation, intellectual property, real estate, trusts and estates, and children and family law. They represented a broad range of practice experience, from relatively inexperienced (one to two years of practice experience) to very experienced (more than 21 years of practice experience). On balance, this group was more heavily skewed toward more experienced lawyers, and roughly 57 percent of the women in this group had upward of 15 years of experience.

In addition to sheer number of years in practice, there was also mix in terms of the number of prior legal positions each lawyer had held, ranging from zero to more than five (and everything in between), although more than half of the group had held only one or no prior legal positions before joining their current firms. When asked about their long-term career plans, just shy of 50 percent of the women said that they intended to stay with their current employers for the duration of their careers, with another

25 percent saying they planned to stay where they were for at least the next three to five years.

In terms of family structure, about 75 percent of the women in this group were either married or in a domestic partnership, and about two-thirds of the women had children. Of those who had children, the range was generally between one and three children; more than half of them had two children. Just shy of 70 percent of the women with children had had their children while practicing law. When it comes to their mothers, we saw a wide range in terms of the highest level of education that they had completed (a statistic that has been shown, in other contexts, to be predictive of professional and academic success). We heard from women whose mothers had completed less than the equivalent of a high school education and, on the other end of the spectrum, from those whose mothers had professional degrees. The average woman we heard from (about 44 percent of the women in the study) had mothers who had completed a four-year college degree and/or a master's degree, which suggests that on balance, and relative to the U.S. population, this group was raised by very well-educated mothers (many of whom were very influential in inspiring grit and growth mindset characteristics in their daughters). As one lawyer shares, "I grew up with strong women who overcame personal adversity to find their own way in the world. There were no silver spoons on our table." She goes on to describe a powerful grandmother, great aunts, and a working mother who was "balancing" all of her responsibilities before that term was even used. Other women we heard from echoed these sentiments as well—referring to strong parents who, like another lawyer's parents "had an extreme commitment to each of their children receiving a college degree."

Finally, in terms of academic performance, we heard from women who had graduated from a broad range of law schools up and down the list of the top-ranked *U.S. News & World Report* law schools. Many of the women did very well in school, and most of them achieved GPAs that were north of a 3.0. Many managed to do this while raising small children and juggling the competing demands of work and family while simultaneously trying to advance their professional goals. A good number of the women in this group ranked at the top of their classes, but there was also healthy representation across the spectrum, including a not-insignificant number of people who ranked in the bottom half of their classes. For most, even if they found the adjustment to law school to be challenging, they ultimately developed ways to improve their performance and made effective adjustments along the way such that their overall academic trajectory was a positive one.

MEASURING SUCCESS

As was the case with all groups that we considered, we spent a significant amount of time trying to determine the right measures of success for women lawyers practicing in law firms today. This undertaking led to conversations with numerous current and former women lawyers in private practice, all of whom provided us with unique perspectives on how they understood and defined success with their respective firms. We heard from a broad range of women of varying seniority and across practices and geographies, in firms both large and small. While many had different ideas about what constituted success in 2016, several themes emerged that ultimately informed our list of success measures.

First, at most law firms, there tends to be what is often described as an "up or out" culture. Essentially, the idea of an up or out culture is that you either continue to move up the ladder toward partnership or another position of leadership and authority or else you are eventually asked to leave the firm. While this is a common practice in the big accounting firms, the consulting world, and the world of Silicon Valley, it is perhaps nowhere more pronounced than it is in the world of large law firms. For this reason, it was important to assess the level of seniority that the women had been able to achieve—the up or out culture suggests that, at least to some extent, longevity is an indicator that a woman was doing well enough that she was not asked to leave. We will pause here to note that we did not assume the reverse was true—that is, that women who stayed for shorter periods of time were not doing well—as we recognized that women in law firms can and do leave for many reasons unrelated to performance, including to tend to the needs of children and other family members, to accommodate a spouse or significant other's move to another city, or to pursue careers in other areas, both inside and outside of the practice of law. Going hand-in-hand with seniority, and arguably a simpler and more direct measure of performance, was whether the women we heard from were on partnership track. While the up or out culture present in many of today's law firms suggests that many— if not most—of those who are on partnership track at any given stage of their careers will not ultimately achieve partnership status, whether a woman was still on track (and could at least in theory still achieve the title) does suggest something important about her performance, past successes, and future career trajectory.

The second theme that emerged from our initial conversations with law firm lawyers (when we were seeking to define the success measures at the outset of this study) was the fact that many firms still rely heavily on the billable hour when internally evaluating the success of their lawyers, both male and female. While there has been much talk of late regarding the changing nature (and perhaps more importantly the appetite for change) of the billable hour approach, it nevertheless remains the industry standard for most firms. Some would argue that it is a proxy for other measures of success, such as the degree to which a lawyer is engaged in and committed to her work or the extent to which the lawyer's skills are in demand. We heard from many of the women we surveyed that the busiest associates are not only hard working but are often the most talented associates (perhaps because the more they do, the more experience they have and the better they become, which then in and of itself becomes a self-fulfilling prophecy).

In any event, it is no secret that many firms use the billable hour as one of the ways in which they reward associates financially. These firms offer bonuses that take into account the total number of hours an associate has billed and set thresholds and billable hours targets that must be met in order to receive the highest levels of compensation. Other firms do not set specific targets but review the entire pool of associates and seek to reward each one based on where she falls with respect to her peers—those at the top of the list earn the highest bonuses and those at the bottom earn much smaller amounts and sometimes no bonuses at all. Based on the conversations we had, it seemed necessary to take into account—at least in some way—the lingering significance of the billable hour. Along those same lines, we also included a measure of performance related to compensation and, in particular, to how much the women we studied earned as a relative measure rather than a fixed dollar amount. Given the dramatic differences in both size and scope of the firms that the women in this group represented, any other measure could and would have been misleading—a woman at the bottom of the BigLaw scale could easily have landed atop a small firm scale, and this would have provided no meaningful measure of success one way or the other.

The final theme to emerge from our conversations around success in this context concerns the nature of the work that the women were involved in. Many told us that the women who were working on the most complex and exciting assignments were the ones the firm placed its faith in. If the matter was difficult and required the hardest workers with the sharpest minds, then it logically follows that the highest performers would be sought out and staffed to those matters. On the other hand, those whose skills and abilities were in question for one reason or another would be far more likely to be assigned to the "safer," less challenging tasks. It should be noted that, as is the case with billable hours, this can and does become a self-fulfilling prophecy in that working on tough matters often has the effect of building skills at a more rapid pace, pushing lawyers to stretch outside of their comfort zones, and to develop a certain degree of comfort with uncertainty (e.g., not always knowing the answer), and this can be hugely beneficial to them down the line. Lawyers who are accustomed to functioning with some degree of uncertainty and are able to navigate their way toward the best possible solutions for their clients tend to be the most valued and sought-after practitioners. In this way, how often a woman was chosen to work on the best and most desirable matters was another key proxy for success in the law firm context.

Although there were some meaningful differences both in how performance was measured and in how it was rewarded within law firms, we were ultimately able to distill it down to a subset of measures that address the fundamental commonalities. Here are those measures of success:

1. Which of the following best describes your current position? (junior, midlevel, or senior associate, staff attorney, specialist or special counsel, nonequity partner, equity partner, equity partner and current or former member of a firm governing committee). *If partner-level title is chosen, skip to question #3; if associate-level title is chosen, go on to question #2*
2. To the best of your knowledge, are you on partnership track? (yes or no)
3. Which of the following best describes the message you received at your last performance review? (your performance was outstanding, very good, average, below average, or poor)
4. On average, how many hours do you bill a year (excluding pro bono)? (various ranges)
5. On average, how many pro bono hours do you bill a year? (various ranges)
6. How often do you get to work on the most high-profile, complex matters at the firm? (always, most of the time, sometimes, rarely, or never)
7. Relative to your peers, your total compensation is: (above average, average, or below average)?

Key Finding #1

Grit is highly correlated to a number of measures of success in law firms of all sizes, including billable hours.

At the outset of this study, and based largely on Dr. Hogan's first research effort in 2013,[1] we assumed that there would be a strong and statistically significant connection between grit and the number of hours a woman bills in an average year. We had seen very powerful results when looking at a population of lawyers practicing exclusively in BigLaw, and we assumed that when we looked at a wider population that included lawyers in firms of all sizes we would see similar results. This was indeed the case.

In order to fully comprehend what the relationship between grit and hours means in practical terms, consider the fact that the average billable rate for a large law firm lawyer can be as high as $540 per hour, and an increasing number of partners now bill their time at more than $1,000 per hour.[2] If you do the math using those numbers, a very gritty partner is likely to bring in close to $300,000 more each year than a moderately gritty partner (assuming grit scores of five and three, respectively). Similarly, even a more modestly billing associate is likely to earn about $155,000 more than her less gritty peer (again assuming grit scores of five and three). When you consider that the average number of lawyers at each *American Lawyer* 200 firm is 578, the earning potential is staggering.[3] It is clear, then, that firms of all sizes (and regardless of the specific dollar amounts at which their lawyers are billed) should be incentivized to hire and develop gritty women lawyers, because having a high number of gritty lawyers on staff will likely lead to increased revenue for the firm.

Setting aside the obvious bottom line implications of employing gritty women lawyers, it is not surprising that there is such a strong connection between grit and number of hours worked. Perhaps more than any other measure of success in this study, number of hours worked is the most obvious and direct way for grit to manifest itself in the law firm environment. When we consider what we know about grit from prior research (discussed in detail in appendix C), it seems to be the case that high levels of grit make it possible for people to log the time needed to succeed—whether they are middle-schoolers studying for the National Spelling Bee, West Point cadets trying to survive boot camp, or women lawyers trying to climb the law firm ladder.[4] Grit is—by definition—a trait that is exemplified by persistence and perseverance not just for short-term gains, but also for long-term goals. One might even argue that if we didn't see a strong connection between grit and number of hours worked that it would be difficult to suggest that grit matters at all in the law firm environment. Indeed, the women we heard from clearly articulated how hard they had worked and the ways in which their grittiness had enabled them to take on and do more than they may have believed themselves capable of. As one law firm lawyer shares, "I had no trouble working hard. In my last two years of college I took 15 units while working 50 hours per week. Law school was completed in two and one-half years, working 32 hours per week to reduce my student loans." She continued to work hard when she joined her first law firm and had to juggle the demands of practice along with two small children, ages five and seven years. Other lawyers echoed this sentiment, and as you will see in the letters at the end of this chapter, they represent a very hard-working bunch that have accomplished some incredible feats. As one of the lawyers noted, grit and growth mindset played an important role not only in her career but in the lead up to her career. As she suggests, grit and hard work matter both at the sunrise and the sunset of one's career, and perhaps nowhere are they more indisputably evident than in the hard number of billable hours worked.

As an aside, there is currently a strong push in certain corners of the legal world to eliminate the billable hour entirely, and some have argued that we are well on our way to doing just that. Any discussion of the significance of the billable hour must take into account that this is a practice that does not seem likely to withstand the test of time. This is true for many reasons, including the fact that it is a practice that tends to reward activity rather than results. While further discussion of the fate of the billable hour is outside the scope of the present research, it is a point that merits further consideration elsewhere.

Key Finding #2

Grit is closely related to the overall quality of the work that a woman receives when practicing in firms of all sizes.

It is somewhat more difficult to quantify the potential impact of the relationship between grit and a lawyer's perception of the quality of the work she receives (i.e., how often she works on the most complex and high-profile work her firm has to offer) than it is to quantify the potential impact of the billable hour. A review of the relevant literature suggests that many employees are less likely to experience burnout if they are satisfied with the content of their work, and they feel that their work both matters and is meaningful.[5] Burnout is defined as a psychological syndrome that involves a prolonged response to chronic interpersonal stressors on the job. The three key dimensions of this response are "an overwhelming exhaustion, feelings of cynicism and detachment from the job, and a sense of ineffectiveness and lack of accomplishment."[6] According to Maslach, the most common consequences of burnout are poor quality of work, low morale, absenteeism, turnover, health problems, depression, and family problems.[7] Given that all of these consequences have dire implications for employers, it seems clear that employers would want to avoid them. Ensuring that lawyers feel good about the quality of their work may be one way of accomplishing this.

Not only are there benefits to having lawyers who feel good about the quality of their work, but there are also dangers associated with having lawyers who do not feel this way. First of all, as discussed earlier in this chapter, assigning a lawyer to low-profile, routine work may inadvertently send a message to her that the firm does not think very highly of her abilities. Given how challenging it is for all lawyers working in law firms, it may very well be the case that such a message would give the extra push to those who are already struggling to integrate work and family responsibilities to opt out of the practice of law altogether. In an environment in which even the most highly committed, ambitious lawyers struggle to reconcile the demands of the job with their lives outside of the office, any evidence that they may not have what it takes to succeed may be just the encouragement they need to pursue a less-demanding career choice.

When it comes to quality of work, the connection to grit may be less obvious than the connection to billable hours. Why is grit so strongly related to this measure of success? As previously noted, gritty individuals tend to be among the highest performers on the job and, therefore, are more likely to receive only the best work. Furthermore, gritty women lawyers tend to embrace challenges and to see them as opportunities for learning, even though—or perhaps precisely because—they tend to be the most demanding in terms of the effort required to successfully complete them. A gritty lawyer would likely to want to push herself and would certainly not shy away from long hours, so the most high-profile, complex matters—the best matters—would be the ones she would raise her hand for. As one lawyer shared with us: "My best move—I volunteered for every difficult trial, often taking the place of a partner at courts in towns that I had to find first on a map." She also agreed to take on matters that she "was guaranteed to lose." These may not seem, objectively, like the best matters, and yet she viewed them in this way because they provided tremendous learning opportunities for her. Similarly, another lawyer suggests that women should:

> Take on challenges gladly—for example, handling the difficult client matter or mastering a "niche" area that no one else is interested in but that could be helpful to your clients and colleagues. This will help you build your confidence, and it will also help your clients and colleagues feel confident in you.

Yet another possibility is that gritty women lawyers are so focused on the work they have, and so committed to working hard and getting the most out of each assignment, that they are more likely to believe that they are working on the most high-profile and complex matters, even if this is not the case. If this were true, the connection found in this research can be explained by the fact that gritty lawyers are just more likely to respond to a question like this one in a particular way. Along those lines, in a study of novice teachers, Duckworth, Quinn, and Seligman found that more optimistic teachers had higher grit and life satisfaction scores, and that grit and life satisfaction, in turn, predicted greater teacher effectiveness.[8] It could be the case here that the gritty lawyers were also more optimistic and, thus, more likely to view their work as the most high-quality work the firm had to offer.

Key Finding #3

Both grit and growth mindset are very closely related to ambition.

It will not come as a surprise to many people that the women we heard from were—for the most part—very ambitious. Given that the pursuit of a career in law is one that takes hard work, long-term commitment, perseverance, and a belief that all of the effort will somehow pay off, it makes perfect sense that it would be a career likely to attract ambitious, gritty women with growth mindset orientations. Indeed, the results we saw suggest that there is an extremely strong, statistically significant correlation between a female law firm lawyer's grit score and where she falls on the growth mindset spectrum. As one lawyer describes it:

> We need to advocate, not just for our clients, but for our- selves. We cannot be afraid to state, clearly and openly, what our goals are—to get a raise, to make partner, to work on a certain case—and just ask what we need to do to get there. . . . I have only gotten those things because I asked for them and worked so hard that "no" wasn't an option. This is not because I am super smart or amazingly skilled—I work hard, I ask questions, and I persevere.

Similarly, another highly successful law firm lawyer shares the following observations about mindset and ambition:

> [Mindset] goes far to explain my own attitude toward human capabilities and potential. . . . Certainly, I never considered, growing up, becoming a lawyer—it meant talking and writing entirely too much. I thought of myself as having more of a scientific and technical mindset, suited to long periods of silent inquiry, lab work, and solitary field work. . . . So I have no explanation, other than the exis- tence of a growth mindset, for how and why I did become a lawyer, and why I love what I do so much.

Finally, a third lawyer shares how she employed a growth mind- set to land a prestigious and high-paying job at a top law firm:

> I got a job as a first-year associate at Skadden Arps in New York. How? I was clear in my mind that I wanted it . . .

and rejected any notion that I didn't meet the standard pedigree for such a firm. I did my research, practiced my pitch, and reached out to my relatively small professional network. In every interview (12 total conducted over three months in four separate visits), I conveyed confidence in my candidacy and a real enthusiasm for the role.

All three of these powerful quotes illustrate the close connections between grit, growth mindset, and ambition. On some level, perhaps you have to be ambitious in order to engage in gritty behavior—grit is hard work and needs to be fueled by passion and a strong desire to improve and advance. On the flip side, you must have a growth mindset orientation—a strong belief in your abilities and your own potential—in order to engage in the kinds of gritty behavior that allow you to exercise your ambition, whether that means standing up and asking for more money, for the plumb assignment that will position you well for future plumb assignments, or even for promotion to partnership.

Key Finding #4

Grit is strongly related to how well women in law firms perform on formal performance evaluations.

In addition to measuring success by looking at billable hours, the majority of law firms also have some formal way of collecting performance feedback on their lawyers. Many law firms solicit reviews of their lawyers' performance on specific matters and then aggregate those into a comprehensive performance evaluation report, which is then communicated to the lawyer, typically in an in-person meeting on an annual basis. Some firms provide written reports to their lawyers summarizing this feedback, while other firms provide only oral commentary summarizing the specific comments. Sometimes the feedback is delivered anonymously and framed as an overview of the general areas in which a lawyer could stand to improve (e.g., in her attention to detail, oral advocacy skills, or written communications) and sometimes it is delivered very specifically (e.g., Sarah thought your summary of the deposition transcripts was good, but you overlooked a significant point and it look longer than expected, etc.). In any event, most of the women whom we surveyed received at least some formal feedback on their performance from firm management, and we were focused specifically on these messages. What we found was that the grittier and more growth mindset–oriented women tended to receive better messages in these contexts. In other words, someone with a grit score of five, the highest possible grit score, was more likely to have received a rating of "outstanding" from the firm than someone with a lower grit score. The same was true of mindset: Those with a growth mindset orientation tended to perform better.

There are several interesting implications of this finding. The first and most obvious is that law firm leaders (and those involved in the recruiting and hiring processes) should be mindful of the importance of grit and growth mindset and may be well served if they seek out such individuals and encourage them to join the firm. (We discuss how a law firm might begin to assess grit and growth mindset in candidates in appendix A.) Our data suggests that these behaviors will influence, at least to some extent, how well lawyers perform once they've been hired. As we've seen in this chapter already, they are likely to be ambitious, hard-working employees who will bill many hours, perform well, and be sought out for challenging and high-profile assignments.

The second implication worth noting is that traits like grit are extremely important when it comes to success because they encourage persistence and perseverance, even when things do not come naturally and require some extra muscle to reach a level of competence and, ultimately, achieve high levels of performance. One lawyer shared a story with us about how she suddenly became the boss of a team, during the middle of the financial crisis, and had to learn how to become a better manager when she discovered that her own boss was unhappy with her management skills. She took his criticism to heart and did what she needed to do to turn things around. Eventually, that enabled her to grow her own management skills and to develop a management style that worked for her but also kept junior team members motivated and engaged.

As her story illustrates, engaging in gritty behaviors is a great driver of performance because it encourages you to do the kind of work that you need to do to make improvements. One could imagine that had this lawyer received a performance evaluation for her work with the team, it might have said something along the lines of the following: "Although she initially struggled with how best to approach her new management role, she responded extremely well to feedback, showed great commitment and determination, and was able to make the necessary adjustments to achieve the desired results for her team and for the firm." This is a great example of how grit and a growth mindset can drive success and lead to great performance evaluations and a reminder that someone who lacks these qualities will be less likely to be able to rebound in a situation like the one that this lawyer faced.

There are countless examples that we heard in our conversations and that are echoed in the letters you will read in this book that underscore the importance of grit and a growth mindset to success for women practicing in law firms. As another lawyer shares, "I believed in doing a job and doing it perfectly and that was always my goal." It's hard to imagine that she would have received poor reviews if that was her focus and her approach to the work she did for her firm.

Key Finding #5

Mindset is strongly related to compensation.

As discussed earlier in this chapter, one of the measures of success we used for women in law firms was total compensation, expressed as a relative measure rather than a fixed dollar amount. We found that there was a strong correlation between the growth mindset orientation and how much a woman earned relative to her similarly situated and seasoned peers (both men and women). In other words, the growth mindset–oriented women were more likely to be earning more than average compensation than the fixed mindset–oriented women. As such, belief in the power of effort, in the ability to succeed in the law firm environment, and in the practice of law seems to be linked to increased compensation.

This could be, in part, because growth mindset–oriented women are more likely to speak up and ask for more money when they need to. For some of these women, speaking up was something they learned to do early in life and then continued to do when they realized how effective it could be. One woman shared the following anecdote with us that illustrates this point:

> As far back as my childhood, I always believed that, as a girl, I should not be treated any differently from the boys in my class. I grew up with three brothers, which taught me the importance of grit and standing up for myself. For example, in middle school, much to my surprise, girls were required to take home economics, while the boys were taught logic and philosophy. I thought this was completely unfair, so I organized the other girls and our parents to demand that we be given the same learning opportunities as the boys. We prevailed, and this early seminal experience made me realize the need to persevere even in the face of obstacles.

Mindset and compensation may also be so strongly related in this context because lawyers' belief in their own abilities tends to lead to high performance, which, assuming the firms are approaching compensation in fair and equitable ways, should lead to salaries, bonuses, and total compensation packages at the higher end of the spectrum. One lawyer describes her own growth mindset–orientation and how that had led to the kind of performance that, in turn, led to increased compensation. She was convinced that her efforts would produce results and that results would lead to more money. For her, however, it wasn't just about the money. In fact, she enjoyed the work itself—and the feeling that she was making progress—so much that sometimes she preferred it to other, social activities.

While it may be hard to imagine that brief writing could trump a social gathering, many of the women we surveyed expressed similar feelings about their work and the passion they felt for it. This also speaks to the fact that growth mindset individuals tend to love learning and working through complex and challenging assignments—they often enjoy "stretch" assignments and hard work that make them better and improves their craft. Not only can you make a compelling case for the impact of a growth mindset on compensation, but—on the flip side—you can make a compelling case for negative impact when a growth mindset is *not* adopted. One lawyer shares her views on what happens when women employ a fixed mindset–oriented approach:

> I feel that my law firm was overly cautious and we did not adopt a growth mindset as quickly as we should have. As women, we were risk averse and did not want to expand our practice too quickly and end up having to lay off people. . . . I think it resulted in us being too cautious to hire associates and grow our firm as we could have. . . . I would caution younger attorneys to learn from this and be willing to consider the risk that is not reckless, but may provide more opportunities.

Key Finding #6

Law firm lawyers believe that grit and growth mindset are important contributors to success.

As we did with all of the women who participated in this survey, we asked the following question of those practicing in law firms of all sizes:

> Have you personally found that being gritty (a gritty person is a person who demonstrates both passion and perseverance in pursuit of her long-term goals) or having a growth mindset (a growth mindset–oriented person believes that her success is based on hard work, learning, training, and doggedness) has been a factor in your overall career success?

Ninety-eight percent of the women who responded said that both of these traits mattered when it came to their own ability to achieve professional success in the law firm environment, and 77 percent said there was "no doubt" in their minds as to its significance and importance. One lawyer summed it up perfectly when she said, "My career is proof that success is far less the product of natural talents and far more the product of grit and a growth mindset." This is consistent with the findings from other groups and lends further support to the overall importance of these traits for women lawyers. This last finding does not require much further analysis, but it is nevertheless very compelling (and often quite moving) to hear the women share, in their own words, why and how grit and growth mindset have played a role in their respective careers. One lawyer noted that you must have grit if you are attempting to practice law while female. Another echoes the point, noting, "I have been very lucky, and I have worked very hard. Enhanced by grit and growth mindset, this is the winning combination." A third lawyer has a similar view, saying, "Women, and particularly women of color, must have grit. We must be persistent in the face of adversity." Yet another explains:

> The advances that we, as women and as professionals, have made in the practice of law, and our contributions to the rule of law in the United States, do all come down to the grit of generations of individual women and their determination to make their way—and to pave the way for others—in the legal profession, in the judiciary, and in public service.

And another lawyer shares:

> It was only as a result of [this] survey that I truly understood that I am someone who has grit and a growth mindset. Lucky for me, although I did not necessarily identify these traits within myself earlier, I followed a path understanding the importance of perseverance, continuing growth, and having a passion for my chosen profession. However, had someone identified these traits for me earlier, or even informed me of the importance of them, I think I may have been even more deliberate in my approach to certain career decisions and goals. . . . As I look back, I now understand that I always had grit—perseverance and passion—and

a growth mindset. I'm just lucky enough now to have a name for it and the ability to pass on the skills to those coming behind me.

Just as the quote above so articulately suggests, sharing these traits with women early on in their careers can be tremendously impactful, and that is exactly our intent with this book. We hope to spread an understanding of their impact and importance, and we hope that this knowledge will be inspiring for women at all levels and in all areas of practice. Along those same lines, one law firm lawyer offers these inspiring words of advice to young lawyers:

> You have everything it takes to succeed as a lawyer so long as you remain tenacious, curious, and sufficiently self-reflective to invest in your own advancement. Every once in a while, you will have some lucky breaks, but for the most part, there will be no handouts. This career is of your making—you are the driver. With grit and a growth mind-set, you are going places!

Notes:

1. Hogan, ML. 2013. Non-cognitive traits that impact female success in BigLaw. Diss. University of Pennsylvania.
2. Jones, L. 2012. Rich lawyers are getting richer faster. http://newsandinsight.thomsonreuters.com/Legal/News/2012/04__April/Rich_lawyers_are_getting_richer_faster/. Accessed in 2012.
3. American Lawyer 200 Report. 2012.
4. Duckworth, A. 2016. *Grit: The power of passion and perseverance.* Simon and Schuster.
5. Cranston, S., and Keller, S. 2013. "Increasing the meaning quotient of work." *McKinsey Quarterly* 1:48–59; Janssen, P., Schaufelioe, W.B., and Houkes, I. 1999. "Work-related and individual determinants of the three burnout dimensions." *Work & Stress* 13.1:74–86.
6. Leiter, M.P., and Maslach, C. 2005. *Banishing burnout: Six strategies for improving your relationship with work.* John Wiley & Sons.
7. *Id.*
8. Duckworth, A.L., Quinn, P.D., and Seligman, MEP. "Positive predictors of teacher effectiveness." *The Journal of Positive Psychology* 4.6: 540–547.

Roula Allouch

I write this letter as a young lawyer on the verge of aging out of that official status per the ABA definition. For those of us keeping count, that means I am 36 and approaching my 10th year of practice. Some days it feels it has been much shorter than 10 years and others much, much longer than that. Reaching a nice round number of years of practice allows one the opportunity to pause and reflect on past experiences both for nostalgic reasons but, perhaps more importantly, to grow and learn from those past situations. In looking back, I hope to implement necessary changes for continued growth in the future. It is not lost on me that I just referenced the concept of growth twice in the last few sentences. Since the time I made the decision to apply to law school, I considered myself embarking on a career path with a purpose and not just taking a step toward a future job or profession.

I have always been a goal-driven individual, as setting goals helps to keep me in focus. In keeping with that habit, as I studied in law school to become an attorney, I also considered what my goals and intentions with my career would be. At the deepest level, I was driven to the law as a means to serve the community and use any knowledge gained to benefit and empower others. I strongly believe that despite our many differences we are all connected. From the outset, I saw the practice of law as a vehicle to unity in our diverse society. I have been privileged enough to have accomplished some of these goals through volunteer opportunities and leadership positions with the American Bar Association and the Council on American-Islamic Relations (CAIR).

I am an American Muslim woman practicing law in Kentucky and Ohio. The parts that define me often appear contradictory to others, but they make perfect sense to me. I have never been anything other than the sum of my parts, and I am proud of each component. I decided to attend law school at a time when members of the American Muslim community were facing increasing violations on their civil rights and liberties. As Islamophobia and its effects have grown and spread, I have found myself devoting more and more time to combating the ignorance and hate that come with it.

What does all this have to do with grit and growth? In order to reach some level of career success and accomplishment, we all must show at least some amount of grit and growth. And female attorneys know we have to exhibit more of these qualities to overcome some of the challenges in our profession unique to us. Adding in my religious faith and background to the mix has called for an additional amount of grit and growth mindset necessary for success.

As a Muslim woman practicing in a post-9/11 world, I have had to persevere through interesting circumstances, both professionally and personally. I am a litigator and could share countless stories of instances when various court personnel assumed I was not an attorney and prevented me access to parts of courtrooms typically open to attorneys. That is an experience I understand to be shared by many of my female colleagues. But I have also had more direct and personal issues.

A few years ago, I was verbally attacked on an elevator in a courthouse by an angry man unhappy with my choice of religion and the manner in which I carried myself. I was surprised and a bit shaken, but had to immediately shake it off and handle a hearing in court. And then there was a time more recently when a judge refused to allow me to speak in court because he did not believe I was an attorney. His continued refusal made it a bit difficult to explain that I was a licensed attorney, hijab and all. My client, who the judge had mistakenly assumed was the attorney on the case, had to speak in my defense to explain that I was, in fact, his attorney and he the party. The judge needed the client's confirmation before finally permitting me to speak and present our case through an awkward hearing. Since that incident, I have appeared in front of that judge again. The civil rights advocate in me wanted to raise hell following the incident, but I had to ask myself what good that would ultimately serve my client. So, I handled the situation as diplomatically as I could. I addressed it not for myself, but for that next attorney who might find herself in front of the judge who doubted her qualifications because of his own misconceptions or prejudgments based on appearance.

So, yes, some grit and growth are essential tools. During the instances noted above, but in many other circumstances as well, I look long-term past immediate challenges. Since law school,

I have had the mindset I would work as hard as I could and leave nothing on the table, so to speak. If I didn't accomplish a particular goal, I would not look back and wish I had tried harder. I may over-prepare, but it would be rare to find me unprepared. At times I find myself on a grit-it-out roll. The challenges seem to present themselves in groups and always when my calendar is full of deadlines associated with a fast-approaching trial date and a number of personal commitments all at once. On those occasions, I try to step out of the situation and focus on the bigger picture. I remove myself and focus on the greater interest. And I often reflect on that comforting principle that has proven itself true time and again: this too shall pass. I remind myself difficulties on the road are simply markers on the path toward the greater goal of fulfilling my purpose through my career. And, as I reflect on the path I have taken thus far, some of those markers are beneficial reminders of challenges I have been fortunate to overcome.

Of course, success does not come with grit and growth alone. I believe all attorneys, but particularly women, must have a support system and network of mentors and advocates. I have been fortunate enough to have found myself surrounded and uplifted by such individuals throughout my career. My network includes fellow attorneys, professors, and friends of all backgrounds, and both genders. But grit and growth come into play here as well. I try to be an equal opportunity networker. For me, that means uplifting others as a part of the goal of improving the condition of the practice of law for women of all backgrounds. I know I feed off of the energy and successes of my colleagues and try to produce that same energy for others. Ultimately, the more we accomplish success in our careers, the less challenges we will collectively face and the better equipped members of our profession will be to serve our clients and communities.

Roula Allouch is an attorney licensed to practice in Kentucky and Ohio, currently serving as the chair of the National Board of Directors of the Council on American-Islamic Relations, the nation's largest civil rights and advocacy group for the American Muslim community. www.cair.com

Dominica C. Anderson

Successful lawyers, regardless of gender, most likely naturally encompass the quality grit. People often ask, "What is grit and how does one learn to have grit?" From my perspective, grit is the primary element of determination, that which makes us get going when the going gets tough; makes us get back up when knocked down; and helps us perceive challenges as opportunities. I personally like to think of combining grace with grit, as grit alone can be perceived as tough—sometimes too tough—whether from a male or female. Grit and grace together provide the building blocks for successful business people, lawyers and nonlawyers alike.

Grit likely has been ingrained in me since birth. When I think of my father, I think of grit and hard work. My father practiced medicine and loved helping people. His desire to help never wavered; he volunteered in the medical arena until his passing at the age of 87. Although he had a successful private practice, he volunteered on the weekends at the inner-city emergency room where gunshot wounds were the norm. And, although he had several setbacks over time (including health issues making practicing medicine a challenge), he never gave up trying to be useful and trying to help others. In fact, I think I inherited the trait of seeing obstacles as challenges from my father. Like him, if I were told I would not likely be successful at something, that would make me want to put more effort into it to prove them wrong.

Although I may have been born with grit, practicing law and working with others for many years have allowed me to hone this strength and use it with grace. Grit makes you want to shout, "You're wrong, I can do it, I can be successful." But, through experience, I have found that grit needs grace or control to be successful. Whether you feel like screaming or not, the grace element helps you control grit. And, regardless, the results of your efforts will surpass any words (or complaints) you might have spoken on the subject. One example from my early years of practice comes to mind.

In the late 1980s, I practiced insurance coverage law, and our firm did a lot of work for Lloyds of London. Historically, women were not allowed on the Lloyd's "floor." In fact, most of the partners I worked with believed our London Insurance clients would not be accustomed to seeing women lawyers on matters in London. Seeing that as an opportunity (i.e., I would be something novel), I set out to make myself indispensable to our London clients. In the end, it was the London clients who contacted my partners asking that they bring me with them on the next trip to London. Once I arrived, as "icing on the cake," one of the elderly London clients looked at me and said to the male partner, "It's about time you brought a female lawyer; I am tired of looking at your sorry face." We all had to laugh. Did I harbor resentment against my partners? No, they were only trying to do the best they could. And that is part of grit and grace, not holding on, but rather letting go. Only in the letting go can you move forward and continue to succeed. The bottom line is this: grit (with grace) is all about how you handle situations. It is not about others providing opportunities. Ideally, you have both, but you need grit to begin with. Again, challenges become opportunities with the grit perspective.

Can one learn the strength of grit? Of course. In fact, I think most people develop grit over time. As a litigator, I do not see how lawyers can survive without grit. When you practice law, there are a few certainties that come with the job. You will lose a case; you will lose a pitch; you will lose a client; you will lose an associate or partner who tries to take a client; and many other unpleasant things will happen, day in and day out. It is purely the way you react to those events that impacts how you will survive. Grit gives you the sense to remember that life goes on and there are many other cases, clients, client opportunities, etc. But each challenge you face is a learning lesson for your next opportunity, so take that challenge on.

Grit will be part of me until the end.

Dominica C. Anderson is the managing partner of Duane Morris LLP's office in Las Vegas and focuses her practice on insurance coverage and complex commercial litigation. www.duanemorris.com

Sheryl L. Axelrod

This letter is dedicated to those many women who are my juniors in the profession, to tell you that as you've read in this book, you can thrive as lawyers, regardless of whatever natural abilities you may think you lack. In fact, my career is proof that success is far less the product of natural talents and far more the product of grit and a growth mindset.

To explain this, I need to set the clock back to when I was in elementary school and first began to exercise grit and a growth mindset. I had a rough time learning to spell. A teacher made me write out around 20 times every word I misspelled. I then repeatedly hand wrote out for myself many words and now consider myself a very fine speller.

My next educational hurdle came in middle school when I had to take a foreign language. I mistakenly chose French. I nearly failed as our teacher marked an entire word wrong if one letter or accent was wrong in it (or missing from it).

I had seen an older sibling struggle, and overcome, a far tougher obstacle. I have two slow-learning brothers, Howard and Kenny. They were in special education classes in school.* The older of the two, Kenny, is the slower of the two. He tests at about the first-grade level.

When Kenny turned 16 years old, he was determined to drive, but passing the written component of the driver's test seemed like an insurmountable obstacle. Still, my parents believed he could learn it.

My dad spent a year teaching him the driver's education manual. In a monumental display of love, belief in his son, and dedication, he read a sentence a night with Kenny until he got that sentence. Then the next night, he read another and went over the

---

* In fact, my mom is the reason the school district has a special education program. She fought the school board to create one. The district now has one of the finest special education programs in the region, not only for students who learn slowly, but also for kids with a wide range of special needs.

sentences from the days before, sentence by sentence until Kenny knew all the material. Kenny passed his driver's test on his first try.

I learned from Kenny that overcoming an obstacle is a matter of perseverance, work, and practice. I figured that learning a foreign language was going to be difficult for me, but I wanted to do it. The next year, I switched to taking Spanish. In Spanish, unlike in French (and English), things are spelled very much the way they sound.

Unfortunately, in my Spanish classes, I was a year behind my peers who had started taking the language the year before, when I had taken French. It was embarrassing to be with them instead of my peers, but I dug in, worked hard, and even spent six weeks over a summer studying in Spain. I spent as much time as I could there speaking Spanish with the natives.

I am proud to say that as a result, I skipped a year and a half of the language in school and wound up in my year's honors class. I kept up the study and now am conversationally fluent in it.

I love Spanish. It's given me the joy of reading books in Spanish and enjoying Spanish songs, and I am a huge fan of dancing salsa, merengue, and bachata. In fact, that's another grit and growth mindset story. I am a good dancer, but I was absolutely horrific at salsa (meaning at salsa, merengue, and bachata) when I first started dancing it. I had never learned a structured dance before, but I loved it and worked hard to become good at it. I have been dancing salsa for years now and feel I am quite good at it.

As luck would have it, I met my husband, Tonio, on a salsa dance floor. He loves salsa and the related dances, too, and is very good at them. (He's been dancing a year longer than I have.) We never would have gotten to really know each other if I didn't keep up with salsa and Spanish. We spoke in only Spanish initially.*

When I started at Temple Law School, I came to the mountain known as advocacy. I had to draw upon quite a bit of grit, and keep a growth mindset, to tackle it, too. You see, I wrote such a poor first paper for my legal writing class that when it was returned to me, it had more of my professor's red ink on it than the black type in which I had written it. I got a failing score.

---

* Now we speak mainly in English, and his English has greatly improved.

I had never written anything like a legal memorandum before, and I had no idea how to write one. I cried thinking I really wanted to be a lawyer but that I didn't have what it takes (the natural talent) to do so. Later I read over my professor's comments and took his feedback to heart. My writing got much better.

What brought my writing to the next level was learning oral advocacy. In my second year of law school, I tried out for Moot Court Team, but I didn't make the team. You could say that I didn't have a natural talent for oral advocacy. Actually, I believe I did, but I didn't yet know how to structure an argument.

The final round of the competition took place in front of the school and was terrific. Afterward, I went up to the winner, Scott Cooper, and asked him if he would teach me how to put on an oral argument. He did so and was a terrific teacher.

He had me try delivering the oral argument I had prepared and gave me great feedback about how I could improve it—how I could better structure my presentation, with a nice introduction (introducing myself, stating who I represent, and raising the issues before the court), the arguments (deciding on my best few arguments and listing them for the court), how to support those arguments (giving a few reasons, at most, for each), and how to wrap up (telling the court what relief my client sought). I worked hard to structure my arguments after that, both in writing and in my oral presentations, and the next year, not only did I make it onto the Moot Court Team, I won the competition.

Not only that, but with the tools Scott had given me about how to be a strong advocate, the quality of my writing skyrocketed. Before launching my law firm, I got hired by Blank Rome, one of the 100 largest law firms in the country. The first brief I wrote there got high praise, and thereafter, I was asked to write briefs in increasingly larger cases. By the time I gave notice of my intention to leave there, I had written the firm's brief in an $825 million case pitting Hewlett-Packard against SunGard.

That brings me to the present. Although I was a terrible speller who struggled to learn a foreign language, although my first paper in law school was a disaster, although I had no clue how to structure an oral argument, and although I was initially a terrible salsa dancer, I now consider myself a very fine speller, conversationally fluent in Spanish, and a rather good salsa dancer. In fact, Tonio and I danced a choreographed salsa and bachata number at our wedding.

As for the rest, at The Axelrod Firm, I'm representing companies in major litigation matters, including in two actions that have been the subject of *Law360* articles—one in a breach of contract action brought by a client to recover $1.25 million and another in an antitrust suit in which the opposing party claims to be entitled to over $66 million. One of my trials in another case, a commercial tort defense victory for my client, was published in "Pennsylvania Jury Verdict Review and Analysis," which catalogs the most significant Pennsylvania verdicts.

As I advocate in my publications and public speaking, as well as over social media, companies must treat women and minorities more equally. We should not have to have so much more grit and so much stronger growth mindsets than our white, nondiverse male counterparts to reach the same levels they do in terms of pay and promotions. That said, I am very pleased to share the news that talent is a far smaller piece of what goes into success than grit and a growth mindset.

Sheryl L. Axelrod is the president of The Axelrod Firm, P.C. in Philadelphia, where she represents companies in their employment, bodily injury, commercial, and appellate litigation matters and provides alternative dispute resolution services. www.theaxelrodfirm.com

Helen Darras Bather

I grew up in the 1960s in a household where sending girls to college let alone law school was not considered. I would have to pay my own way in order to pursue any dreams I had of a career, something I knew would be needed to take care of myself and any children I might have after watching my mother struggle when her marriage ended in divorce.

I had no trouble working hard. In my last two years of college I took 15 units while working 50 hours per week. Law school was completed in two-and-a-half years, working 32 hours per week to reduce my student loans.

After a couple of years, I found a home with a growing law firm. In order to get a higher paying position and perhaps a partnership, I learned how to attract clients, as well as the attention of partners. My best move: I volunteered for every difficult trial, often taking the place of a partner at courts in towns that I had to find first on a map.

Single motherhood became a reality after my divorce, when my children were five and seven years old. A few partners suggested that my kids would be a bar to becoming partner. I told them they needed to understand with CAPITAL LETTERS, **bold face type,** and underlined, that the only reason I cared about making money for the firm was to provide a future for my children. It took grit to speak up, but I was emphatic and they were quieted.

But hard work and an education were not enough to put me in position to control my own destiny. I needed a progressive plan or mindset, so I had to branch out by doing things outside of my firm and comfort to become well known in the industry.

I began teaching a paralegal class in legal writing in the evenings. My firm held seminars as did the industry, and I became a regular speaker at these events. When asked to write material for a continuing education class, I did so and was invited to teach one. The latter also saved money, since I received three hours of CEB credit for each hour I taught rather than paying for those hours.

My relationships with clients grew as these activities gave me more notice. People appreciated my teaching, knowing that I was always up to date on the law. By then, our firm had grown to seven offices and I had appeared at all but two courts in the state. A client who wanted only one or two lawyers to handle their cases state-wide could send them to me, and they did.

While still at the old firm, one of our largest clients was brought in by a partner who was later assigned an expensive case that allegedly could not be defended. I agreed to handle the matter even though I was guaranteed to lose. The client was not that familiar with me and would likely continue to send cases to my partner even if I lost.

The bills at the time of trial were over $500,000 and growing. My client gave me no settlement authority and argued about the witnesses I intended to call. When I went to trial, I was sure it would be my last for that insurance carrier.

However, I was able to elicit testimony showing the injured worker had a family history of his condition, a point I made at my seminars. Amazingly, I won the case, and the owner of the insurance company was so grateful that he placed the court's decision on the bulletin board at their office, earning me and our firm many more cases in the future.

I became partner, adding managing duties while continuing to handle my regular case load. The economy slowed down in early 1993, and several partners at our firm had difficulty getting business. Years of collection problems had caught up with us as well. After several missed paychecks, and numerous contentious partner meetings, three lawyers and I left to form a new firm.

I had to save for my share of new expenses, such as rent and equipment for the new firm, as well as paying our employees. We received no pay for over three months and had to fund payments for cars, health insurance, and other bills our old firm used to pay. It took guts and a lot of faith to make this move, especially as the sole support of my children. I was grateful to have continued to be a working lawyer, because these cases I was handling became our first billings.

Eventually, two original partners went on to other firms, which was best for all. My remaining partner and I continued at our firm, which I now run nine years after his retirement.

I know that I was lucky to have been hired with my old firm at a time of great growth. I was also fortunate to have left there before the financial situation worsened. And at my current firm, I had the best partner anyone could hope for.

However, my determination and perseverance would not have been enough to allow me to exceed my career goals, nor would my hard work. The fact that I was doing it for my children was an important factor, but given that, I should have been risk averse.

Instead I took chances by agreeing to accept cases in multiple and unfamiliar venues, volunteering for difficult trials, and branching out to do speaking and teaching assignments. By doing so, I became one of three women partners in a large firm and went on to be successful in my current firm, having put two kids through college and on trips to many countries.

My advice to any lawyer is to work hard, learn new things, pay attention so that problems become opportunities, and speak up on your own behalf. And make sure to take chances!

Helen Darras Bather has been partner/owner of Callopy & Bather in Chino Hills, California, where she focused on workers' compensation defense, discrimination, and serious and willful actions associated with workers' compensation cases.

Laurel G. Bellows

Don't Be Afraid of Spiders

When I think of grit, I think of my outer confidence, which inspires me to accomplish what my inner voice aspires to achieve.

I grew up with strong women who overcame personal adversity to find their own way in the world. There were no silver spoons on our table. My grandmother was a concert pianist who taught me to play with love not terror, yet her heart condition forced her to refrain from playing herself. My great aunts ran the businesses their families could not run well and received no credit for their success. One aunt was an adventurer who preserved her independence by remaining single and traveling the world on her own in the late 1800s. My mom was a model, an actress, and a caring, always present homemaker. Looking back, I have no idea how she "balanced," a word never used at the time.

Their inner toughness was invisible to me until adulthood. I experienced the attention and love devoted to an only child, me. And I grew up believing, at least on the outside, that I could be anything I chose to be.

I chose to be a lawyer after college. I knew only one lawyer and had no idea what lawyers did or the discipline required. I only knew that I sought a way to earn a living, other than as teacher or nurse.

Then WHAM! Law school in the 1970s. A seating chart. Being singled out each day because I was a woman taking a man's place, thrown into survival mode, into the discipline of being super prepared, forced to prove my competence day after day, imbued by that challenge with the will to succeed, igniting a force that was dormant within me, inherited from those strong women who pushed through without complaint.

Then, I chose to be a trial lawyer. Interesting choice for a 4'11," smiling blond when the image of a trial lawyer was tall, slim, silver-haired with horn-rimmed glasses and a "bring it on" demeanor. Every day, several hundred white male, seemingly arrogant, trial lawyers crowded the trial assignment courtroom. Today as I write,

I physically recall the feeling of smallness and inadequacy when the judge leaned over the bench each time I appeared to ask where the lawyer on my case was . . . and his doubtful expression when I pronounced that **I** was that lawyer.

How did that bright, smiling, petite lawyer develop the grit, the savvy, the competence, the confidence in herself, and the confidence of others to run her own law firm; become president of the Chicago Bar Association, the National Conference of Bar Presidents, and the American Bar Association; and successfully advocate for gender equality and for the eradication of modern day slavery?

My mantra is an old Chinese proverb: "Those who say it can't be done should get out of the way of those doing it."

Here is my recipe for cooking your personal grit:

Dare to win. Learn to persevere despite the odds, because it is your performance that will win the day.

Identify your strengths: Plan in advance where and how to use your expertise to greatest effect.

Prove your competence every day, playing offense, not defense. I am a senior lawyer. Still I must prove my competence every time I walk into a room of strangers. The greatest compliment is the reaction of those who meet me for the first time and say "I pictured you to be tall." I am always over-prepared on the subject and the background of the people at the table. But the preparedness is for my client or the cause, not for other people. Plus, there's the benefit of knowing that some folks will underestimate me. Voice your opinion, succinctly, confidently. Feel the room, but don't wait for others to say what you know to be true.

Don't be afraid of spiders. There is too much big game that requires your focus. Don't anticipate a fear. Never been bitten, and afraid of the bite? Spiders rarely bite. Why lose focus by looking under rocks for those that do?

Years back, I took our nine-year-old daughter to meet Dr. Tarantula and his pets on Halloween. Orange, blue, gray, and very few are venomous. In fact, the tarantula's main defense is to spit fur into the eyes of its pursuer, giving the tarantula time to move in another direction . . . a good legal tactic. And, yes, I allowed a tarantula to crawl up my arm. Soft, furry, *with claws.* YES, my daughter and I enjoyed a boost of self-confidence from our close encounters with spiders, proof of courage that carries me through tough deals. After all, if I can hold a tarantula, I can deal with any situation.

Name your fear . . . then step over it. Name your fears if you are going to move past them. Are you afraid of confrontation, public speaking, big groups at meetings, negotiation, the isolation of mediation, the first client interview, your first connection with opposing counsel? Are you able to identify what is frightening and tear the fear into small pieces, each new piece easier to digest and overcome? Do you believe that you are the only one afraid of failure, mistakes, or success?

Own the doorway. I am an introvert, contrary to appearances. But networking is essential to rainmaking, and rainmaking is a matter of survival. Get comfortable with talking to strangers about your business. Airplanes, bathrooms, movie lines, any opportunity to use your practiced 30-second elevator speech . . . even in an elevator. Big crowds bring clients, referrals from other attorneys, and an opportunity to shine. Outside the room, take a few deep breaths and stretch out posture perfect. Focus on small groups, not the mass. Introduce yourself to a group that has a space so you won't need to push to join. Bring a few conversation starters: "Did you hear what they discovered in Alaska?" and "What do you think about. . .?" Bring along your 30-second elevator speech about what you do for a living. Rainmaking IS a game . . . so learn to play it!

Make it smaller. Any huge goal is daunting. Break your strategy into little pieces, complete each smaller objective, and, POOF, you've accomplished the entire huge goal. Confident in your accomplishment, you are open to collaboration. Sharing passions and work is energizing and cements relationships that started as a passing connection.

Listen and learn. Listening is an underdeveloped skill. How do you know what the other side values if you don't listen to the words they use and the priority they give each issue? Grit does not mean uncompromising. Grit means the confidence to focus intently on what the other side is conveying to you, consciously and unconsciously.

Learn to negotiate. Being able to articulate needs, support your objectives, understand, and incorporate the interests of others into a mutually beneficial agreement is a power skill that builds grit.

Pick your battles. Then stick and stay.

When the going gets tough, and pressure feeds your doubts, there is always your song—a song that energizes you to take on any challenge and any challenger. Santana's "Black Magic Woman" is top on my playlist. Choose yours and play it loud.

Still need inspiration? Consider this: "If you don't build your own dream, someone will hire you to help build theirs."—Tony Gaskins

Women with grit take control of their own future.

Laurel G. Bellows is the founding principal of The Bellows Law Group, P.C. in Chicago, where she focuses on executive compensation, business disputes, human resources, and corporate risk assessment in compliance with new anti-human trafficking regulations and policies. She served as ABA president in 2012–2013. www.bellowslaw.com.

Kelly M. Bonnevie

I am the co-founder of a small, women-owned law firm established in 1996 in a Boston suburb. The three of us had worked together and decided that we wanted to go out on our own in the hopes of having more control over the cases we selected and the income we earned. That was 19 years ago, and we have never looked back. The ability to select clients and cases has made all the difference. I enjoy my professional life and private practice and see myself continuing to work in a profession that, unfortunately, has a high misery index. Not all of my law school classmates can say the same.

I can think of instances where grit and a growth mindset have helped:

➤ *The initial decision to go out on our own.* That was a risk, but we did it in a way that was well planned and researched. The daughter of a janitor who didn't finish high school, I was the first in my family to attend college, and my poor parents were horrified that I hadn't applied for a nice, secure government job. My law partners and I tried to minimize risk where we could by keeping our overhead costs low initially (our first office was small and located in the basement of a converted church, and we had one, part-time receptionist on our support staff). Taking that initial leap of faith and having it be successful was empowering since I had absolutely no one in my family or family friends who was a lawyer or entrepreneur. My law partners and I had male allies our age and a bit older who believed in us and coached us in terms of legal advice and practical office planning advice. As we move into the mature phase of owning our law practice, we now have several female mentors who have coached us in practice management issues pertaining to what comes next, and that has been enormously helpful.

➤ *Deciding to switch practice areas.* After 10 years of working in litigation with an emphasis on difficult race and sex discrimination plaintiff-side cases, I made the decision to switch to a different practice area that was more transactional and family-friendly: real estate. I was encouraged to do this by a male colleague (nonlawyer) who remarked that I had worked really well on a complex nonlitigation project, and had I ever thought about that kind of work? Hearing him say this spurred me to contemplate my unhappiness in litigation and my desire to use my legal skills in a different way. I had to learn an entirely different practice area and adapt to life as a lawyer who was not a litigator—this change initially involved having to overcome feelings about abandoning work as a "real" lawyer, but this change was for the better, and I have not regretted it.

➤ *Dealing with a health and family issues while overseeing my law firm.* At age 41, I was diagnosed with breast cancer. I was the family breadwinner (my partner, Karen, was home with our children, then ages six and three), and this required me to face worries about my own mortality and my family's future. I was fortunate that it was early stage, and for me, working during my treatment was a helpful, productive outlet. I had to make decisions about what and how much to tell clients about my treatment and health status, and I learned how many other colleagues had their own health issues that they were facing. In addition, I have aging parents who require help managing their care, and I am raising a niece who has come to live with us. Again, I have learned that many of my female colleagues are in the same boat in terms of caregiving responsibilities, and I have learned how to be very specific in asking for help from my other family members and protecting my time. I can speak to a client while waiting to pick up a child or parent from a doctor's visit without the client needing to know that I am not currently calling from the office. As long as I am doing high-quality work for them on time and within budget, my clients don't necessarily need to know what else I am juggling (although at times, those conversations with clients have been relevant and helpful).

➤ *Expanding our practice.* This is the one area of minor regret. I feel that my law firm was overly cautious, and we did not adopt a growth mindset as quickly as we should have. As women, we were risk-averse and did not want to expand our firm too quickly and end up having to lay off people. I understand that mindset and motivation, but I think it resulted in our being too cautious to hire associates and grow our firm as we could have. I see that male law school classmates who founded their own practices did not seem to have the same concerns, and I have watched one classmate, in particular, grow his firm to a level that has allowed him to earn more and take on more complex cases successfully in ways we could have as well. In retrospect, we could have expanded earlier, and we were probably too cautious in that area. I would caution younger attorneys to learn from this and be willing to consider risk that is not reckless but that may provide more opportunities. Many male attorneys feel "ready" to take something on when they are about 60 percent prepared to do so; for women, they often feel that they have to be 120 percent ready. That mindset means we miss out on certain opportunities, and I would love to help women change that and be willing to throw their hats into the ring when they are 60 percent ready as well.

Kelly M. Bonnevie is the founding partner of Wilson, Marino & Bonnevie, PC in Newton, Massachusetts, where she focuses on residential real estate matters, representing buyers, sellers, and lenders. www.wmblawfirm.com

Jocelyn Cara Bramble

An openly gay black woman in a notoriously difficult practice group, after 10 years of hard work I did what many times seemed impossible: I became a partner in my law firm as of January 1, 2012. Instead of running a long victory lap, I quickly stumbled as my large, international firm publicly imploded. I was devastated, heartbroken, and temporarily immobilized by fear, until I remembered (with some help) what got me that partnership in the first place.

Like many associates, I joined my first law firm with strong skill sets I, quite naïvely, thought would be sufficient to succeed. A few years in BigLaw disabused me of that notion. Even so, to my surprise, I found the work (mostly) engaging and challenging and I decided I wanted to become a partner.

Committing to a partnership run was a defining point in my career. I took failure off the table and determined that going forward I would find a way to overcome any obstacle in my path and would work relentlessly to achieve my ultimate goal. That seemingly simple shift in my thinking led me to a new way of working and approaching the world.

Banishing the Thought: "I am not that kind of person"

I no longer reflexively dismissed certain actions because of unexamined assumptions about myself or others. I quickly discovered that "talent truly is overrated" and that much of what I previously saw in others as talents that I did not possess were instead skills that I could learn and master with deliberate practice.

I knew, for example, that if I wanted to make partner, people and business development skills would be important. I could not hide behind my natural introvert tendencies or plead that I just wasn't a people person. I started with books, moved to seminars, and then used those as a basis to start internal conversations at my firm around these issues. These conversations, in turn, led to the creation of a firm committee dedicated to training young lawyers in personal communication and business development skills and providing them with opportunities to develop them in real-world situations.

I co-chaired the committee as a senior associate. This work led to additional opportunities within the firm that allowed me to deepen relationships with my colleagues at all levels of the organization. My successful management of the committee and my resulting higher profile within the firm were only possible because I changed my mindset.

Moving from "I cannot do that" to "What steps must I take to do that?"

I began to take the same approach with many other projects I would previously just have assumed I could not do. I was terrified of public speaking, but the success of my partnership quest required that I speak well in public. Once I changed my mindset, the question became, how do I make myself a better public speaker? That is, what specific step-by-step process do I need to undertake to get myself from where I am now to where I need to be? Breaking it down into concrete steps always made doable what at first blush seemed impossible.

Learning to Be Flexible

I still struggle with this one. Trying to control everything is always a losing battle. Despite our best efforts, we do not get a say in many of the things that happen in our lives. I was forced to confront this professional reality as a senior associate, when the work in my litigation practice group slowed down just as I was about to be put up for partner. At the same time, I had, for separate reasons, grown increasingly impatient with many of my firm's management decisions. I decided to leave.

My firm made me a counteroffer. Rather than permanently leave the firm, they asked me to do a secondment for six months at one of our large insurance clients. When originally presented, the idea struck me as utterly bizarre. I was a securities litigator who knew nothing about insurance law. The company was a regulatory client rather than a litigation client, and it would require that my family and I move thousands of miles away for six months.

Skeptical, I agreed to at least visit the client's corporate head-quarters, meet relevant staff, and learn more about the work I would do, should I choose to accept my firm's proposal. Once there, it did not take long for me to appreciate the opportunity I had been presented with, and it turned out that the secondment is one of the professional highlights of my career. The experience changed the way I think about my work and how I service my clients and, I believe, made me a better lawyer. I returned to the firm with additional business from the client and this important client's full support of my partnership bid. I also formed some of my most important professional relationships, including with the client's then general counsel, who remains a valuable mentor and friend.

Asking for Help and Building Authentic Relationships

At various points throughout my career, and most acutely as my firm imploded, I found myself needing to ask colleagues, friends, and mentors for help and guidance.

BigLaw culture is not known for its compassion. Because most of us wear our mental toughness as a badge of honor, we find it hard to share our vulnerabilities with others. I believe successful women and people of color take particular care to avoid any appearance of appearing whiney or weak, particularly at work. The same is true for me. As such, learning to ask for help required the most personal growth.

But knowing when, who, and how to ask for help is one of the most important professional skills one can learn. I learned that obtaining help from the best sources is more easily accomplished when you have created genuine and authentic relationships with diverse types of people. As I was once told, "build the bridge before you need it." It is actually better built before you ever imagine needing it.

My relationships have served as an important professional resource—and perhaps my most important professional lifeline. I have tapped members of my professional network for help, knowledge, support, and a (I believe all too often undervalued) sense of community. Carla Harris aptly calls this resource "relationship currency."

Relationship currency, Harris explains, empowers people to make requests, gain access to other people, and recover from mistakes. Based on my experience, I would add that relationship currency also affords you:

➤ Opportunities (e.g., training, business development, jobs)
➤ Understanding the "unwritten rules" of an organization
➤ Benefit of alternative perspectives to assist with help with problem-solving

Harris wisely advises people to build networks and relationships both vertically and horizontally. This point bears repeating. I am always amazed at how many people fail to understand what a vital potential resource people equal and "beneath" them on the pay scale and staff roster represent. A resource I have, unfortunately, witnessed all too many BigLaw attorneys neglect or, worse, abuse. They do so to their own detriment. As I often tell those I mentor, good relationships with all colleagues from the mailroom to the executive suite can make the difference between success and a professional disaster at any particular moment.

★★★★★

I will not say the devastation caused by the largest U.S. law firm to collapse to date was for the best. As is often the case, too many of the blameless paid the price for the failures of others. Even today, many continue to suffer the consequences. My partnership at Dewey & LeBoeuf did not last long. Yet, in my relentless pursuit of it, I transformed. I now know that I am more capable than I imagined—provided I seek out the right information or help, remain flexible, and follow the right process. That knowledge and the skills I developed as a consequence drove and sustained me through the dark days of 2012 as they do to this day.

Jocelyn Cara Bramble is general counsel of the District of Columbia Department of Insurance, Securities and Banking in Washington, D.C., where she focuses on issues involving insurance, securities, and banking products and services. https://disb.dc.gov

Paulette Brown

"We're here for a reason. I believe a bit of the reason is to throw little torches out to lead people through the dark."

—Whoopi Goldberg, comedian

This letter is written during an unprecedented era of female leadership at the American Bar Association. The top leadership ranks of the ABA have never been more diverse. When I pass the baton at the end of my term in August, all four of the ABA's top leadership positions (president-elect, chair of the House of Delegates, secretary, and treasurer-elect) will be women, including three women of color. This progress is significant and should be celebrated, but so much more remains to be done. Although the percentage of law school graduates of color has almost doubled in the last two decades to just over 25 percent, women and lawyers of color have made almost no headway in recent years in increasing their ranks at major U.S. law firms. For instance, among all employers listed in the 2015–2016 NALP Directory of Legal Employers, just 2.55 percent of partners were women of color. We also know that diversity can never be measured through numbers alone. Real gains are achieved when diverse lawyers feel valued and included in their organizations.

Suffice it to say we know we are not yet living in a world in which everyone gets the same, fair opportunities. Even when overt discrimination is not at play, the impacts of micro-inequities and implicit bias toward women and women of color, in particular, affect our trajectory and success in life. Further, we know that diversity and inclusion will not happen on its own. Our efforts toward a more diverse and inclusive legal profession must be intentional.

Women, and particularly women of color, must have grit. We must be persistent in the face of adversity. Women of color face negative effects in our professional lives that can be directly linked to our perceived "invisibility" at work. In 2006, I co-authored an important ABA Commission on Women in the Profession report, "Visible Invisibility: Women of Color in Fortune 500 Legal Departments." The report described the difficulties faced by black, Hispanic, Asian, and Native American female lawyers in law firms and found that they were leaving the legal profession at an extraordinarily high rate. The report also found that female lawyers and lawyers of color were subject to demeaning comments and harassment, were skipped over for client development opportunities and desirable assignments, and lacked networking opportunities and access to significant billable hours.

Unfortunately, not much has changed over the past 10 years. In a 2016 survey of young women lawyers by the Florida bar, 43 percent said they had experienced gender bias in their careers. Of the 464 women surveyed, 40 percent said they experienced insensitivity by their employer and 17 percent said they experienced harassment. The reported examples of gender bias included being mistaken for court reporters, being "drunk dialed" by senior partners, and being punished for assertiveness. In addition, 21 percent of the women surveyed said they believed they were not paid the same as their male counterparts with similar experience.

Gender bias is not just a problem for young women. Women of color of all ages often face biases and low expectations. When I started practicing law in 1976, you could count on one hand the number of lawyers who looked like me who were in court. Often, I was asked whether I was the court reporter—or even the defendant—everything except whether I was a lawyer. Forty years later, these kinds of wrongful assumptions, unfortunately, still happen. For example, I was in a courtroom, standing in front of a judge, and as we were being introduced, a woman talking to the judge said, "We have several lawyers here . . . including the president-elect of the American Bar Association." The judge looked around the room until finally I said to him, "She's talking about me." The judge looked in every direction with the exception of mine, despite the fact that the woman had pointed to me during her introduction. But perhaps he was looking for his perception of what the ABA president-elect should look like. Oftentimes, people actually have no idea what they are doing. Some of the most prevalent discrimination these days is unconscious, and when you tell the "guilty" party, many times they're horrified.

I like to think I got to where I am today because I did not conform to some people's expectations. I recall, many years ago, when
one of my co-workers said at my law school going-away party,
"Don't feel badly when you flunk out of law school your first year;
I hear 50 percent of first-year law students do," that comment made
me even more determined to succeed. Sometimes, there is power in
being underestimated. Just as I had received little encouragement
to consider a career in the law, later on as a law student of color
it was not uncommon to be channeled toward legal services or
public defender positions assisting the disadvantaged—certainly a
noble calling—rather than more prestigious jobs in major law firms
or even the prosecutor's office. I figured I would show them that
I was more than capable. And I did. I set out on a career that led to
positions as in-house counsel for several Fortune 500 companies.
My first job was with National Steel, then the nation's third-largest
steelmaker, and I became an expert in ERISA. Sometimes our most
serious challenges in life are what builds our character most.

But a grit and growth mindset is more than fighting our way
to the top. Once we have a seat at the table, it is our responsibility
to empower others. It is imperative to take risks and use our influence. I have the great privilege of being the first woman of color to
lead our association in 136 years. Because I believe opportunities at
all levels should be available to all, my presidential appointments
committee worked hard to ensure we reached historic numbers of
women and diverse leaders selected to lead the ABA's many standing committees, commissions, entities, and other initiatives. When
our committee was told there were no women or people of color to
fill certain positions, we pushed back. We refused to take no for an
answer. As a result, women made up 55.12 percent of presidential
appointments while 49.8 percent of those appointed were people
of color, a nearly 13 percent increase over the year before.

Once we have established and recognized that we have grit,
we have to ensure that we pay it forward. We have to own it. To
do that, we must be willing to allow those coming behind us an
opportunity to shine, and we have to ensure that all women know
they have to accept and take responsibility for their brilliance and
the contributions they make. It provides encouragement for the
next generations. They will see us as someone to emulate.

We must see ourselves as mentors at all times. There are so many good and talented female lawyers ready to shine, if only given the chance. Many top legal officers set aside time for mentoring. As we know, mentoring and sponsorship are critical tools to achieve diversity and inclusion and to guarantee a healthy future for the legal profession and justice system. I have been privileged with many insightful mentors, both men and women and those who were older and younger. I founded the New Jersey Women of Color Mentoring Group, drawing attorneys from large and small firms throughout the state, and a decade later we're still going strong, albeit as the 2006 report predicted, most have left their firms.

Likewise, during my term as the first woman of color to lead the ABA, I made a conscious effort to be visible in communities that do not typically get visited by the ABA president. I visited Boys & Girls Clubs around the country because it is hard to aspire to be something you don't see. It is important to help our young people fulfill their potential and imagine better futures for themselves. As president-elect and president, I invited young people with local Boys & Girls Clubs to attend the ABA's Annual and Midyear meetings. A young lady from a Boys & Girls Club wrote a heart-felt Youth of the Year speech in which she told the audience that her experience with the ABA taught her to "believe in achieving the impossible." She was so inspired to become a lawyer that she secured a summer internship at a local law firm.

As a woman, especially a woman of color, in a leadership position, it is imperative to be more than a figurehead. You have a real responsibility to pave the way for others to be successful. As my mother taught me, "to whom much is given, of much is required" (Luke 12:48). There is an inherent obligation of everyone to share knowledge with someone else. A grit and growth mindset can be taught and learned. I share with people both my good and bad experiences so they can learn and grow from them.

Paulette Brown is a partner at Locke Lord LLP in Morristown, New Jersey, where she focuses on labor and employment litigation. She served as ABA President in 2015–2016. www.lockelord.com

Ingrid Busson-Hall

You have opportunities to seize, foundations to build, and examples to set. The path you are on is well trodden. You are one of us—a woman in the law. Margaret Brent arrived in the American colonies in 1638 and became the first woman lawyer. She and many pioneers since have made your steps on the path possible. You have everything it takes to succeed as a lawyer so long as you remain tenacious, curious, and sufficiently self-reflective to invest in your own advancement. Every once in a while you will have some lucky breaks, but for the most part, there will be no handouts. This career is of your making—you are the driver. With grit and a growth mindset, you are going places!

Here are a few things I've learned along the way to guide you as you write your own playbook.

Be Intentional, but Adaptable to Change

I didn't want to practice law at all. I studied environmental law at Vermont Law School to get a firm understanding of policy and regulations. I envisioned a career as a treaty negotiator at the UN or the World Bank. Somewhere between Civil Procedure and Corporations, I changed my mind. During my third year, never having summered at a firm, with no moot court trophies and no experience with a law journal, I decided I wanted to go to a big firm. Despite my good grades, I wasn't the preferred candidate. This was unceremoniously and repeatedly confirmed by the 100 plus rejection letters that filled my mailbox. After taking the New York bar exam, with no job, I moved to Washington, D.C. I landed on a generous friend's couch and found a job at a legal placement firm. Over the next nine months, I worked on various document reviews, making $20 to $25 an hour.

Then I got a job as a first-year associate at Skadden Arps in New York. How? I was clear in my mind that I wanted the job when I heard about it and rejected any notion that I didn't meet the standard pedigree for such a firm. I did my research, practiced my pitch, and reached out to my then relatively small, professional network. In every interview (12 in total, conducted over three months in four separate visits), I conveyed confidence in my candidacy and a real enthusiasm for the role.

Remain Perpetually Curious and Challenge Convention

While at Skadden, I bucked the trend and switched practice groups. I went from products liability litigation into financial services regulation. I had no idea what I was doing; the FDIC-insured stamp on the checkbook in my wallet was the extent of my awareness of banking. Any insecurity resulting from my lack of substantive knowledge, however, was mitigated by a keen sense that I was unsatisfied in my existing role and needed a change. I thought, "a good lawyer can learn anything" and threw myself into this new area with focus and determination. In the years since, I've become an expert in a field with few players. My curiosity gives me an edge in understanding the fast-changing fabric of rules and regulations so that I can best advise my clients in a highly competitive industry that is under significant pressure.

Be Bold

Constantly stretch the outer edges of your frame of reference and don't expect to be "ready" when opportunities to shine come your way. After five years in private practice, I went to work in-house at Crédit Agricole, a French foreign bank. I had a great boss who made sure I had a lot of challenging work. Only two years into it, she decided to leave. What would this mean for me? What would a new boss be like? What would the transition be like? The uncertainty felt heavy. The day after she announced her impending departure, she suggested I ask the general counsel to promote me into her role. I wasn't ready for this for so many reasons: I had far fewer years of experience, I didn't have her gravitas, I would have my neck on the line, etc. None of these were sufficiently compelling to hold me back once she had pushed me in the right direction. There was no guarantee I would get the job, but I had to ask. I got the promotion.

Identify and Address Blind Spots

The learning curve was steep. Suddenly, I became the boss of a small team. Proving the point that there is no better time to learn than when you're drinking water from a firehose, all this change happened at the outset of the global financial crisis, which affected me and everyone I worked with professionally and personally. I thought my team was doing a great job handling the stress. My boss thought differently and told me I needed to learn how to motivate and manage my team more effectively. Without the luxury of spare time, I built out a strategy for success. I spoke with friends and colleagues who managed teams, read some management theory books, and most importantly, listened to my team. Eventually, I built out a management style that fit my company's needs and my personality.

Embrace Fear and Take Risks

Control and comfort aren't signs of fulfillment, rather they are warnings of boredom and frustration. You can't grow and thrive in a career without taking a chance that things might not work out. After eight years at Crédit Agricole, I was well respected and well known throughout the bank's global network. I was advising clients on major changes to the regulatory landscape that affected nearly every aspect of how we did business and with whom we could do it. In my personal life, I had gotten married and had a baby. This was the perfect time to sit back and enjoy. Unfortunately, I couldn't remain still and become complacent; I needed a new challenge. So, just after my daughter's first birthday, I started a new job at Morgan Stanley.

Invest in Yourself

Building your professional brand and network, learning a new skill, and discovering a new area of the law all require significant commitments of time and, often, money. In an era of cost containment, you may have to pay your own way. Once you've prioritized your development goals for the year, decide how much you are personally willing to invest to realize them. I'm an active member of the ABA Section of International Law. I've never had an employer who covered the full cost of my dues or attending meetings. My engagement in the section has been invaluable in terms of networking and leadership training. I pay for it. A few years ago I decided I wanted to overcome my fear of public speaking and become a recognized speaker. I found a coach and paid for it myself.

Find Your Voice and Recognize Its Power

If you are in the room, someone put you there for a reason. Maybe it was your boss, a sponsor, a colleague from the bar association, or maybe it was you, because you didn't want to miss out on the conversation. So, why do you remain silent? You are smart, thoughtful, and have good judgment. Have confidence in these things and speak up when you have something to say. I know what it's like to agonize at meetings and presentations, searching to find exactly the right words to make a point or ask for clarification. My mantra is this: engage and always ask the question. You will be amazed at the reaction. People won't remember the precise words you chose, they will remember you for your insight and your courage.

Regardless of the accomplishments that ultimately define your success, getting there will take passion and perseverance. I wish you good luck and great adventure!

Ingrid Busson-Hall is senior director, financial regulation at PayPal in New York City, where she advises PayPal's global businesses on U.S. and international regulations related to consumer protection, licensing, anti-money laundering, sanctions, and anti-bribery. www.paypal.com

Elizabeth J. Cabraser

I am so very honored to be included in the ABA Commission on Women in the Profession's "grit book." The advances that we, as women and as professionals, have made in the practice of law and our contributions to the rule of law in the United States all come down to the grit of generations of individual women and their determination to make their way—and to pave the way for others—in the legal profession, in the judiciary, and in public service.

I have been in private practice, on the plaintiff's side, for my entire career. Indeed, I can accurately say that I have had only one law job: an attorney at the plaintiffs'-side firm now known as Lieff Cabraser Heimann & Bernstein, LLP. Lieff Cabraser had its genesis in 1977, when my still-partner, Robert Lieff, offered me a job, during my last year in law school, as a clerk and research assistant. I kept that job, upon graduation, and found myself in court the day after my admission to the bar. Bob Lieff never had the slightest doubt that I could, and would, be a good lawyer. That utter confidence in my abilities nourished my own small stirrings of self-confidence. It was a new experience for me, to have the trust of a senior professional who was absolutely certain of my professional abilities—even those that I did not then possess. That confidence spurred me to demonstrate that it was, indeed, well-placed. This is where a little bit of grit comes in. I soon found that Bob Lieff's confidence in me as a young lawyer was the exception, not the rule. As the first child in my family and the oldest of five, I had always been the leader, the path-maker, the one whom my brothers and sisters looked to for guidance and to take risks. I had, quite simply, throughout my schooling, never experienced being second-best. The practice of law, then a very predominantly male profession, was quite a wake-up call. I was sometimes belittled, and often underestimated.

Condescension, if not the norm, was a frequent occurrence.

My first reactions to these rebuffs were hurt, anger, and resentment. I soon learned, however, that, while justified, these emotions were simply making me miserable and were not doing anything for me in terms of achieving advancement or respect. Somehow, I managed to internalize a mindset of regarding myself the way I wanted others to regard me. I strove always to treat others with the respect and consideration that I desired. Reciprocity did not always happen, but it happened often enough to re-charge my resolve. I must admit that I did, also, incorporate some of the more stereotyped tricks of gaining credibility in a man's world. I learned to deepen my voice, and to speak more slowly and in more measured terms. I curbed a bit of my enthusiasm. In the days before the Internet and email, I destroyed far more letters than I actually sent. Sometimes, grit meant pretending that the little slings and arrows wafted my way by snarky or rude male "colleagues" simply did not exist. True grit is like sandpaper: It smooths, not roughens, the surfaces with which it interacts. So, I found that a little diplomacy—without ever giving in on my truly core values and objections—also went a long way. It has now been nearly 40 years since I got my first, and only, law job. The path has been gritty, but I have tried to make the way a bit smoother for my younger women colleagues and to support women in the profession wherever, and however, I can. Along the way, I have been continually astounded by the achievements of women in the law, especially by those who have shown far more grit than I could ever imagine.

Recently, I was introduced to the concept of "growth mindset." Amazingly, it goes far to explain my own attitude toward human abilities and potential. I do believe that we arrive upon this earth each as our own person, with unique characteristics and a singular personality. Otherwise, what would be the point? As Oscar Wilde famously said, "Be yourself. Everyone else is already taken." But there is a lot of room for growth within each self. Certainly, I never considered, growing up, becoming a lawyer—it meant talking and writing entirely too much. I thought of myself as having more of a scientific and technical mindset, suited to long periods of silent inquiry, lab work, and solitary field work. Never was I one to speak out in class, to engage in the debating society, to star in plays, or to put myself out on any stage. I loved music, and did consider a professional career as a musician, but that career would be spent, safely, at the back of the stage, behind a set of drums. To be both seen and heard at the same time, I considered, was a bit much. So, I have no explanation, other than the existence of a growth mindset, for how and why I became a lawyer and why I love what I do so much. An orator I am not. No golden pen have I. But I care about my clients and my cases, I love to work collegially with other lawyers and with experts, and I have the utmost respect for the remarkable women and men who serve on our judiciary. For me, the work of litigation, which I still do every day, is itself a journey of growth, toward solutions, and toward justice.

Elizabeth J. Cabraser is a founding partner of Lieff Cabraser Heimann & Bernstein, LLP in San Francisco, where she focuses on representing plaintiffs and plaintiff classes in securities and financial fraud, product defect, consumer, civil rights, and antitrust litigation. www.lchb.com

Alissa Chambers

I didn't know I had grit until I found myself sitting across from one of my first-year law professors, about one month into my first semester of school. I received another "R" for "rewrite" on a legal writing and research assignment. In college, I had done well and I had never worked as hard as this. What was expected of me in my first year? I was out of my element, convinced I was just not smart enough to hang with the crowd I found myself surrounded by in law school. Professor Harri's kindness when I walked into his office opened up the floodgate of emotions I was working so hard to hide from everyone. I began our discussion with my conclusion that getting an "R" in his class was proof of what I already knew—I was not cut out for this. I proceeded to list my grievances, expressed how incredibly stressed I was, and bemoaned I was not as smart as this group of first-year lawyers and I did not stand a chance.

When I was done, Professor Harri asked me if I believed I was giving school my all and I was trying my best. When I assured him I was, he paused for a few minutes before calmly saying, "Maybe it is time to talk about your back-up plan." His question was sincere and compassionate, but it felt like the floor had dropped out from beneath me. In the past year, I had invested more effort than I ever had in my life just to get to law school. I had only been in school for a few weeks, and I was finding myself asked whether I was ready to give up. The realization that I did not have a back-up plan was sobering.

Professor Harri let it sink in for a few minutes and then told me that, although he did not know whether my classmates were smarter than me, his experience as a professor was the students who did the best in his class tended to be the students who spent the majority of their time at the library. You see, Professor Harri was famous (or notorious?) for walking around the library late on Friday nights before a big research project was due and observing which students were researching *American Jurisprudence* or the

American Law Reports (he strictly prohibited Westlaw research for first-year students).

I was not sure what to do with myself when I left his office, so I went to the library. I chatted with my classmates who were there. I started looking at the books with them and venting about how hard this assignment was. It was so shocking to hear they were also having a hard time and they thought the project was hard, too! I had always been so intimidated, figuring that everyone else had some innate ability making them immune to the pressure I was experiencing. I was not sure how to figure out the legal research and writing problem, but if other folks could figure it out, I could probably figure it out. I made some great friends in the library, and the feeling of not going through this process alone helped a lot. I figured until I found a back-up plan, I was going to commit myself to my studies. Putting one foot in front of the other, things started to turn around.

I was in the top 10 percent of my class my first semester. I am grateful to Professor Harri; his kindness, concern for his student's well-being, and life lessons—not to mention the fundamental skills of legal research and writing—have shaped where I am in my career today. Professor Harri taught me that knowing the answer is less important than knowing how to find the answer. In my career, I have welcomed all kinds of research projects and not shied away from complex or novel questions, which I also credit to Professor Harri.

Out of law school, I took a job in the commercial department of Crowley Fleck in Helena, Montana. My supervising partner, Jason Loble, has a practice focusing, in part, on mergers and acquisitions and private securities offerings. I was excited to have a job and determined to put in the work necessary to find out if these practice areas were my calling. I jumped feet first into this unknown field and once again felt the growing pains of the learning process. A few weeks into my first job, I wished I had listened to my mother and tried harder in my math classes. I found myself reviewing contracts with complicated purchase price adjustment mechanisms and Googling questions on algebra to figure out dilution percentages for private stock offerings. I was a bit freaked out—I had become an English major, so I didn't have to take the higher level math classes.

I drew on Professor Harri's library refuge and decided I needed to go to my "library" for some help with math. I called my mom, who is a proud, self-proclaimed math nerd—a former math teacher turned entrepreneur who has built a career around for her love for math. It killed me to call her and tell her that she was right, it was cool to learn math, and I needed some help. My mom was so excited to hear I wanted to learn math, she forgot to say, "I told you so!" My mom sent me some fourth grade extra credit workbooks on fractions and recommended some mental math exercises. For the next few months, I worked through the elementary school math books, sometimes cursing the author (my mom), sometimes finding myself having fun and experiencing satisfaction when I figured out a word problem. I am excited to say I now welcome any math challenge presented to me and relish the opportunity to use my freshly relearned algebra skills! I have been sought after in my firm for my math abilities.

I have found my passion in pro bono work. I have learned so much about perseverance and strength working with my pro bono clients who demonstrate strength in times of true adversity. I am now on the board of Montana Legal Services Association (MLSA), a nonprofit law firm that empowers low-income people by providing legal information, advice, and other services free of charge. The grit exhibited by the MLSA staff attorneys inspires me and gives me hope for our future.

I take heart in knowing I do not need to be the smartest or the best to find fulfillment and reward in the practice of law. I believe that effort and attitude have contributed more to my experiences and opportunities than any pre existing skill or talent. Our challenges are there to lead us to greater awareness. Grit does not come from the times in our life when we are on top of the world; it comes from painful and uncomfortable experiences. If you are reading this and are a law student, I would encourage you to keep a journal. I think you will find if you look back on it years later you will be surprised how much you have grown and how much you have learned. You are what you are seeking. If you can have the courage to look inside when things are challenging on the outside, if you can embrace obstacles as a learning opportunity, you will come out on the other end stronger for it.

Good luck and good cheer.

Alissa Chambers is an associate at Crowley Fleck PLLP in Helena, Montana, where she focuses on mergers and acquisitions, employment law, and private securities offerings. www.crowleyfleck.com

Antoinette M. "Toni" Jackson

As a child of the civil rights era, I was moved to make a difference and believed that lawyers had the ability to impact lives. I remember as early as the fifth grade that I wanted to be a lawyer so I could help people and change lives. However, I did not always know the path that I would take to accomplish my goal. In fact, other than television, I had not met nor been exposed to a real-life attorney until my last year in college.

I was not prepared to go directly to law school after college for financial reasons, but I knew that I was going. So, I set out the steps for my plan. At least, looking back on it now, I realize it was a plan. I always told everyone that I wanted to be a lawyer, and I was fortunate to have a friend introduce me to a lawyer who gave me a chance to work in his small firm. The experience from that job enabled me to get my second job as a paralegal in a mid-size firm. These jobs gave me a chance to gain experience and learn about different practice areas while I saved money for law school. Each year I would apply to law school so that I would stay on track and remain focused, but each year money was still an issue. Unfortunately, while I was going through this off period, there were people around me who told me I would never go back. Fortunately, those voices were drowned out by those who encouraged me and the even louder voice inside me that was determined to prove the naysayers wrong.

While in law school, I realized that I essentially had everything working against me for entry into a white, male-dominated profession that valued Ivy League and elite pedigree. I am African American, a woman, was attending an HBCU law school, and at that time I was wearing my hair in braids, and my jewelry staple was six, very ethnic looking brass bangles. To further illustrate my personality, I once wore a royal purple suit to a job fair and almost gave our career placement director a heart attack because I didn't wear the traditional black, gray, or blue suit. Despite her misgivings about my attire, I came away with two job offers. Many asked how, but I knew how: I was personable, determined, and confident, but more important, I was prepared. I knew about the companies and firms I was talking to, and I engaged the interviewers with probing questions that showed both interest and knowledge. This was the beginning of how I handled myself and represents the overall gist for how I practice.

After pursuing job options that weren't as glamorous but provided a solid foundation for my ultimate practice, I was offered an opportunity to join a majority firm. This was an unexpected direction for me and never where I had envisioned myself, but it was exactly the path for which I had prepared. BigLaw was not my plan, but my path had prepared me for this opportunity and, more importantly, had given me the tools to succeed in the BigLaw environment. Even still, there was a lot I did not know about practicing in a firm. I had no frame of reference and no one who sat me down to give me the ins and outs of billing time, developing business, or just handling the day-to-day life of being in BigLaw. This was a different world and I had to figure it out fast.

Although there were few black partners at that time, I identified a number of people whom I wanted to emulate, and many became mentors from afar. When I was attending meetings, conferences, and even social events, I watched and learned. I became a sponge for information but was more like a piece of unmolded clay waiting to be shaped. I also learned from my clients. I learned about their interests, their business styles, and even their lifestyles. Then I began to work on me. I took golf lessons, learned about wine and fine foods, and broadened my travel horizons. I did all of these things while continuing to sharpen my skills in my chosen practice area. I understood that even though I had a law degree and a bar card, it was important to my success that I continue to learn and grow both personally and professionally.

Now I am often invited to speak to young lawyers and students of all ages from middle school to college. One of the things that I often tell them to remember is that each of us is a product. Those hiring, be that person a client or employer, are looking for the best product that their money can buy. When we remember that we are a product, we also have to remember that new or improved models, whether a new lawyer or other competition, are always available with more bells and whistles (knowledge). Therefore, you must always be willing to learn and improve your product to ensure that you have the best product to offer to the buying public.

Another thing that I try to stress is being your true and authentic self while pursuing your goals. Remember the description I gave of myself and my worries about being the right fit for the legal club? Despite my concerns, I remained my authentic self and never stepped away from who I am. By doing this, I was able to stay focused on my goals without being distracted by trying to become someone that I wasn't. I remember a lawyer I worked with once criticized how I had handled a matter even though I had handled it successfully. I reminded him that I had been successful in achieving a positive outcome for the client while explaining to him that he and I simply had a difference in style on how to achieve the desired outcome. I chose to handle the matter in a way that stayed true to my authentic self.

As I continue my process of learning and improving my product, I responded to an ABA survey about women attorneys. It was only as a result of that survey that I truly understood that I am someone who has grit with a growth mindset. Lucky for me, although I did not necessarily identify these traits within myself earlier, I followed a path understanding the importance of perseverance, continuing growth, and having a passion for my chosen profession. However, had someone identified these traits for me earlier, or even informed me of the importance of them, I think that I may have been even more deliberate in my approach to certain career decisions and goals. This year I celebrate my 25th year of practice, and 18 of those years have been in BigLaw. As I look back, I now understand that I have always had grit—perseverance and passion—and a growth mindset. I'm just lucky enough now to have a name for it and the ability to pass on the skills to those coming behind me.

Antoinette M. "Toni" Jackson is a partner at Jones Walker LLP in Houston and focuses on affordable housing financing and community development law. www.joneswalker.com

Elaine Johnson James

Grit and a growth mindset root and ground us in ourselves, repelling fiery darts from people who do not acknowledge women's talent and capacity or fear that our perseverance, passion, and ability will expose their ineptitude. Among the gritty, growth-minded principles that have helped me remain happy, and relatively sane, during 34 years in BigLaw are:

1. Conflict is a natural and predictable part of life. Don't give your adversary power by getting angry—just excel. Living well is the best revenge.
2. Don't absorb the badness, madness, or sadness of your detractors. Their conduct reveals who they are, not who you are.
3. Never let anyone who is not wholly invested in and completely supportive of you define you, not even one whit.
4. The law is a competitive environment. Strive to get respect and fairness, not love, from your professional colleagues.
5. Choose your friends *very* carefully. Include only people who share your vision and values in your posse.
6. Occupy your space. Don't be intimidated when a man brands you "aggressive," "difficult," or, my personal favorite, the "B word." Remind him that clients pay for your zealous, energetic representation, not your aptitude for kowtowing, rolling over, or playing dead. I've been called the B word so often you'd think it was my middle name. Conjuring up a zinger helps me cope, even if I don't utter it. I've often thought (and once said), "If I were a B-----, I'd have a pedigree. You, sir, are a mutt."
7. While you can have it all, you definitely cannot have it all at once, so establish priorities regularly, expect them to shift as life's seasons change, and be fully present and engaged wherever you are.
8. Be receptive to constructive criticism, even when it stings. Like fertilizer, it will help you grow.

Hopefully, the following personal vignettes provide strategies for avoiding (or, at least, overcoming) obstacles I encountered as the only, and often the first, woman or black lawyer in BigLaw firms. Rest assured—you're not the Lone Rangerette. Many women have faced similar challenges.

Tenacity, faith, opportunity, and exemplars all are elements of grit. My focus and belief about who I am and what I can do were instilled and undergirded by amazing, adoring, no-nonsense parents, who taught my sister and me that our options were limitless. They also were realistic about, and careful to prepare us for, the challenges of life in our working class, Chicago neighborhood in the 1960s. I vividly recall my mother telling me to check my homework *again* when I was eight. I balked, and she said, "You're a Negro; you must work twice as hard and perform twice as well in order to get half as much as a white girl." When prejudice or unfairness reared its ugly head, our parents reapplied our invisible Teflon coating, so insult and sorrow would not stick, kissed and hugged us, then sent us back into the fray. As a result, my sense of self seldom has been vulnerable to others' preconceived notions or opinions.

I integrated a public high school, walking from the bus past unkempt, unruly picketers shouting "NIGGERS GO HOME" through bullhorns. At age 12, I felt unsafe, but not for long. Daddy, a strapping policeman, drove me to school in his squad car every day until the picketers left.

With familial support and grit, I focused on academic achievement instead of wallowing in or reflecting upon the horror of bigotry. Inexplicably, when recounting those events to a friend 40 years later, I sobbed, even though experiencing them hadn't generated one teardrop.

A cohort of mentors and sponsors, fabulous people and accomplished lawyers, blessed me early in my legal career. Some demand mention, like Honorable Clifford Scott Greene, a black man, who earned the highest score statewide on the Pennsylvania bar exam in 1952 but could not find a job. Judge Greene gave me a federal clerkship, taught me innumerable, invaluable lessons about law and life, and never displayed a scintilla of bitterness about his long journey up the rough side of the mountain.

Drinker Biddle & Reath gave me opportunity. I was its first black female lawyer. Kenneth Frazier, now chairman of Merck, was the only black associate until I joined DB&R in 1983. Kenny welcomed me when I routinely (i.e., daily) intruded on his early morning solitude to ask questions or just sit in a safe place. He remains among my dearest friends, and he mentors my beloved children.

As a young partner at DB&R, my rabbi, Lawrence Fox, the ABA ethics guru and Yale law professor, made Kenny and me join and actively participate in the ABA, let me—a first year lawyer—take depositions and argue motions, and took me to client meetings (after one of which, he literally leapt into my lap while flying through a hellacious thunderstorm). Years later, Larry included me on the faculty of his nationally televised ethics seminars. He's still my muse.

Bobbi Liebenberg, former chair of the ABA Commission on Women in the Profession—on which I now serve—and JoAnne Epps, the Temple University Provost, inspired and guided me. The respect these young women lawyers garnered in the male-dominated, Philadelphia legal community in the early 1980s showed me that I, too, could succeed, despite male lawyers who mistook me for a court reporter or a secretary who hadn't made coffee. In each instance, I noted that court reporting (or coffee-making) was not on Harvard Law School's curriculum and inquired whether that course had been offered by his alma mater.

Every BigLaw firm has at least one jerk; many target women. In an otiose attempt to usurp client control, my partner publicly accused me of failing to file a brief for a client. Instead of responding to him, I emailed the firm's manager a note from the client's general counsel, thanking me for the "best brief she had ever read," and the opinion affirming judgment in favor of her company.*

At another firm, partial origination credit for one of my cases was given to a paralegal.** As a result, I—the first and only black female partner—received a smaller share of the substantial contingent fee I had won. I appealed, to no avail. The handwriting was on the wall. If the pie shrunk, I would not get a slice. Eleven

---

* Of course, I cc'd the prevaricating partner.
** This is not a typographical error or an Aesop's Fable.

months later, I started my own firm with all my clients (and some of theirs) in tow.

Life affords ample stimuli to generate bitterness or anger almost every workday. Although you cannot change the stimuli, you can control your response. I typically choose gratitude over resentment and service over strife. I have, however, openly declared war when bad conduct affected others, as well as me. Thus, after years of mistreatment by a misogynistic partner, an inexperienced, not gifted, but very powerful man from Kentucky, I forwarded one of his more abusive emails to the firm's management. He was forced to apologize to me, but retained power and continued to cause women to leave the firm in droves. The support and encouragement I received from my sister partners, Paulette Brown, immediate past president of the ABA, Pamela Robertson, and Lynn Wright, were crucial. We are friends for life, no matter where we practice law. Mature lawyers need mentors and sponsors too.

Imagine my joy when bidding that partner adieu and informing him that I was joining another BigLaw firm and every client I originated or served (including those who had stayed with the firm when another partner left) had chosen to follow me. Red-faced, he raged that I had taken advantage of the firm. I responded, "The same talent, work product, and personality that led our clients to stay when John Doe left the firm last year are causing them to leave with me." I didn't have long hair to fluff, so I robustly batted my eyelashes for punctuation.

Your Teflon coating won't keep naysayers' sick stuff from sticking to you if you scratch the coating with self-doubt. Climb on your big sisters' mature, sturdy shoulders. Be gritty and growth minded. Believe in yourself, for greatness is in you. Dear Sister-in-the Law, I pray that life and the practice of law will be as joyful, rich, and fulfilling for you as they have been, and are, for me.

Elaine Johnson James is the president of Elaine Johnson James, P.A. in West Palm Beach, Florida, and a commercial litigator, focusing on trials and appeals in federal and state courts, administrative law, and arbitration. www.elainejohnsonjames.com

Nancy E. Joerg

By way of personal introduction, I am presently 70 years old. I have been happily married for 47 years, have three wonderful adult children, and seven amazing grandchildren.

I am still in the full-time practice of law and enjoy it tremendously. Our law firm, Wessels Sherman Joerg Liszka Laverty Seneczko P.C., is a management-side labor and employment law firm with five offices: St. Charles, Illinois; Chicago; Minneapolis; Davenport, Iowa; and Oconomowoc, Wisconsin. This is the only law firm in which I have worked.

I am the managing shareholder of our St. Charles office. I am also a long-time member of our law firm's five-person executive committee.

I was a stay-at-home mom for 12 years. Our home was in Batavia, Illinois. Then, I went to Northern Illinois University College of Law in DeKalb, Illinois, for its close proximity to my home. I graduated law school the day after I turned 40 years old.

I was very scared about going to law school in the first place. I eventually went because my husband had such tremendous faith and belief in me. Walter, my husband (who is retired now), was a school psychologist and assistant superintendent of schools. He had remarkable insight into who I am as a person. Walter said to me, "Nancy, it's up to you, of course, whether you want to go to law school, but I strongly feel that if you plan to be a housewife and a mother and never develop your own career, that is a prescription to eventually becoming unsatisfied and depressed. In my opinion, it is not a good long-term plan."

I would say, "Well, I will wait until the kids graduate from college." Walter would counter, "Nancy, that is not a way to use your full potential. Don't blame me if some day you come to me and say you are depressed." Walter further observed, "You love to help people, you love to write, you love to read and study, you should be a lawyer." He negotiated. He suggested that I try taking the law school admissions test, and, if I didn't do well, he would never again bring up the subject of law school.

So, I went to a prep class for the law school admissions test, and I studied very hard (I've always been a hard-working student). I did well on the law school admissions test. My husband felt very triumphant and urged me to apply to law schools.

I went ahead and applied to law schools and was accepted by several. I selected the Northern Illinois University College of Law because it was the closest to my home. But I didn't go to law school right away. I waited a few years. I remained doubtful about my ability to do well in law school despite all evidence to the contrary.

Surprising to me, the head of admissions at the NIU College of Law would call me every year and ask me if I was ready to go to law school yet. I would say, "No, not yet, George." After three years of his gracious and encouraging phone calls, I accepted his invitation for me to start full-time law school.

I was so nervous about going to law school that I had my oldest child (my son) accompany me on the orientation day of law school. I was one of the older students in my class. I felt that everyone else was younger, smarter, and more confident. Some of the students even asked me if I was at law school "as a hobby" or if I actually planned to become a working attorney. Happily, I ended up doing very well in law school (winning a book award in constitutional law and graduating with honors).

I loved the intellectual stimulation of law school. I never missed a class. Many of the professors were brilliant with a wonderful sense of humor.

Studying for the bar exam terrified me. I went to another prep class and passed the bar on my first attempt (to my great relief).

Getting a job as a lawyer was difficult. When I looked for work, I was 43 years old and had not one day of experience working for a law firm. I went on many job interviews but was not selected. I interviewed for jobs as a lawyer for legal aid, the public defender's office, and a wide variety of private law firms.

Finally, I was hired by a management-side labor and employment law firm just a few miles from my home. I gratefully accepted that job offer and worked under the supervision of the founder of the firm, Dick Wessels. Dick has been that mentor to me whom every new attorney wishes they had. From day one, he encouraged me to use all of my talent, skills, and abilities. He was as happy with my successes as I was. He cheered me on from challenge to challenge. He modeled how to deal with clients.

When I won my first big employment law case, Dick Wessels said, "Wonderful! Now write about this legal victory." I wouldn't have thought of using my writing skills in that manner. However, when Dick Wessels told me to write about it, I didn't question his judgment. (He has never steered me wrong.) So, I found a news-paper to publish my article about the legal victory, and that article brought many new clients.

I continued to write about employment law matters and now have hundreds of articles on the Internet. Because I am in a niche practice of helping employers with independent contractor issues, I have phone calls from all over the United States about this issue. This has allowed me to do an unusual amount of rainmaking for a woman who started her legal career in her mid-40s.

Dick Wessels made me the first woman partner in his law firm. He had to convince the other male partners that I should be a part-ner as well. I gained slow acceptance over the years as a legitimate partner with the other partners.

Over the years, when I would get discouraged by an obstacle involving a client or a fellow attorney, Dick Wessels would tell me "shake it off." Likely a term from Dick's impressive career as a high school and college football player. Dick would say, "What are you going to do? Go home and sit in the closet and suck your thumb!?! Shake it off and keep going."

I've wondered if I would have been better off by participating in team sports when in high school instead of being an editor of the high school newspaper. There are certain qualities in athletics that I see in Dick's self-confidence, leadership, and the ability to keep going despite the obstacles. I've tried to learn these attitudes of grit and growth from him. I'm so grateful that he has mentored me for my entire legal career, which is now 26 years.

Dick's attitude of both supporting me and urging me out of any discouragement or self-pity has enabled me to develop an atti-tude of grit and growth. This did not come easily to me because of my many years of being a stay-at-home mom where I was extremely sensitive and highly empathetic. Those skills can help as an attorney dealing with anxious human beings, but you also have to develop a thick skin and a perseverance as a lawyer that may not have been natural to you as a nurturing mother and wife.

As you can see from my story, I have been very lucky to have such belief in me from both my husband and the founder of our law firm. I feel that I have taken advantage of the opportunities that were presented to me and worked as hard as I can. There's an old Jewish expression, "When opportunity knocks, give it a seat." I feel that I have done that with all of my heart and mind. But I am also very aware as I write this letter of how very fortunate I have been. On top of all of that, I have had the blessing of a very talented, dedicated, and skilled legal assistant through all of those years. The same individual has assisted me day in and day out for my entire legal career. I could never be grateful enough to her as well.

I have been very lucky, and I have worked very hard. Enhanced by grit and growth, this is the winning combination.

Nancy E. Joerg is managing shareholder and senior attorney at Wessels Sherman Joerg Liszka Laverty Seneczko P.C. in St. Charles, Illinois, where she focuses on management-side labor and employment law with a particular emphasis on assisting companies using independent contractors and representing companies at Illinois Department of Employment Security (IDES) audits and hearings. www.w-p.com

Linda A. Klein

Presented by Wendy Huff Ellard

This letter is not at all about me. Rather, I was invited to write about Linda Klein, a partner in my firm's Atlanta office and president of the American Bar Association in 2016–2017.

As an associate in the Jackson, Mississippi, office of Baker, Donelson, Bearman, Caldwell & Berkowitz, PC, and vice president/president-elect of the Mississippi Women Lawyers Association, I am honored to write this letter describing the impact of grit and growth mindset on Linda's professional and personal lives. I knew I would learn a great deal from her approach to work and career. What I did not know is that I actually would learn far more from the way she handled her contribution to this book and her invitation to me to join her in this effort.

Linda maintains a very active general dispute resolution practice while she serves as our senior managing shareholder, all while preparing to serve as president of the American Bar Association. She also serves on numerous public and private boards and committees. To say that Linda Klein is busy would be a severe understatement. However, when I asked for time to meet with her, she replied immediately and we scheduled an interview for the next day.

In speaking with Linda, I immediately agreed with the impressions of others—her voice is almost serene, but commanding. she made me feel at ease, and she spoke every word in a thoughtful and sincere manner.

I first asked Linda what the concepts of grit and growth mindset mean to her and asked her to explain how she may have used these principles to advance her own career and what she has learned along the way.

She replied that her advice is to stay focused on the mission, no matter what you are doing. And always be a very good listener and make sure you are accessible. Linda has developed a reputation to always answer emails and calls, no matter the time. Clients appreciate the dedication and feel more at ease knowing she will always be there. Linda also finds it very important to be inclusive, to build and keep a very diverse team. But, once you do this, you must be accessible to all team members—you want everyone on your team to feel valued. When someone feels appreciated, they are more likely to feel a personal dedication to the project and work harder to achieve a great result.

Linda mentioned a saying she often thinks of in tough situations: "The harder I worked, the luckier I got." When you are a young lawyer, you want to be the one with a reputation of providing great work each and every time. Start with small projects and grow from there.

After Linda moved to Atlanta in the early 1980s and did not know anyone, she joined the local Young Lawyers Division to make friends and soon joined the board of directors. As the chair handed out assignments, there was one job no one wanted—and Linda took it. She was tasked with polling the bar about the new rules of court. The results of her work were published in *Atlanta Lawyer* magazine, which caught the attention of the State Bar Committee on Uniform Rules. Linda eventually would chair the Commission on Uniform Rules of Court. It was soon suggested that she run for a seat on the State Bar of Georgia Board of Governors, which she did and won. A few years later she was elected state bar secretary. A few years after that, she was elected as the first woman president of the State Bar of Georgia.

After Linda's service as state bar president ended, she became more active in the American Bar Association. She was elected chair of the ABA Tort Trial and Insurance Practice Section and later chair of the ABA House of Delegates. She is now preparing to serve as president of the world's largest lawyers' organization. All a result of doing a great job with a "job that no one wanted." All of this demonstrates how perseverance, hard work, and a laser focus on each mission—no matter how small or "unwanted" it may be—can get you closer to where you ultimately want to be.

I asked Linda if she felt she had always had grit and growth mindset traits or if she had developed these at some point along the way. She replied that she only realized she has these traits now that she looks back on her life. She always completed her homework first. She viewed her teacher as always right, and her parents valued education over playtime. Even then, focus was very important to Linda; she says, "I believed in doing a job and doing it perfectly and that was always my goal."

I next asked Linda if she has any advice for a young attorney who is apprehensive about taking those "unwanted" assignments or those that do not have any obvious or immediate benefits. To which she replied, "Always take advantage of opportunities." Take assignments that are the toughest and you will become the go-to person for these types of projects. Make sure the person who gives the assignment understands that you have worked hard and always do what needs to be done to present a great end product. You will develop contacts that will be available to you throughout your career and will earn the reputation of being a person willing to take on the toughest or worst job and doing it well. You never know when a project could lead to much greater things. You never know who may see your work and appreciate the job done, even on a small task.

Linda explained that you sometimes get great rewards from things when you least expect it. She described one case that involved an injury on state-owned property. Three other law firms refused the case, believing sovereign immunity would likely prevent any recovery, but Linda wanted to help. She made one phone call and discovered one fact regarding the property that allowed a significant recovery. "This call took very little effort or time on my part but changed someone's life," she said.

Through the entire process of preparing this letter, I had intended to capture Linda's thoughts in a draft letter for her signature. But Linda told me she did not want to handle her submission in this way. Instead, she wanted me to receive recognition and prepare our letter as a joint product. Linda's selfless instruction as to how she wanted me to prepare the submission provided much more insight regarding her character. As my mother would say, Linda practices what she preaches. She supports the work of her fellow women attorneys and is happy to share the spotlight. She has worked very hard to get where she is today and expects others to do the same. Linda Klein is a true leader in our profession and a role model for us all.

Linda A. Klein is senior managing shareholder at Baker, Donelson, Bearman, Caldwell & Berkowitz, PC in Atlanta, where she focuses on business dispute resolution, including contract law, professional liability, construction, higher education, and the pharmaceutical industry. She served as ABA president in 2016–2017. www.bakerdonelson.com

Wendy Huff Ellard is a shareholder at Baker, Donelson, Bearman, Caldwell & Berkowitz, PC in Jackson, Mississippi, and focuses on administrative law with a strong emphasis on disaster recovery, government relations and public policy, and federal contracting compliance. www.bakerdonelson.com

Roberta "Bobbi" Liebenberg

In 2013, I had the good fortune of hearing Dr. Angela Duckworth present her cutting-edge research on the importance of grit, as well as the research of Dr. Carol Dweck concerning growth mindset. What resonated with me was Dr. Duckworth's fascinating conclusion that the possession of these traits is a far better predictor of professional success than IQ, class rank, GPA, or what school you attended. Shortly after hearing Dr. Duckworth, I met Dr. Milana Hogan, who discussed with me her own studies of grit and growth mindset and their strong correlation to the success of women lawyers.

I was impressed by the work of Drs. Duckworth and Hogan and realized that it would be both interesting and beneficial to other women lawyers as well. Therefore, in order to shine a spotlight on grit and growth mindset, we made them the focus of a signature initiative of the ABA Commission on Women in the Profession when I started my second tenure as chair in August 2013.

Because grit and growth mindset can be learned and enhanced, my vision was to create a comprehensive training program that would teach women lawyers to master these traits, empowering them to navigate everyday challenges and barriers. The Commission's Grit Project Toolkit allows women lawyers to take charge of their careers and dispel the inner voices of doubt everyone has heard, making you think you won't or can't succeed or that you will be exposed as an impostor. At the same time, the Toolkit provides law schools, law firms, corporate legal departments, and bar associations with specific steps and guidance to teach women how to develop these valuable skills.

My Childhood Experiences Taught Me to Be Gritty

As far back as my childhood, I always believed that, as a girl, I should not be treated any differently from the boys in my class. I grew up with three brothers, which taught me the importance of grit and standing up for myself. For example, in middle school, much to my surprise, girls were required to take home economics, while the boys were taught logic and philosophy. I thought this was completely unfair, so I organized the other girls and our parents to demand that we be given the same learning opportunities as the boys. We prevailed, and this early seminal experience made me realize the need to persevere even in the face of obstacles.

I attended law school in the early 1970s, when women were just beginning to enter the profession in larger numbers. I had the first of my three children during my second year of law school, which was very challenging. I also needed all the grit I could muster when I began my job interviews in Richmond, Virginia, which had very few women lawyers in private practice.

Prospective employers asked me questions that are not only shocking by today's standards but are also now impermissible. For example, I was asked whether I planned to have more children, and, in one interview, I was even asked whether I would cry if a judge yelled at me during a hearing.

Having a growth mindset helped me to find my niche in antitrust law. When I started my career at a large law firm in Richmond, I learned that it was creating an antitrust department. I immediately expressed an interest in joining that group even though I had not taken a single antitrust course in law school. I taught myself antitrust law by reading cases and treatises at night. It was not easy, but I stuck with it and soon realized how much I enjoyed this practice area, which involves complex factual, legal, and economic issues. Having grit was also important because the antitrust field was and continues to be dominated by male attorneys. For years, I was the only woman in almost every hearing or deposition in which I participated. But persistence, passion, and a good sense of humor helped me overcome the many hurdles I faced.

Becoming Partner, Starting My Own Law Firm, and Lateral Moves

When my family moved to Philadelphia, I joined another large law firm, where I ultimately became one of only five women partners. Grit and growth mindset were indispensable to my attainment of that goal. By that time, I had three children and my cases required extensive travel around the country. I loved what I was doing and had wonderful sponsors who made sure I had interesting cases, and I dug in and took each case and each day one-at-a-time. I did not let setbacks deter me. I was often required to juggle car pools and attendance at school conferences with briefs, depositions, and trials. In retrospect, all the sacrifices and hard work were well worth it.

Several years after making partner, I decided to take a risk by co-founding the first women-owned law firm in Philadelphia that concentrated its practice on complex commercial litigation. I wanted to have more control over the types of cases I was working on and greater flexibility and autonomy in making my own work-life balance decisions. Because I had developed grit and a growth mindset, I felt confident in my vision of starting a firm. I realized that there would be difficult times, but I also knew that I had overcome daunting challenges in the past and could do so once again.

Eight years later, I took advantage of the opportunity to become a partner in one of the country's premier antitrust boutique firms. This lateral move also entailed risk, but it provided me with a platform to handle significant cases and also afforded me even greater latitude to work on behalf of advancing women in the profession.

What I Have Learned

Application of grit and growth mindset have taught me the following:

> ➤ *Don't Try to Be a Superwoman*—Many women feel unduly pressured to attain "work-life balance." The truth is that a perfect balance is impossible, and, therefore, I recommend setting realistic priorities, recognizing that your goals may change over time as new opportunities present themselves. Take ownership of your choices, don't second-guess yourself, and try not to feel guilty when you leave your family as you head off to work or out-of-town.

> ➤ *Take Risks*—To fulfill your dreams, don't be afraid to try something new. If you are dissatisfied or stymied in your

current practice, don't settle for the status quo. I have always found that taking risks, although nerve-wracking, can be energizing and prove well worth it. By being flexible, proactive, and receptive to change, you can create new pathways to success on your own terms.

> *Be Amenable to Constructive Criticism*—Try to get as much feedback as you can from the people with whom you work. While it is sometimes hard to hear criticism, look at it as a means to continue to learn and grow.

> *Have Fun and Enjoy Your Career*—Being a lawyer provides you with a wonderful passport that enables you to chart a career that best suits your own interests and passions. I hope developing grit and a growth mindset will help you find professional success and personal fulfillment, just as I have over the past 40 years!

Roberta "Bobbi" Liebenberg is a senior partner at Fine, Kaplan and Black, R.P.C. in Philadelphia, where she focuses on class actions, antitrust, and complex commercial litigation. www.finekaplan.com

Heather Macre

"If you have to cry, go outside."

—Kelly Cutrone

When asked to write about grit, this quote from MTV's faux reality hit, *The Hills*, leapt into my head. As some of you may recall, *The Hills* and its ilk chronicled the (largely invented) lives and (likely staged) loves of a small group of tan, wealthy, and feckless kids trying to make it in the urban jungle that is West Hollywood. Our not quite plucky heroine, L.C., found herself "working" for self-proclaimed public relations maven Kelly Cutrone, who hurled that little bon mot at L.C. after she had yet another breakdown in the open-plan office.

While the show was likely fake, Ms. Cutrone's guidance works in the real world. To me, this is the essence of grit—persevering even when it's difficult, picking yourself up when you have fallen down, and going back in for another round. Being a lawyer is tough; the hours are long, the work can be tedious, and sometimes, even when you shouldn't, you lose. You cannot let those losses define you; they are a part of the job, and I am quite sure that even the Notorious RBG—that is, Ruth Bader Ginsburg—has had a few motions denied.

You also must have inner grit, especially if you are practicing law whilst female. This is a profession where I, a partner at my firm, have been asked, on more than one occasion, if I am the court reporter when I arrive to take a deposition. And I am supposed to take some solace from the follow-up, that while I am not the court reporter, I sure am pretty enough to be one.

Of course, this is a trap, too. Women in the legal profession have to be "office pretty"—i.e., not so overly glamorous as to look unserious but not so dowdy as to look too serious. Entire law school discussions, corporate training seminars, and Above the Law message boards tell women how to dress, how to talk, how to be the right balance of smart, but not intimidating, commanding but not bitchy. I am always shocked by the amount of ink spent debating whether peep toe shoes are appropriate for a courtroom.

So how does one navigate this world? Grit. Perseverance. No one has ever made a comment about my looks *after* I have finished taking their deposition. You cannot let it break you. I know because a male partner almost broke me when I was barely out of law school. His constant berating and his insane demands almost drove me from the profession. I watched as my ideas were constantly belittled while my male colleague was praised when he presented the exact same strategy. I cried outside, a lot, until one day I just quit. I walked out the door and thought hard about walking away from the law, but I decided that I could not let one person take away my career. In retrospect this seems clean and simple; at the time I can assure you it was not.

As women in the law, we do have to work harder and smarter than the boys just to be respected equally; we have to be grittier. We have to speak louder and worry less about perception. We should not be afraid to ask questions, because if you have a question everyone else is probably thinking about it, too. We can't let other people defeat us, and we have to stop being our own worst enemy. The analytical, see-both-sides skills we learn in school can make us our own worst enemies. We have to get out of our own way.

We need to advocate not just for our clients, but for ourselves. We cannot be afraid to state, clearly and openly, what our goals are—to get a raise, to make partner, to work on a certain case—and ask what we need to do to get there. We have to hold ourselves accountable and demand our just rewards when we meet the metrics. We have to fight to be treated equally and call out bias when we see it. I have gotten a lot of things in my career—the aforementioned partnership, the ability to handle cases that matter to me but don't bring in a lot of money—but I have only gotten those things because I asked for them and worked so hard that "no" wasn't an option. This is not because I am super smart or amazingly skilled—I work hard, I ask questions, and I persevere.

I am also mindful that while I have reached the milestone of partnership, I need to reach a hand down to other women, to help them get here, too. We are never going to be treated equally or be given paid maternity leave or have our work valued at more than $.77 to the $1 unless there are more women behind the doors of the partners' meeting or in the C-Suite. When you are in management it is easy to get bogged down with other things plus your case load, but we all have the same number of hours in the day as Beyoncé, a woman who exudes grit. Tellingly, you never hear anyone say that you have the same number of hours in the day as Jay-Z.

I rest my case.

Heather Macre is a shareholder at Aiken Schenk Hawkins & Ricciardi P.C. in Phoenix, where she focuses on bankruptcy and commercial litigation. www.ashrlaw.com

Patricia Nemeth

I've never really thought about my career in terms of grit or a growth mindset. Like most people, I suspect, we just do; we don't analyze the traits that propelled us forward—to do or keep doing. Taking the time to reflect has been educational. Both played a large part in where I am and doing what I'm doing.

Grit for me developed out of necessity. To say that my childhood was chaotic would be an understatement. Suffice it to say, it was not a rosy one. The first divorce happened when I was around seven years old. Luckily, also at seven, I stumbled upon an old movie—*Adam's Rib* starring Katherine Hepburn and Spencer Tracy. If you've never seen the film, it's about two attorneys who are married to each other and litigate a case against one another. This was the first time I realized a woman could be an attorney. There were no attorneys in my family and, in fact, no college graduates.

Perry Mason had not piqued my interest in becoming an attorney, but Katherine Hepburn's on-screen role did. From that day on, I knew I wanted to be an attorney. Whatever I did, it was done with that goal in mind. Through the chaos, I studied. I studied because I wanted to get good grades so that I could get into a good college and go to a good law school. When asked what I wanted to do when I grew up, I responded that I wanted to become an attorney. When I considered running away from or leaving home, I was stopped because of one thought. I needed to stay in school and graduate so that I could eventually go to law school. When asked what year I would graduate, I would say 1984. I never said 1977, the year I was to graduate from high school. Nor did I say 1981, the year I was to graduate from college; 1984 was the year I was to graduate from law school. I graduated from high school one semester early, moving out of the house at the age of 17, so that I could work full time at McDonald's. I knew I had to earn money for college and law school. My passion for becoming an attorney was my true north for many, many years. It's what kept me grounded. It's what kept me in school. It's what kept me focused. I'm happy to say I did graduate from law school in 1984.

All the schooling, like other things, did not come easily. That's where having a growth mindset was invaluable. Some people, it seems, are just naturally smart—you know the ones. They never have to study (at least they say they don't) but still ace a test. I was not one of those people. I didn't struggle in school, but I did work hard—very hard. I earned all A's, honor roll, etc., but that only came with a tremendous amount of effort. I learned very early that if I wanted something I was going to have to work hard. I also learned that if I worked hard where it mattered most to get me to where I wanted to be, I would be rewarded. And I still believe that.

Having grit and a growth mindset has helped me in my career in a number of ways. One of the quotes lying beneath the clear plastic blotter sitting atop my desk reads "Intellectual growth should commence at birth and cease only at death," credited to Albert Einstein. I'm always looking for ways that I can grow intellectually. It happens naturally to a certain extent, because the law is always changing and you need to be aware of those changes. But I also look at ways that I can improve by learning, by growing intellectually. That's what led me to become certified as a mediator, an arbitrator, and an investigator. By having these additional skills, I'm able to better serve my clients. I continue to learn. I read books about running a law firm, best practices for businesses in general, managing employees, emotional intelligence, how people make decisions, spirituality, cultural diversity, etc.

Without grit and a growth mindset, I doubt that I would have ever opened my own firm. When I decided to do so, I had no delusions about it being easy. Being persistent and having the goal of running a successful law business was somehow not overwhelming to me. Whatever I did, I did with that goal and the goal of serving clients in the best way possible. I knew it would be hard work—very hard work—but I was used to working hard. I knew it would not happen overnight, and I was used to that, too. I knew that it would take time to develop relationships with people and earn their trust before they would feel comfortable assigning me work. Persistence and hard work do pay off. People remember you. It may take a while for the reward, but the reward does come.

Starting a firm is one thing; running and sustaining a firm is quite another. There were so many upheavals I never could have anticipated—a server crash where our contracted computer company had not backed up our information, and attorneys leaving, to name a few. One time three attorneys left to start their own firm and began contacting our clients. Another time, the husband of one of our partners went missing and was found one month later deceased. There was a lot of media attention surrounding the disappearance and discovery. A few years ago, one of our named partners left. In all of these situations, the attorneys and nonattorneys in our firm worked together, stepped up, and stepped forward. We kept moving forward, moving ourselves forward and moving the firm forward. We worked through the adversity together with the end goal in mind. Righting the ship. Maintaining a good place for employees to work. Patience. Persistence.

> You will meet me often as you work—
> In your companions, who share your risks . . .
> In your friends, who believe in you enough
> To lend their own dreams
> their own hands
> their own hearts
> to your building . . .
> In the people who will find your doorway,
> Stay a while,
> And walk away knowing they, too, can find a dream.
> There will be sun-filled days,
> And sometimes it will rain—
> A little variety!
> Both come from me.
> So come now—
> Be content.
> (Excerpt from *God's Dream* by Charles Peguy)

Patricia Nemeth is the president of Nemeth Law, P.C. in Detroit, where she focuses on management labor and employment law, serves as an employment and commercial law arbitrator, and mediates all types of civil disputes. www.nemethlawpc.com

Susan I. Paquet

It is because I thought I had failed that I became a lawyer.

I was born in 1946 (yes, that makes me older than your mother; perhaps even your grandmother). Women of my generation were given a pink blanket at birth and a specific set of goals. They were to be beautiful. They were to attend college for the sole purpose of finding a husband with an education. They were then to have three kids and become an excellent housewife. I failed. I was average looking, attended college because I enjoyed learning, and was terrible at housekeeping.

I confess, I did meet some of society's goals for my generation. I found a wonderful husband who has not only put up with me for 48 years but provided me with encouragement to be my own person. I also had a child, a fantastic daughter. She somehow managed to grow up healthy and happy despite my lack of parenting skills.

It is now a different world. It is 2016, and I am considered a success. I am a partner at a prominent, well-respected, 25-attorney law firm. I am proud to work at the law firm. However, I measure my success in terms of the goals I have set for myself as a lawyer and a person. In my career and personal life, I have strived—and usually succeeded—to be honest, dependable, hardworking, and caring.

It is difficult to analyze how I moved from the 1946 pink blanket to where I am today. In looking at my life, I am certain that it was struggles and adversity, not the easy times, that resulted in grit and growth.

Sometimes the struggles and adversity were my own, and sometimes they were what those around me had experienced. My parents were from the era of our country's Great Depression. One of the favorite family stories was about my father when he was 18. He desperately wanted a job—at a time in our country's history when there were no jobs. He wore a starched white shirt and a tie and went to apply for a job as a janitor. They hired him, and he worked his way up to district manager of the company. I recently found an entry in my grandmother's diary for a Sunday afternoon. It talked about everyone going "over to town to see a picture show," except my father. He was a janitor but wanted to go into work and do extra cleaning. He did not earn extra money for this work. He wanted everything to look nice for the office staff on Monday.

These family anecdotes were not given to me as a learning tool. However, in reflecting on my legal career, I can see the impact they had on me. Primarily, they taught me that having a job is a gift that has been given to me. Being a lawyer is a privilege, not a right. My law firm hired me because they believed in me and wanted me to be part of their team.

I also learned that all jobs, including that of a janitor, are important. I think it is easy for new lawyers to forget that court clerks, bailiffs, receptionists, secretaries, and the night cleaning crew have important jobs. They deserve our respect. We are not better than them because we are lawyers. I cannot count the number of times people in these positions have come to my rescue. I am certain that I would have never made partner if it had not been for secretaries. They humbly, time after time, made my mess of pleadings and correspondence into professional documents.

My father dressing in a white shirt and tie emphasized to me the importance of a professional appearance. It is easy for male attorneys, as they have a uniform of a suit, starched shirt, and tie. It is much harder for women attorneys, as we have many choices in clothing. It is crucial to use those choices wisely. Remember that judges and managing partners in law firms are probably of an older generation. They appreciate and expect conservative dress. Someone told me once that it is important that people remember what you said, not what you wore.

I also need to mention my father going into work on the weekend rather than the movies. A successful lawyer is one who goes the extra mile. Being an attorney is not an 8–5 job with an hour for lunch. It is hard work, night work, and weekend work. It is writing a legal brief when your friends are going to a party. On the plus side of this is that most legal work is fascinating. The attorney writing a brief may actually be having more fun than the friend at the party.

I have digressed. Let me return to me as a baby in a pink blanket. My parents had thought I would be a boy and had even picked out the name Sam. However, they quickly adjusted to a Susan. I don't think my father ever saw me as a girl or a boy. He just enjoyed being a parent. From my early childhood to my teen years I would often go to his office, where he had become a district manager. I went for the fun, like using the railing on the loading docks as monkey bars. However, I also saw my father's style of professionalism and was allowed to ask questions about the business world.

One question I asked was why only men were salesmen and managers. I knew my father respected the intelligence and ability of women and never thought of men as superior. This was in the 1950s, and he answered as a man of that time. He told me it was because the company could not afford to spend the time and money training a woman and then have her leave to take care of a baby. I asked, "What if her kids are in school?" My father answered, "Who is going to take care of the kids when they are sick?" In 2016, men are not allowed to think like this, but they do. A law firm loses money on a young attorney during the first couple of years. It is disappointing for them to then leave the firm for whatever reason. It may not be acceptable for me to say this in 2016, but think of my father's questions before you decide to have a baby. It will be beneficial to both you and the law firm to be prepared with a specific plan of handling the responsibilities of a child before you announce your pregnancy.

I have now been practicing law for years. I do, however, remember my early days of struggle and adversity. I thought I would not succeed as a lawyer. I was successful because of two men who were the firm's senior partners. One was warm and encouraging. He saw me in a positive light and taught me how to see myself that way. The other was a task master. He would meet with me every Friday morning and rip my work to shreds and not give up until I had sewn it back perfectly. I hated Friday mornings. I now understand that he demanded perfection because he believed I was capable. He gave me his time and expertise, for which I am forever grateful.

I will close by saying this to everyone: work hard, learn from those around you, and enjoy the gift of a legal career.

Susan I. Paquet is a partner at Brown Pruitt Wambsganss Ferrill and Dean, P.C. in Fort Worth, Texas, where she practices exclusively adoption law and assisted reproduction law. www.brownpruitt.com

Thomasina Real Bird

I first learned the importance of grit and a growth mindset early in life. I was born in Martin, South Dakota, near the Rosebud Sioux Reservation and raised on my family's allotment in the Choteau Creek Community on the Yankton Sioux Reservation. I am proud to be *Ihanktonwan Nakota*, *Sicangu Lakota*, and an enrolled member of the Yankton Sioux Tribe.

My childhood was spent immersed in the culture of both of my tribal nations, and I tried my best to observe the behaviors and actions of everything and everyone around me. Because I am not a fluent speaker of Dakota, I would later learn that this is a traditional Dakota concept expressed as *He Wadaka He*, which translates to "Did you see that?" And the next questions is, *He Dakuaya Bleza He*, which means "What did you see?" or "What was the observation once you saw it?" While many of my observations were beautiful and still bring back fond memories to this day, there were many observations that stand in stark contrast—poverty, social ills, fragile health profiles, and challenging housing conditions seemed almost overwhelming. While I cannot say that these conditions were solely caused by the patchwork of federal government policies that were imposed upon tribes, I do know that the imposition of a foreign mindset and outside values nearly decimated many tribal nations and eliminated many other tribal nations. However, we as tribal nations also owe accountability for allowing ourselves to embrace much of the negative. Unfortunately, this dichotomy of opposing life ways nearly strangles our ability to sustain the values of our ancestors. Whatever the source or perpetuation, these conditions would linger in my mind and serve as sources of motivation throughout my life and, in particular, my career path as areas to improve for the benefit of many. I learned early in life that I could carry and utilize the important skill of observation.

Also at a very young age, I realized that I would need to persevere in the face of seemingly insurmountable obstacles if I wanted to not only survive an upbringing where these conditions were prevalent but emerge to live a life that contributes to improving conditions for tribal nations and tribal members, while at the same time finding joy and passion in my life. These turned out to not be mutually exclusive goals, and my path would eventually include law and the legal profession.

I did not grow up always wanting to be a lawyer, however. I initially dreamed of becoming a medical doctor because that seemed like a productive way to address the fragile state of health and seemingly absent health care for tribal nations and their members. However, I soon realized that I wanted to affect systemic improvements rather than individual improvements, and I did not want to be limited to only the medical field, although I admire the few doctors who are truly working on improvements in our tribal communities. It did not take me long to realize that the legal profession was where I would develop the tools to pursue my life-long goal of improving conditions for tribal nations and tribal members. After all, I spent my childhood observing and later learning in my professional training that Native Americans are the most regulated, politicized, and codified group of people. We are the only race mentioned in the U.S. Constitution, and Title 25 of the U.S. Code is devoted exclusively to "Indians." Sometime in college, I learned that in addition to being a racial classification, the U.S. Supreme Court had declared that there is a political status tied to being Native American.

I was fortunate enough to have parents and family members who exposed me to larger tribal and national matters that affected tribes and tribal citizens. These experiences validated the complex thoughts that flooded my mind. These experiences also allowed me to learn about some incredible professionals who would later serve as mentors, whom I observed and who inspired my career, whether they know it or not. I am fortunate to follow in the footsteps of true trailblazers who pioneered what is now federal Indian law and tribal law. I grew up with the benefit of their ground-breaking efforts, as well as their accomplishments on behalf of Indians and tribes. When I learned there were Native Americans with whom I could identify who were practicing law and making a difference for tribal nations and their members, I knew in my heart that it was possible for a Native American to achieve success in the legal field because these individuals were paving the way. I knew that I had found my path.

However, I still had to attend college, graduate school, and law school, as well as pass two bar exams—Colorado and South Dakota—which meant a lot of sacrifice, dedication, and an investment in myself. It is not enough that we have great mentors and a support network, although it is certainly very important. The practice of law is challenging, difficult, and sometimes daunting. In my practice, I am often faced with insurmountable tasks but I persevere not only because it is my passion but because I believe my work is worthy. The opportunity to utilize my talents and training to assist clients is worthy because I believe that my work contributes to my lifelong goal of improving conditions for tribal nations and tribal members. I consider it an honor and a privilege to serve as general counsel to my own tribe and to represent many other tribal nations and tribal interests.

I am grateful to work for the largest Native American–owned law firm in the nation that devotes itself exclusively to the representation of tribal nations, tribal members, and tribal corporations. Fredericks Peebles & Morgan LLP is a law firm whose slogan is "tribal law-tribal solutions." Approximately half of its attorneys are Native American, and all of its attorneys are dedicated to the practice of Indian law and tribal law. Each of us has grit and a growth mindset. It takes consummate professionals with incredible talents, focus, determination, and intelligence to so dramatically affect Indian law and policy in positive ways. I am also blessed to walk on this journey with my husband of 13 years, Ken Henry Real Bird, and receive the support of my mentors, in-laws, *tiwahe* (family), *tiyospiye* (extended family), and *oyates* (tribal nations).

My advice, dear colleagues, is to continue to observe and use your talents for good, represent your clients with integrity and grit, be true to yourself (unless your true self is a bully, in which case don't be a bully), and be a good relative. I am proud to be *Ihanktonwan*, proud to contribute to improving conditions for tribal nations and the lives of tribal members, and proud to carry on the great legacy of my culture, my ancestors, my mentors in the legal arena, and my chosen profession.

Thomasina Real Bird is a partner at Fredericks Peebles & Morgan LLP in Louisville, Colorado, where she focuses on tribal and federal Indian law. www.ndnlaw.com

Sandra Brown Sherman

Although I am pleased to offer my insight and advice, I would begin by suggesting that there is no fail-safe or must-do method for achieving success in the practice of law. Furthermore, I think that success should be broadly defined as a career that one can look back on with pride and satisfaction. Success is too often measured in economic terms or with reference to other factors that do not necessarily show that one's work was truly fulfilling or beneficial in a larger sense.

I've worked in a variety of law firm environments. I started private practice in a firm with only five attorneys—all partners, and all men—and I worked there on an hourly basis. It was a high-quality, boutique practice, and I had the privilege to be particularly guided by the most senior partner. He was very understanding of the predicament of younger professional women, despite his age, because he had two daughters with very active professional careers who also had young children. This was not the first time that I got encouragement from men who had daughters pursuing professional careers.

I then went into a slightly larger, but still relatively focused, practice that grew to as many as 20 attorneys and which, at its best, was a very happy place to work. That was the first firm where the male attorneys made an active effort to include the female attorneys as colleagues in a general sense. And it was very helpful to have other female attorneys working with me for the first time in my career. The women I have had the privilege of working with have been a great source of support and strength for me, and some of them have been particularly invaluable in helping me through the invariable rough spots that present themselves both professionally and personally.

I ultimately left that practice, though, to go into one of my state's largest firms, and one that had a deserved reputation for being one of the better large firms in which to work. By sheer serendipity—and serendipity turns out to be a bigger factor than some might admit—I began my tenure there with a young male partner with whom I built a very nice practice. We were similarly minded in terms of how we grew the practice, serviced our clients, and treated the people who worked with us in our practice, whom we both viewed as essential to our ultimate success.

The time came, though, when it made more sense for us to take our practice elsewhere with some of our other colleagues at that firm, and so we only recently started a new firm. That was probably the biggest professional challenge I had ever confronted. It gave me great admiration for attorneys who also have to function as business people. It's also given me an opportunity to be a more vocal participant in policy-making that could help the interests of women.

If I could offer some observations, although I'm reluctant to call this advice, to other women in the profession, let me say that it's vitally important, if you have a family, to have the strong support of your spouse and children as your career evolves. I'm not sure that happy personal and professional lives can exist without it.

You will also see things that occur, sometimes very subtly, within your firms and the profession generally, that still are not completely fair to women in the profession—or to men in the profession who want to be actively involved in the day-to-day care of their children. In retrospect, I think there were times when I should have agitated about these concerns sooner than I did. And although agitation needs to be done carefully, if an egregious situation presents itself and it's only right that it be rectified, you will feel some satisfaction at the end of the day to know that you made your voice heard.

Be mindful of the fact that support and opportunities can come from anywhere. Sometimes it's just a more senior attorney who is willing to discuss a problem and has weathered a similar experience as a younger attorney. Or maybe it's an older attorney who would like some quality help from a junior attorney, and who would be more than happy to mentor that person if he or she had confidence in the quality of the work and the dedication of the younger person to serving the clients.

Take on challenges gladly—for example, handling the difficult client matter or mastering a niche area that no one else is interested in but that could be helpful to your clients and colleagues. This will help build your confidence, and it will also help your clients and colleagues feel confident in you. In all events, you will need to work hard, on a sustained basis, to do as good a job as you can to serve clients well, so that you can be satisfied with yourself and the small part you played within the legal system to make life better for others.

And remember, sometimes this journey may seem like a struggle, but your steadfast pursuit will serve you, your clients, and the advancement of the profession—including the women of the profession—well.

Sandra Brown Sherman is a founding partner of Sherman Wells Sylvester & Stamelman LLP in Florham Park, New Jersey, where she focuses on trusts and estates and tax law. www.shermanwells.com

Elizabeth Lee Thompson

I felt compelled to submit this letter because, honestly, anyone who knows me would attribute 100 percent of my success in my career to true grit. It is the one quality that carried me through law school and practicing law in a large firm for 30 years while being a wife, mother, and now a grandmother.

The youngest of five children of blue-collar parents, the options presented to me were somewhat limited. My parents had an extreme commitment to each of their children receiving a college education. Graduating from an all-girl Catholic high school, I was expected to go into nursing or social work like my three older sisters. My daddy was a mechanic and body man. He was a good and loving man, but if you picture Archie Bunker in your mind, you won't be far off. One night I was home from college for the weekend. Mom fixed my favorite for dinner—corned beef and cabbage. As we were eating, I told my parents that I was thinking about going to law school upon graduation. My father looked over his glasses from the head of the Formica and chrome table, as if an alien had landed in my chair, and uttered in complete disbelief, "Where do you get this shit???!!!"

Gosh, I had such wonderful mentors. My economics professor secured a position for me with the V.P. of Public Affairs at a publicly traded restaurant company. The V.P. said that me working as his secretary was "the Peter Principle in reverse." I had been demoted to a job for which I was totally incompetent, but I persisted. Truly, my typing, shorthand, and telephone skills left something to be desired. He could count on me, however, to report on daily news regarding industry important issues from *The Wall Street Journal*, *The New York Times*, and *The Washington Post*. Three years later, that V.P. secured an internship for me as a congressional staffer.

My congressman met me on a Delta flight from our home state to Washington, D.C., as I arrived for my internship. Being a true Southern gentleman, he insisted on carrying my two bags to the taxi and seeing me safely off to my lodgings. Little did he know that my hard-sided Samsonite suitcases weighed about 100 pounds each. Without the wheels we now take for granted, inherited from my older sister, still bearing her initials, and heavy in their own right, they were now weighed down with an electric clock radio, an iron, a comforter, and a three-month supply of shoes. He walked through endless concourses, a bag firmly gripped in each of his meaty fists. As his face reddened, and the sweat poured from his brow and between his shoulder blades, headlines formed themselves in my overactive imagination: "Congressman slain by law student with shoe fetish." Mom and Daddy had never been to D.C. until they visited me there. Not sure what Daddy thought about the internship, but by then he was at least relieved to know he wouldn't have to support me for the rest of my life.

My law school didn't allow first-year students to work, but I was low on funds. So, on the sly, I interviewed with a firm headed up by Tom Cruise's uncle, William Mapother. He spoke all over the country on the "new bankruptcy code" and self-published a book for creditors. One of my jobs for him was to summarize the bankruptcy decisions reported since enactment of the Bankruptcy Code in 1978 for annotation of the latest version of this publication. At the same time my bankruptcy professor, Judge Joe Lee, was the sitting bankruptcy judge in the Eastern District of Kentucky. His class was at 8:00 a.m. so that he could arrive at court in a timely fashion. He was from Arkansas and had a lovely soft, slow Arkansas drawl guaranteed to render the most energetic student into a senseless stupor before he could get from section 101 of the Bankruptcy Code (with over 55 crucial definitions) to section 102 (crucial rules of construction). At the time, I also worked as a night watchman in a college dorm and was exhibiting signs of narcolepsy, falling asleep often and easily. So I sat right in front of him each class morning for fear I would fall asleep and tumble from my chair, which would have been so embarrassing! I gazed up at him, willing my eyes wide open, forcing myself to attend to each soft utterance. In the end, he began introducing me as one of his best law students. So, I became a creditors rights and bankruptcy lawyer. What else?

A group of female lawyers and I have been having a potluck once a week for years. They call us the good old girls now. Our female friends include state supreme court justices, federal district judges, state circuit judges. But this is now and that was then. We all have the same stories, showing up at opposing counsel's office for a deposition and being told where we should set up our recorder and how many copies of the transcript we were to deliver—being told that it was absolutely imperative to wear a skirt, hose, and heels to court, even in the snow. One jury trial early on, the trial judge called me honey throughout the proceedings. He didn't mean a thing by it. After I appealed the adverse jury verdict and was given a summary judgment on appeal, he sent me a letter of apology. Not for the "honeying." But for not listening to me when I knew the law better than he. I still have the letter.

Raising two sons while practicing law full time is not for the faint of heart. It is the best and most impossible thing you will do in your whole life. Without dependable child care and a fully contributing husband with a regular work schedule, I wouldn't have survived. Practical decisions like having a full-time housekeeper/ child care provider who came to my home each day and my husband and I staggering our schedules when possible kept the balls in the air, but just barely. I have painful memories of my son's second grade teacher calling me at work because he cried at school when we failed to show up for an open house. The same son, I am ashamed to admit, was allowed to wear his school clothes to bed for a few years in grade school because he was a slow riser and it facilitated on-time school delivery. A current female bankruptcy judge, then attorney, helped avoid my emotional meltdown when held very late in bankruptcy court one evening. She sagely whispered, "It's perfectly fine to buy your three-year-old's cake at Kroger tonight. He won't know you didn't make it."

Back then, I was given four weeks' maternity leave and took two additional vacation weeks. Each matter had to be worked to a holding point before departure and then picked up quickly on return. The first pregnancy I went three weeks overdue. The delay may have been caused by the scheduling of an important U.S. District Court argument on my due date. My body, prepared for war, refused to deliver. The hearing was on Christmas Eve. A local dealership had been selling out of trust leading up to the holidays, so an immediate writ of possession was required. The district judge, old and wizened, bald on top, and looking not unlike the Wizard of Oz, peered down on me from his high podium and bellowed, "Ms. Thompson, what is this all about?" Tremoring a bit Dorothy-style, I stood with my file firmly held to the top of my protruding belly (the podium was out of reach, because my son's full 20" length seemingly stretched in front of me). The district judge began laughing, and laughing, and laughing, until tears streamed from his eyes. After removing and wiping his glasses on his white handkerchief he said to me, "Who are you, Ms. Thompson, the ghost of Christmas Future?" Who am I indeed? And where did I get this shit?

Elizabeth Lee Thompson is a member of Stites & Harbison PLLC in Lexington, Kentucky, where she focuses on creditors' rights, bankruptcy, and business litigation. www.stites.com

Julie M. Walker

What constitutes a grit and growth mindset, and how/when does it come into play? As I reflect on the last 21-plus years of law practice, I can pinpoint several points in time that grit and growth may have influenced my choices.

The first occasion was early on in my career. At a time when legal jobs were not easy to come by, I was lucky enough to land a second-year clerkship at an established 75-year-old law firm in Denver. The firm offered a wide variety of practice groups, which for me was very appealing. My mentor at the time told me I was set—a clerkship from that firm would certainly turn into an offer to join as an associate.

Three days into the clerkship, the firm announced it was closing its doors. The office was stunned. The firm was kind enough to let the summer clerks stay on, work as much as we could, and continue to earn our summer stipend. I don't remember much about the work I did that summer, but I distinctly remember observing the senior partners in the firm moving about the halls like ghosts, or sitting behind their desks, staring out the window with a blank look on their face. The stress in the office was palpable. Now, as an owner of my own law firm, I can imagine the range of emotions they must have been feeling—from loss to resentment to instability to resolve.

Thanks to my mentor, I landed another clerkship at the Denver office of a large national law firm. I worked there during my third year of law school and then received a coveted offer to join the firm as an associate. I was one of only a handful of my fellow law school graduates in 1994 who had a big firm position prior to graduation.

Here is one of the points in my career where grit and growth mindset came into play. The law firm that offered me a position had a reputation for only hiring top-tier law school graduates at the top of their law school class. I did not attend a top-tier law school. I was not in the top 10 percent of my law school ranking, either. In fact, when I came onboard at the outset of my third-year clerkship, a more senior associate at the firm told me straight out, "Don't expect a job offer here, because this firm will never hire an associate from your law school." Challenge accepted.

I was assigned to work for one of the senior equity partners in the firm who handled complex commercial litigation. There were at least two or three attorneys (associates and/or junior partners) between me and the senior partner on any case. I was asked to prepare legal research memoranda on various topics that would then be distilled and incorporated by more senior associates into a motion or a brief that would then be passed up the chain to the more senior attorneys on the case.

I had worked as a litigation paralegal for a couple of years prior to law school, so I had a general idea of what a litigation matter case file looked like—file drawers with folders marked Pleadings, Discovery, Research, Documents, Indexes, etc. Mind you, this was in the days of hard copy files; emails were just starting to be utilized.

Once assigned a research project on a specific case, the first thing I did was hunt down the file and review whatever I could get my hands on. The complaint, answer, any factual background memoranda, matter opening memos—whatever. I wanted to know as much as I could about the case before I starting doing research. I made a point of trying to focus my research to the type of case at hand.

The Denver office made only two first-year associate offers that spring—one to a Harvard Law graduate and one to me. I knew it was in large part because of the extra effort I put into my work for this particular senior partner.

That summer, I took the bar exam at the end of July. I was getting married three weeks later—and would then begin my associate position in early September. A week after I took the bar exam, I received a phone call from one of my colleagues at the firm; they had just announced they were closing the Denver office. Déjà vu!

Once again I had a front-row seat to attorneys at all levels of practice coming to terms with a sudden and unexpected shift in their career. What I observed and took away from this experience left an indelible mark on my career. In essence, those who had clients of their own or portable business landed on their feet very quickly. Those who did not struggled and took huge pay cuts. Many of them are still struggling today—20 years later.

I made a point from then on of learning how to develop my own book of business. I observed those around me who had their own business. How did they go about developing it? How did they interact with their clients? What worked for them? What did their clients like or dislike?

I then spent a number of years trying out different business development methods to see what fit for me—because not all methods work for all people. For example, I was at first very uncomfortable with the standard large ballroom full of strangers with drinks in their hand. I would awkwardly mill about until someone took pity on me and brought me into their conversation. But I watched others interact in those settings and learned how to do the same.

Over the years, I had the good fortune to work for several highly successful rainmakers—most of them men. Some were more willing to share their secrets than others. Some were far better mentors than others, and finding good mentors along the way is critical. But all of them offered the opportunity for observation. Take advantage of those opportunities.

There are, without question, certain business development methods and opportunities that work for men and not for women—and vice versa. Women need to be aware of the traits and skills that they naturally possess—that men do not—that give them an advantage in the right business development circumstance. A rather obvious example: on one occasion, my firm participated in a pitch for work to a group of in-house counsel. One of the in-house attorneys came to the meeting visibly pregnant. One of my firm's associates at the meeting was also pregnant at the time. The two of them bonded in a way that no man in the room could, and we landed the work, in large part because the in-house counsel felt so comfortable with the female associate on the work.

On the other hand, women also need to be mindful of the traits we possess that hold us back in certain circumstances. The biggest example of this for me was to learn how to ask for work—not wait for it to come to me. Men are more inclined to simply come out and ask the client to give them the opportunity. This is not a trait that comes naturally for women—but one that should be adopted. Clients understand and expect that you are looking for work to drive your practice. Don't be afraid to ask for it.

And do not lose sight of one of the key factors in becoming a rainmaker—once you land the client, give them excellent service within the parameters that they desire. Make sure you understand whether the client wants a scorched earth approach in a case or a "do the minimum to get to mediation" approach. Wherever their desired goal is on the spectrum, identify it and provide the best services you can to get them to their goal.

My grit and growth mindset has driven me from that point to where I am today—the founder of my own law firm with a steady seven-figure book of business. I attribute much of my success to the excellent mentorship I received along the way. However, my observations early in my career of attorneys whose careers suffered because they relied too much on others to provide for them, in contrast to successful rainmakers who demonstrated right in front of me business development means and methods that had clear results, contributed greatly to the independence and control that I am fortunate enough to possess over my own practice.

Julie M. Walker is a founding partner of Kelly & Walker LLC in Denver, where she focuses on commercial litigation, professional liability, and products liability. www.kellywalkerlaw.com

Marguerite S. Willis

Recently, my law firm asked each lawyer to develop a personal slogan. It did not take me long. Today, if you go to my webpage, you will read the following: "If it is easy, you don't need me."

As I sat down to write this letter, I realized that my slogan really tells the story of my career. At no time has my path been easy. At every turn, however, I found a way to overcome, to push through, to carry on. My destiny, as it turned out, was to deal with things that were not easy—professionally, personally, and otherwise. So, when faced with hardship, I turned overcoming adversity into a marketable attribute.

All of this may seem silly and perhaps it is. But I figured if I could solve my own problems, then maybe I could solve the problems of others. And so, over time, easy problems were no longer interesting to me. It was the tough situation, the complex disaster that drew my interest. I learned to take a difficult issue and turn it on its side or at an angle. Over and over, I found myself taking different vantage points to solve complicated issues.

Along the way, I learned a couple of helpful lessons. First, I learned that there is no problem that cannot be addressed—and usually fixed—if you act quickly. The people I work with know the only mistake I will not forgive is the failure to admit a mistake in a timely fashion.

Second, I learned that when life gives you lemons, you really can make lemonade. Almost every situation which seems at the time to be a negative can be turned into a positive. For example, on occasion, I have been fired as counsel. Instead of arguing or sulking, I have used the event to show how generous I can be as a lawyer. I have extended courtesy to the new counsel and shared with him or her not only my work file but also my thoughts on how best to move the matter forward. And, in every single instance, the client has returned to me, either in the same matter or for another case, at a later date.

Finally, I leave you with this thought. The practice of law, particularly for women, requires courage, diligence, and creativity.

Although today there are many more women in the practice than when I began my career, there are still important issues of gender discrimination and pay inequity that confront us all.

So, get up, get dressed, and get started. Face each day with the determination to turn your obstacles into attributes and your setbacks into opportunities. And remember, nobody said it would be easy. After all, if it were, you would not be reading this letter.

Marguerite S. Willis is a partner in Nexsen Pruet, LLC in Columbia, South Carolina, where she focuses on antitrust and complex litigation. www.nexsenpruet.com

Patricia Wise

So grit is what we're calling it now. Everyone talks about it, and it is an admirable quality. I first heard it as a young child, when it was personified by Kim Darby as Mattie and John Wayne as Rooster Cogburn in the original *True Grit* movie. But you have to be of a certain age to know that and not think that the Coen brothers version in 2010 was the original. But I think that grit as personified in that movie was the same then as it is now for women in the profession. And for me that means that you do what you have to do to survive. As to growth, you get a little smarter about how you survive.

So, how do you survive? Sometimes you just have to jump in and pretend to know what you're doing. With clients, with opposing counsel, and even with judges. And the growth comes when one day you wake up and realize you're not pretending, and you actually do know (at least most of the time!) what you're doing. And you have to do the hardest things, the things that most scare you—giving a client bad news, challenging what a judge tells you, trying your first case solo. And sometimes the hardest things are harder because you are a woman.

Specifically, for me surviving has meant literally concealing my pregnancy from clients who might have discounted my advice. A month before one of my due dates a long-time client called to ask how to discipline a female employee with performance issues, who might take it badly due to her pregnancy. The manager shared that women were emotional during that time and wouldn't be able to understand the constructive nature of the criticism, or to process the information properly until after the pregnancy. When I was called to a meeting with that manager a week before my due date, I carried my briefcase and my raincoat in front of me until I sat at a conference table so that I would not be perceived that same way. They were quite surprised to learn that I was in the hospital the next week after delivering my daughter, but by then, fortunately, the period of my perceived "disability" had passed. Sadly though, practicing in a small office at the time, the next week I was sitting in day-long depositions. Sometimes you have to overcompensate, because you are held to a higher standard. Grit? Or survival?

Similarly, when the managing partner at the large firm where I started my career announced the firm "record" for a return to work two days after delivery, I laughed along with all of the other female attorneys. And we joked and tried to ignore it when the male associates got invited to golf outings and lunches in the men's grill. Same as when you are referred to as "honey," "dear," or "girls" by clients and men in positions of power. It's just what you do as a woman in a profession still dominated by men. Grit? Or survival?

Hopefully, in the best situations, you have a female role model or a mentor. And as you grow, if you are fortunate, you get to be a role model or a mentor. Because you learn how much more fulfilling it can be to collaborate, even when you might already know the answer or the best strategy. Unfortunately, collaboration is missing for some women, by choice or due to circumstances they can't control.

I also think grit is just about getting up and doing more things than are humanly possible, then getting up the next day and doing even more. Are there people still debating whether women can have it all? That's nice. I know the answer to that. Some days you can watch a daughter's basketball game, read another daughter's essay, have dinner with your family, and still get a decent amount of work done. Some days you let someone down. Some days you feel that you fail at both family and professional obligations, but the next day you get up and try again. So, the clear answer is, some days "yes," some days "no."

And, if anyone reading this letter thinks that it is written with regret, read again. This has been a fabulous career, and I wouldn't change a thing. What is grit? Taking the time to write this letter when I have a trial to prepare for and one million other things to do!

Patricia Wise is a partner at Niehaus Wise & Kalas Ltd in Toledo, Ohio, where she focuses on employment law. www.nwklaw.com

Valinda Barrett Wolfert

A career that you love is a gift. I always say that it is one of the legs on the stool of life. I am a firm believer in four-legged stools: faith, family, friends, and work. All will be down at some point, but it is very rare for all four to be down at one time. It's best to keep all of them around and available as needed. I have needed each of them to be my primary support at some point along my journey. I hope that you will love practicing law as much as I have. I didn't love it on day one. I often didn't love it during the first two years. I stuck with it as a means to an end, which initially was a paycheck. I grew to love it as I became comfortable with (and began to enjoy) the work and learned that the relationships being developed were great assets for my life.

As a banking associate at a fine regional law firm in Dallas, in 1984, I was in one of the first groups of women to enter large law firm life. There were three of us in the class of about 15 that started work out of law school. There were two in the class ahead of us. There were two or three women who had been around for a while, but they showed little interest in us. We were still an oddity, but we knew we had the knowledge and skills to be successful. We were confident because in undergraduate and law school, no one distinguished between men and women, so we believed we were just as capable as the guys. It took a lot of grit to get through those early years. It still does today. I encourage all of you to give yourselves time to grow to love it if you don't already. Look for things about it that you love and build on those.

Grit was key along the way. Many older male partners didn't know how to treat women as peers—a necessary component of a successful law firm team and key to the success of the individual team members. As male partners have become fathers to daughters with careers, their perspective has shifted, because they want their daughters to succeed. We just kept showing up each day, doing the work, and taking it when we were told to read *The Wall Street Journal* when, of course, we were already reading it. We used the strengths we had to persevere and find our niches. I love business and the banking world, and that love showed to our banking clients. Every client prefers a lawyer who is genuinely interested in his or her success and who is happy and thankful to work with them. The world of banking in 1984 was populated with men and women coming out of undergrad and business school, all anxious to learn and build relationships. My new best friend and fellow first-year female lawyer—from Erie, Pennsylvania, whereas I was from Griffin, Georgia—and I were in many ways united by our aloneness in this new world. She later married one of those bankers.

My career was a rollercoaster ride with lots of ups and downs, both personally and professionally. I had great successes, and I made mistakes. I served on my law firm's management committee. I served as a practice group leader and on recruiting and other committees. What was the hardest role? My three-year service as chair of a women's initiative in the early 2010s. How could we still need a women's initiative when women had comprised approximately 50 percent of law school graduating classes for many years and were recognized as being at the top of their classes, and when women had been in BigLaw for over 25 years? The numbers tell the story. Women are underrepresented in partner ranks, as are women in management and leadership roles. I remain committed to helping women achieve more parity. We must acknowledge that if a woman gets a prime role or a partnership, that means a man has not gotten that position. It is a competitive marketplace, not only for women but for all other underrepresented groups. I am confident that everyone wants women to succeed, but no man wants to give up his seat at the table. Every seat a woman gets (other than designated seats for the underrepresented) is taken away from a man who badly wants it and will fight for it.

I was fortunate to have a father who encouraged and pushed me to understand business just as much as he pushed my brother. It stuck. I am recently retired but spend time each day reading and keeping up with the loan markets; I want to be ready in case I choose to go back to work in some capacity, and by the way I love it and don't want to let go. I always believed that I was just as good as the guy next door. I simply kept pushing forward. If I had to name my magic ingredient in addition to grit and growth mind-set, it is that I always cared. Everyone knew, especially the clients. I prepared for their deals by staying up to speed on market conditions and legal issues. I always had an agenda for meetings that I was leading, so we were organized, efficient, and thorough. That agenda included introductions of new attendees, so that everyone's role was recognized, each face had a name, and we knew why they were there. I never backed down just because a more senior lawyer tried to bully me into his position, and I readily explained to our client why. I was always prepared and thoughtful in my positions.

I retired in 2015 after 30+ years of practice to spend time with my family, including an adult disabled son with health issues. I hope that each of you will find success and happiness in your careers and lives. I am always here to support and help you.

Valinda Barrett Wolfert is a partner (retired) at Vinson & Elkins LLP in Dallas, where she represented arrangers, commercial banks, and businesses in loan transactions, focusing on acquisition financings, other syndicated credit facilities, and complex restructurings. www.linkedin.com/in/valindabarrettwolfert

Kareen Zeitounzian

Have you ever credited an encounter with a stranger for being the reason you learned or better learned an invaluable life lesson? If your answer is yes, you might relate to the story of how I was introduced to the grit and growth mindset in the context of my career.

One day in the late 1980s or early 1990s—before "Take Your Child to Work Day" became an observed tradition—I had the pleasure of accompanying my father to his office in Eastman Kodak Co. in Rochester, New York. I viewed it as a momentous affair, even at the time, for it was one of the only occasions in my childhood my parents permitted me to skip school for a reason other than being ill. The only other occasion I recall to fit this description was my attendance at a 1988 ceremony where my parents, late brother, and I were naturalized as U.S. citizens.

Many details of my previously mentioned parental work visit are now, decades later, vague to me. Two aspects, however, still distinctly stand out in my mind. The first is the less significant of the two, namely the fact that a friendly security guard in the lobby of the building had issued me a laminated visitor's pass on a lanyard. The purpose of the pass was not for safety, but rather to bolster my sense of self-importance for the day. In hindsight, I can report the security guard's objective was met. The second, more noteworthy detail I remember from this visit is a brief exchange I had with one of my father's colleagues as we made our way to his office.

The exchange was with an administrative assistant who, based on my beginning assessment of verbal and nonverbal cues at the time, hardly knew my father. I don't know and I likely will never know why this assistant chose me—a complete stranger and child of age 13 or 14—to impart career advice, but she did so in no uncertain terms. She took one look at me in my electric wheelchair and proceeded to assert that, when I grew up, I could be anything I wanted to be. More specifically, she indicated I could hold any job I wanted to hold. She advised me to view my brain as the muscle I didn't have in my arms and legs and train it to persist in achieving my career goals. She relayed her foresight that I would have many struggles, but as long as I embraced them as challenges and stayed the course, I would come out stronger on the other side. Several times throughout her passing motivational pitch, she repeated the choices were mine to make.

You may be able to understand how, at first blush, this woman's message to me came across as rather odd. I wondered why she felt she could determine what I could or should do based solely on my physical appearance. It wasn't the first time my unrevealed abilities or personal beliefs were judged by a person not familiar with me, but it was one of the most blatant instances of it.

As years passed, the conversation with my dad's former colleague stayed with me. I would even say it somewhat nagged me. I experienced no shortage of setbacks on the path leading to my career, and every time I did, the conversation seemed to creep into my thoughts. I recalled it the few times in high school I received a grade less than what I desired. I recalled it when I was struggling with grief and fear my last semester of college, after my brother, with whom I was extremely close and who had the same diagnosis as me (spinal muscular atrophy), suddenly passed away in his sleep. I recalled it my first semester in law school, when I spent over a month in the intensive care unit and was struggling for my own life. I also no doubt recalled it every time I did not pass the New York State bar exam, before I realized a minor testing accommodation could be granted to level the playing field and allow me to succeed.

Each time I recalled the conversation at issue, I recognized more and more the value of its message, which I later identified as a message about grit and growth mindset. I came to understand why it is helpful to tie effort, more than present ability, to success. I began to appreciate the importance of viewing setbacks or failures as an opportunity to learn. In doing so, I noticed one can create a positive feedback loop that fosters continued scholarship and improvement. This, in turn, fosters a greater sense of free will. In a world where limits exist in many forms, including those physical or social in nature, what could be more precious than a fortified sense of free will?

When I realized my answer to the latter question is "very few things, if any," I deemed my dad's former colleague's message a very insightful one. I determined her comments were not made with a rude or illogical intent but instead with a positive intent to impart valuable life advice to someone she remarkably selected worthy of it. I, thereafter, chose to adopt the concepts of grit and growth mentality in my career, as my dad's former colleague urged years prior. Her objective, like the friendly security guard's objective, was ultimately met.

In closing, I want to note the conversation at issue in the above story was by no means my only introduction or exposure to the grit and growth mindset, nor was it the only basis upon which I developed my use of its concepts. Throughout my life, I have had the great fortune to know and learn from numerous family members and friends who have applied the grit and growth mindset in their own lives. The success of these relatives and friends unequivocally serve as a critical source of inspiration and information to me. By sharing this story, however, I hope to demonstrate that lessons on how to nurture and apply the grit and growth mindset—like many other of life's lessons—can be leveraged from a wide variety of sources, even strangers!

Kareen Zeitounzian is a senior associate at Harris Beach PLLC in Rochester, New York, where she focuses on business and commercial litigation. www.harrisbeach.com

4

In-House Lawyers

KEY FINDINGS

➤ In-house practitioners believe—almost to a person—that grit and growth mindset are important contributors to success.

➤ Grit is strongly related to the message that in-house lawyers receive in their performance evaluations.

➤ Grit influences the point at which women lawyers are brought into the decision-making process, as well as how long they will stay in the game.

➤ Mindset predicts seniority within the organization.

THE WOMEN WE SURVEYED

More than 450 women who are currently practicing in-house participated in our research efforts. As was the case with the solo practitioners in our study, the in-house women we heard from practiced many different kinds of law, with the greatest concentrations practicing corporate, labor and employment, banking and finance, health, and real estate law. They all came from almost every industry, from agriculture to electronics to private equity to venture capital. The industries with the most representation included, in order: financial services, health care, energy, banking, real estate, service, and technology.

189

The women represent a broad range of practice experience, ranging from relatively inexperienced (one to two years of practice experience) to very experienced (more than 21 years of practice experience). On balance, this group was more heavily skewed toward more experienced lawyers, and roughly 67 percent of the women in this group had upward of 15 years of experience. The fact that so many of the women in this group were so experienced is not surprising—indeed, many companies do not hire newly minted lawyers and instead prefer to hire those who have already learned how to be effective practitioners—most often at law firms or in other environments where they have had an opportunity to build the necessary and relevant skills to succeed as counsel in-house. Seventy-one percent of the women in this group had held at least two legal positions prior to the current position, and 43 percent had held three or more positions. For 13.5 percent, the number of legal positions held was greater than five.

In terms of seniority within their organizations, we also saw a broad and healthy range—more than 25 percent held the senior-most legal position within their organizations (either general counsel or another c-suite equivalent), 55 percent fell somewhere in the middle, and another 20 percent occupied more junior legal positions on the organizational chart. Roughly 35 percent were officers.

In terms of family structure, roughly 77 percent of the women we surveyed were married or in a domestic partnership and 72 percent of the women had children. Of those who had children, the majority had two children (52 percent) and 95 percent had between one and three children. Roughly 5 percent had four or more children. Ninety percent of the women had had children while working as a lawyer, and the remaining 10 percent had had them at another time—generally before practicing, or they had taken a short (or long) hiatus and then returned to practice sometime later. In terms of family history, the women in this group were fairly evenly split when it came to the level of education achieved by their mothers. About 26 percent of the women had mothers who had achieved at least a high school degree, 44 percent had achieved at least a four-year college degree, and the remainder—30 percent—had achieved an advanced degree of some kind.

Lastly, in terms of academic performance, we saw a broad mix. Roughly 26 percent attended top-tier law schools, and another 48 percent attended law schools in the second tier. The remaining 26 percent attended schools in the third and fourth tiers. GPA was relatively evenly distributed, with a mix of top performers (including a few with perfect 4.0s) and a healthy number of those who fell into the bottom half of their classes. This group also had strong undergraduate and high school academic performances in terms of GPA, and 50 percent of them attended a top-tier undergraduate institution. That said, there were also women in the survey who had less than stellar academic performance in either high school and/or college.

MEASURING SUCCESS

As discussed in earlier chapters, the most challenging part of the study was trying to accurately capture and define success for each subset of the women we surveyed. To do this, we surveyed women at varying stages of their careers, across industries and practice areas, and up and down the organizational chart. Some of the women we heard from defined themselves as successful and some did not; some were currently practicing law in-house, some had moved on to other areas of practice, and some were no longer practicing law. All of their perspectives were helpful as we sought to understand more about what it means to be a female, in-house lawyer today and how that group weighs and measures their own accomplishments and the contributions they make to their organizations.

As was the case with the solo practitioners and law firm lawyers, a few themes began to emerge from our discussions with women in-house. First of all, while there were some overarching commonalities, each organization had its own way of measuring the success of its employees internally. These methods included, among other things, performance evaluation processes and talent management metrics that were often very unique to their culture. For example, one of the women we spoke to worked at a company that relies heavily on nautical themes. The company, Vanguard, is named after the HMS *Vanguard*, the British admiral Horatio Nelson's flagship in the Battle of the Nile in 1798, and buildings on the corporate campus—which is shaped just like a ship—are named after Nelson's other ships, such as *Victory, Zealous,* and *Goliath.*[1] There is also a ship incorporated in the company's logo, employees are called crew members, the cafeteria is the galley, the gym is named ShipShape, and the company store is referred to as the chandlery.[2] Jack Bogle, Vanguard's founder, apparently got the idea for the name from a book he received from an antiques dealer about Great Britain's naval achievements. While the abundance of nautical references may seem odd to those outside the walls of the Vanguard campus, the nautical terms resonate with its employees. As one employee notes, "The crew of a ship has to work in tandem, in union, otherwise you're going to go nowhere," and an employee's ability to participate in and contribute to this culture of collaboration is an important part of how they conceive of success.[3]

The Vanguard story provides a good example of how specific measures of performance can be within any given organization, and the differences expand beyond questions of culture to include specifically defined benefits. For example, some companies offered long-term incentives to their most successful employees, whereas others tended to reward top performers with significant year-end bonuses, or a combination of the two. Some companies offered tuition assistance or sent their high-potential employees to industry conferences in attractive locations, and one company even proffered the use of a company-owned time-share. Although there were significant differences both in how performance was measured and in how it was rewarded, we were ultimately able to distill it down to a series of central measures that resonated with most of the people we surveyed. Here are those measures:

1. Which of the following best describes your current title? (general counsel/c-suite, deputy general counsel, associate/assistant general counsel, senior counsel, or counsel)
2. Are you an officer? (yes/no)
3. Do you have significant signing authority? (yes/no)
4. Do you currently have any leadership responsibilities (e.g., responsibility for making key decisions and influencing policies) (yes/no)

5. Do you have managerial responsibilities for other attorneys? (yes/no)
6. At what point in the process are you generally brought into discussions about important business decisions? (the planning phase, the execution phase, when legal advice is needed, or not involved in these discussions at all)
7. How important is it to you to be included in the planning phase? (top priority, very important, somewhat important, or not important)
8. How often do you interact with senior executives and decision-makers at your company (nonlawyers)? (never, less than once/month, once/month, two to three times/month, once/week, two to three times/week, or daily)
9. Did you receive a formal, written performance review within the past 12 months? (yes/no)
10. If yes, which of the following best describes the message you received at your last performance review? (your performance was outstanding, very good, average, below average, or poor)
11. If your employer provides you with a talent profile or future potential rating, which of the following best describes your most recent rating? (high potential, some potential, no potential, or this has not been communicated to me)
12. Have you been told by decision-makers that you are part of a succession plan? (yes/no)
13. Relative to your peers (coming from similar markets/employment backgrounds) your base salary is: (above average, average, below average, or not sure)
14. Relative to your peers (coming from similar markets/employment backgrounds) your bonus is: (above average, average, below average, or not sure)
15. Have you been offered Long-Term Incentives (LTIs)? (yes, no, or my company does not have such a plan)

The second theme to emerge when we reviewed this list is that, for many practicing in-house, both women and men, success is often measured by how frequently they are able to interact with the senior-most decision-makers (often nonlawyers) within the organization and the extent to which they are sought out as business partners early on in the decision-making process. As one in-house lawyer explained:

> It's all fine to be a competent lawyer who knows how to draft just the right turn of phrase for an essential contract, but at the end of the day, if this is all you are bringing to the table, then all you are is a cheerful processor. And there is nothing wrong with that, but, for me, when I am brought into the very early stages of the discussion—the point at which we are trying to figure out whether it even makes sense to explore the idea of a contract—that's where it gets exciting and where I know I am tremendously valued. What you really want is to have a seat at the table from day one of the discussions, not day 40, or even day five or day ten.

The third theme to emerge is that no matter what organization you work in, money matters. It is not the case that there is a specific number or a threshold beyond which you are or are not successful. As industry reports make clear, specific numbers vary tremendously by company, industry, and geography, but what does seem to matter is how much you are bringing home relative to your peers. As a plethora of other studies—including those published by the ABA Commission on Women in the Profession[4]—have made clear, women fall significantly behind their male counterparts when it comes to measures of compensation, and this is a critical issue that warrants further exploration, analysis, and action. That said, for purposes of this study, we were focused on compensation—specifically base salary and bonus—as a measure relative to one's similarly situated peers (e.g., those coming from similar markets/employment backgrounds) rather than as a fixed number or as a measure relative to similarly situated peers of the opposite gender.

Key Finding #1

In-house practitioners believe—almost to a person—that grit and growth mindset are important contributors to success.

As we did with all of the women who participated in this survey, we asked the following question of those practicing in-house:

> Have you personally found that being gritty (a gritty person is a person who demonstrates both passion and perseverance in pursuit of her long-term goals) or having a growth mindset (a growth mindset-oriented person believes that her success is based on hard work, learning, training, and doggedness) has been a factor in your overall career success?

Ninety-nine percent of the women we surveyed said that these traits had played a role, at least to some extent, in their ability to achieve career success in the practice of law, and only 1 percent suggested that they had not played a role. As anyone familiar with surveys and data analysis will confirm, this is an overwhelming response to this question and underscores, in some ways better than any of the more nuanced analysis that will follow, how central grit and growth mindset are in this context. Here, in their own words, are some of the ways grit and a growth mindset shaped the careers of some of the in-house women we heard from. First, one in-house lawyer provides a great description of the application of the growth mindset orientation:

> Why did I continue? I am pretty stubborn. I would not admit to the world that I could not cut it, that the city kids were smarter than I was. In fact, I was convinced that was not the case and that I was brighter than them, more hard working than them, and I would succeed.

Another lawyer addresses both traits in her letter, noting that grit and growth mindset were critical components of her legal career and have been essential from the start. She goes on to describe how she used the elements of both traits to turn "yeses" into "nos," surprising her colleagues with her tenacity and perseverance.

> "I cannot believe it," a senior partner said to me one day when starting to observe the changes. "Top leadership in

the firm keeps telling you, 'No!' and you keep coming back again and again. Over time, you have turned their 'no' into a 'yes.' I never thought it would happen."

As both of these women—and the other 452 in-house lawyers in our survey—make clear, these traits matter when it comes to success within U.S. companies and, indeed, are mission critical when it comes to professional satisfaction and advancement.

Key Finding #2

Grit is strongly related to the message that in-house lawyers receive in their performance evaluations.

As discussed earlier in this chapter, specific ways of measuring performance differed greatly among corporations and across industries. That said, the vast majority of corporations do provide some form of annual or semi-annual feedback to their employees, including those working in their legal departments. In an attempt to make an apples-to-apples comparison among processes that likely involve distinct questions specific to each organization's mission and culture, we asked survey-takers to respond to the following question: *Which of the following best describes the message you received at your last performance review?* Responders could then choose one of the following answers in response:

1. Your performance was outstanding
2. Your performance was very good
3. Your performance was average
4. Your performance was below average
5. Your performance was poor

We had a high degree of confidence that asking the question in this way would resonate with most in-house lawyers and that, furthermore, it would give us a legitimate sense of the relationship between grit, growth mindset, and the level at which the women lawyers in our survey were performing. It also has the added benefit of providing us with information about their most recent performance evaluations—in other words, how are these women doing right now (or at least within the past 12 months). The timing is important here because we are interested in measuring their current grit scores against their current performance levels in order to understand as much as we can about how one measure influences the other.

What we found was that the higher your grit score, the more likely you are to receive a higher—or better—overall performance rating. The grittier you are, the more likely your company will be to see you as an outstanding performer, or at least one who is very good. One could certainly point to a number of flaws—some systemic, some process-oriented, some having to do with implicit bias and other psychological factors that may come into play—in almost any evaluation process. Those flaws may lead some to question how much emphasis companies (and law firms) ought to place on the performance evaluation process, but regardless, it is telling that grit is a statistically significant factor and, one could argue, a predictor in how well women will perform in this context.

What can and should we take from this finding? In our view, there are a couple of important implications. The first is that, for better or for worse, gritty women tend to be extremely focused, hard-working, and committed to their work. Moreover, they tend to have a long-term investment in the practice of law and to be driven to achieve mastery in their specific areas of practice. They also tend to be persistent and to not let setbacks deter them or throw them off course. Given these common, gritty characteristics, it is hard to imagine a company that would not want employees who behaved in this way and, more specifically, a company that would not reward individuals for demonstrations of these tendencies. Who doesn't want a dedicated, driven, and self-motivated lawyer on staff? Certainly no organization that we can think of. Of course, part of the problem companies face is identifying gritty employees at the hiring stage—some initial thoughts about how this might be done are included in appendix A.

Second, as discussed in more detail in appendix C, gritty individuals tend to be the kinds of individuals who perform well on a number of different measures, such as in academic settings and physical or athletic endeavors (playing an instrument, surviving cadet basic training at West Point). Therefore, it makes logical sense that they would also perform well when it comes to professional measures of success. Not surprisingly, there was a statistically significant relationship between the grit scores of the women practicing in-house and their law school ranking, meaning that the higher the grit score, the more likely the women were to have attended a top-ranked law school. Furthermore, the higher the grit score, the more likely these women were to have graduated at the top of their classes. These findings suggest that many of the women in-house discovered the importance of grit, or at least demonstrated grit-like tendencies, prior to becoming lawyers. Many were already using these concepts to achieve success in law school. As one in-house lawyer explains in her letter:

> I used grit and growth mindset tactics in law school to help me succeed . . . when I needed it the most, my grit and growth mindset went into overdrive. Instead of being defeated, I worked really hard, and I only missed one question on the final exam. This small success made me feel vindicated and helped give me strength when dealing with clients and co-workers later on in my career. Over the coming years, as I started my career, I looked back to this moment when I needed a reminder that hard work yields results.

Similarly, another lawyer, following a difficult divorce, made the decision to attend law school as a means to support her two young daughters and faced the doubly difficult challenge of juggling her academic workload alongside financial needs and the needs of a 15-month-old baby. She worked during the day (part-time), went to classes in the evenings, and, with significant support from her parents, managed to graduate. Both of these lawyers learned early on that their grit could fuel their academic success, in spite of some pretty daunting challenges, and both relied on grit later in life when building successful legal careers. Having healthy amounts of grit allowed them to stay in the game, even when quitting seemed like an appealing option. As one lawyer shares:

> During those early years of practice, there were plenty of times when I thought about throwing in the towel. There are certainly easier ways to earn a living. But I knew I had to push through for my children, so that they could see the importance of setting and achieving a goal. I think this mindset has served me well throughout my career and has helped me achieve a level of professional success that I never would have expected.

Once again, gritty women like these two discovered early on that grit is a powerfully effective tool and then continued to use it strategically to fuel their career success—whether in law school or later on in their careers—and this allowed them to accomplish both their personal and professional goals. It also helps to explain why gritty women tend to do so well on performance measures in-house—and why this is so closely correlated with their ability to thrive in law school. That said, it should also be noted that not all women lawyers, including the subset practicing in-house, discover grit at the same point in life. Indeed, while many women practicing in-house seem to have done very well in law school— which suggests that they became aware of the importance of grit relatively early on—there are countless others who did not discover the significance or the power of grit until much later in life. There is no set path, and one can benefit from grit at any stage of the journey. Regardless of when one makes the discovery, grit can and does lead to success.

Key Finding #3

Grit influences the point at which women lawyers are brought into the decision-making process, as well as how long they will stay in the game.

As noted earlier, one of the measures of success that we used for women practicing in-house was the extent to which they were consulted in the decision-making process. Specifically, we asked them: *At what point in the process are you generally brought into discussions about important business decisions?* The women could then choose one of the following responses: (1) I am involved at the planning phase, (2) I am involved at the beginning of the execution phase, (3) I am involved when someone thinks they need legal advice, or (4) I am not involved in these discussions at all. As noted earlier, our rationale for this question was that many of the in-house lawyers we interviewed mentioned the importance of being thought of as a strategic business partner rather than as someone who should be brought in, potentially as an afterthought, to clean up messes or to execute on decisions made by others. The women who were the most engaged and passionate about their work tended to be the ones who felt like they were valued not only for their technical legal ability but also for their ability to be forward-thinking and to understand the needs of the business. As Brian Woram, executive vice president and general counsel, KB Home, points out, "To be effective means being someone who is not only a good attorney, but also someone who has an appropriate influence on the overall activities of the business—someone whose advice is sought out and heeded."[5] Some of the top-performing female general counsel we surveyed reported that they were regularly consulted by senior leaders, including the CEO and the CFO, on matters related to the organization's core business strategies. A few even reported that, at a very high level, the work they did felt less about the practice of law and more about the issues facing the business, although they were always mindful of bringing to bear their unique legal perspective and insights. As *Harvard Business Review* noted, "The general counsel is now a core member of the top management team and offers advice not just on law and related matters but helps shape discussion and debate around business issues."[6]

The strong connection between a woman's grit score and the point at which she is brought into the decision-making process is an important one and suggests that the grittier the woman is the more likely she is to be seen as a top performer. Moreover, she is more likely to be relied upon to help drive business results and to be thought of as a core member of the organization's leadership. When all of these elements align, the experience of practicing law in-house can be tremendously rewarding and enjoyable. As one in-house lawyer recalls, when she transitioned to her first in-house role with a large, multinational automotive company, she got immediate, direct access to business leaders. These leaders were not interested in her legal theories, however. Their focus was on solving problems and delivering results. Now that she is comfortable with these expectations, it is the approach to practice she enjoys the most. This lawyer went on to accept another in-house role as associate general counsel for an international organization. Her experience at her second in-house position, as a woman and an attorney of color, taught her that she could bring her grit to bear in a number of different ways within the organization. As she describes it:

> I have learned that the complexities that exist within corporate culture and in-house legal departments are by no means a perfect model for women and attorneys of color. In 2016, the ranks of general counsel could stand to be more diverse. This is where grit and growth mindset materialize as helpful tools for navigating the mercurial waters of corporations. I remain confident that even greater leadership and growth opportunities are within my reach.

This lawyer's experience effectively highlights both elements of this finding—first, that grit can influence the nature of the role that one plays in-house, which is an indicator of how one is viewed and valued within the organization, and second, that the same application of grittiness that drives this form of success can also influence how long one ultimately practices law. Her optimistic view of the opportunities that exist for her, in spite of the obstacles that she faces, suggests that she is committed to her practice and willing—and indeed eager—to either stay with her organization and to continue to develop and flourish or rely on her grittiness to help her make a bold move if and when necessary. (Editor's note: Since writing her initial letter to us about her experiences, this lawyer did, in fact, end up making a "bold move" and went to work for a law firm, providing us with a terrific example of grit in action!) This optimistic outlook is a perfect example of a healthy and robust growth mindset, and coupled with the grit that she so clearly has, it is hard to imagine that she won't continue to progress in her legal career (in whatever iteration makes the most sense for her long-term).

When we consider the results of the survey, it is clear that there is a strong and powerful connection between grit and how long one practices law—in other words, as grit score increases, so too does the number of years that a woman is likely to have practiced. One of the profound implications of this research, then, is not only that grit predicts some measure of longevity within the practice of law, but also that life experiences teach us the importance of grit. Even when we don't consciously think of it or define it, we know, on some fundamental level, that grit is an effective way to achieve your own personal and professional goals, whatever they might be. As one lawyer shares, "I couldn't and wouldn't even contemplate giving up my work. . . . I am always working toward something. I am always prepared, focused, and committed. I do what I say I am going to do." It is easy to see why someone that gritty would be committed to the practice of law for the long haul. On the flip side, when giving advice to more junior lawyers, another lawyer cautions:

> Don't whine. I mean that in two ways. In one sense, attitude is everything. If you cannot find positive value in your work and in your contribution to the company, why would anyone seek you out for your counseling and your expertise? Suck it up. In another sense, your co-workers all have their own challenges and life experiences. Some of them are far more horrific than yours, and even if they aren't, the person who is living those experiences doesn't see it that way.

Although this may come across like tough love, her point is an important one. Remaining optimistic about your practice and being the kind of lawyer who views challenges as opportunities for learning, growth, and development—a gritty lawyer—is the kind of lawyer who is likely to be sought out by other lawyers and nonlegal members of the organization. On the other hand, a lawyer who does not display these kinds of characteristics is less likely to be included in important, high-level decision-making. As one lawyer points out, "The choices I make today can open doors, or close doors of future opportunities." The important takeaway here is that demonstrations of grit, whether it be an unwavering commitment to the practice—both in terms of the number of years spent devoted to it and the commitment to achieve mastery within specific areas of practice—or an optimistic future outlook, are likely to make you the kind of lawyer who is really "more than a lawyer."[7] Importantly, those lawyers who bring more than just technical legal skills to the table are exactly the kinds of lawyers who thrive in corporate settings.

Key Finding #4

Mindset predicts seniority within the organization.

The final finding of this chapter is a relatively straightforward one: Those with a growth mindset orientation are more likely to occupy more senior roles within the organization. In many ways, this finding is consistent with the other findings discussed in this chapter. Believing in your own ability to succeed appears to be, for many women practicing in-house, a self-fulfilling prophecy. As one lawyer explains, having a growth mindset has assisted her in excelling in various professions. Whenever she encountered a challenge, she focused on what she could do to improve her situation, adopting a mantra that she has carried with her throughout her career: "The more you learn, the more you earn." This is a perfect example of the growth mindset orientation and how it can position you for success, both in terms of your progress within a specific organization and in financial terms. When asked to give advice to more junior lawyers, another lawyer offers a like-minded mantra: "Keep trying and keep asking—maybe the next time you will be successful."

Notes:

1. https://about.vanguard.com/who-we-are/
2. *Id.*
3. http://www.marketwatch.com/story/5-things-you-dont-know-about-vanguard-2014-10-31
4. http://www.americanbar.org/groups/women/publications.html
5. http://www.kornferry.com/institute/general-counsel-senior-leader-more-just-lawyer
6. https://hbr.org/2012/09/the-rise-of-the-general-counsel
7. *Id.*

Toni Camacho

One must first believe in growth before being able to adopt a gritty mindset. Like building blocks, growth is only possible through confidence gained from success in prior experiences. In other words, you need to believe that you can achieve your goals before you can believe that working toward them is realistic, and you can gain the confidence to set those goals by looking back at prior success.

How Did I Get Here? A Few Personal Examples

Engaging the grit and growth mindset played an important role in the circumstances leading to my career in law as much as it has played in the circumstances I've faced in my career. For starters, I am a statistical anomaly. I'm a first-generation college graduate, a first-generation American, a Mexican American woman, and a woman working in corporate law. In short, it was statistically improbable that I would graduate from high school, college, and law school, and perhaps even less likely that I would pass the bar exam or work at a large international law firm. Even with diversity efforts in recent decades, Hispanic people still hold only about 4 percent of all law licenses despite being about 18 percent of the population.* But somehow, I'm here—an M&A lawyer in New York City who has practiced at some of the largest and most prestigious law firms in the country.

A lot of people helped me along the way, and, although I've been able to succeed, in part because of a mixture of luck and opportunity, imagining where I could go and working to get there (i.e., grit and growth) are the reasons I'm here today. I have never felt that I couldn't overcome my circumstances or shortcomings. I made it by being persistent and feeling that I could work at being better, even when I wasn't successful on my first try. Oftentimes, just letting people know that you need help is the best way to help yourself. More often than not, women aren't good at vocalizing their goals. Women tend to be less self-serving and more self-conscious about asking for resources and support that they

---

*http://www.americanbar.org/content/dam/aba/administrative/market_research/lawyer-demographics-tables-2015.pdf

need and deserve. Women need to be more confident, and this confidence can come from looking back positively at your prior success. By way of example, I used grit and growth tactics in law school to help me succeed and found that the general lack of gender and racial diversity made implementing those tactics difficult. Although my law school class was about 60 percent women, the courses I took at the business school didn't mirror that percentage at all. When I took courses at the business school, I was nearly always the only woman, or one of a few women, and almost always the only student of color enrolled in any given class. One particular instance at the business school stands out from my new venture finance class. The professor encouraged us to form study groups, and, after politely being told that there was no more room in each of the two study groups I approached, I began to feel like it was me they were really saying no to. I didn't know why I was rejected by my classmates but could only guess that it was either because I was a law student in a business course, a woman, a student of color, or some combination of all three. Perhaps when I needed it the most, my grit and growth mindset went into overdrive. Instead of being defeated, I worked really hard, and I only missed one question on the final exam. This small success made me feel vindicated and helped give me strength when dealing with clients and co-workers later in my career. Over the coming years, as I started my career, I looked back to this moment when I needed a reminder that hard work yields results, even when disparaging people are around you.

Law Firm Life: What Can Be Learned and What Needs to Change?

Law firms are hard places to work. Associates must devote huge amounts of time to work to become successful. While the grit and growth mindset might be sufficient to get women a seat at the law firm associate table, real change is needed in the profession before women can get equal seats at the partnership table. An article* from the *Harvard Business Review* notes that "high-achieving women experience social backlash because their very success— and specifically the behaviors that created that success—violates

---

*https://hbr.org/2013/04/for-women-leaders-likability-a

our expectations about how women are supposed to behave." Although women have advanced professionally, gender bias is still very real and continues to hurt women in law firms. Although I can think of many female partners, I can think of three times as many female associates whose law firm careers were stunted or cut short far too soon. However, I truly believe that women can increase their chances of success by using the grit and growth mindset; after all, law firm life is really just a mix of working really hard and making yourself available to client demands. Implementing the grit and growth mindset can be challenging at times, so here are my top tips for finding success at a law firm: (1) seek out mentors who will advocate for your career; (2) actively set tangible and achievable goals every fiscal quarter; (3) write a personal business plan and work it and then go back and reevaluate yourself often; and (4) don't give up when something doesn't work—just change your approach and move on (hence the "reevaluate" step in number 3). Breaking down associate development into tangible parts will give you a clear path to measure your progress and implement the grit and growth mindset into your daily tasks.

While I continue to work at developing myself professionally, I think one thing remains true: Organizational change is needed at law firms before women can expect grit and growth alone to elevate them to partnership. Partnership at all major law firms steadily remains largely male and white, and, even when women make it to partnership, they are often out-earned by their male counterparts. While women can use the grit and growth mindset to pave a path to success, that alone won't allow more women to succeed in law firms. What women really need is for the men in law firms to meet us halfway by recognizing and acting to correct the implicit gender bias that female practitioners face. We need these men to work with their female counterparts to help create an environment where hard work, above all else, determines success. Finally, women need to look at their male colleagues and not only demand the same treatment, but, more importantly, believe that they are deserving of the same benefits and treatment afforded to their male colleagues.

Toni Camacho is an attorney in New York, New York, where she focuses on corporate, capital formation, and securities law and cybersecurity and data privacy. www.linkedin.com/in/tonicamachoesq

Stephanie Goble

Grit and growth are critical components of my legal career and have been essential from the start of my legal practice. Many years ago, as a young attorney with a large law firm, I learned firsthand about the importance of grit and how it pays off into growth opportunities. During my tenure at that firm, I worked to convince senior leadership to amend certain processes. After two years, things started to change.

"I cannot believe it," a senior partner said one day when starting to observe the changes. "Top leadership in the firm keeps telling you, 'No!' and you keep coming back again and again. Over time, you have turned their 'no' into a 'yes.' I never thought it would happen." This was quite a surprise to the senior partner. Over time, he had repeatedly assured me that the firm had a long history of doing things in only one way, these processes helped bring success to the firm, and there would never be openness to change.

But I wasn't buying his limitations. I wondered if maybe things appeared stuck simply because no one pushed for positive change. Maybe the top partners were waiting to see if any of their associate attorneys cared enough to keep asking. Or, maybe the other partners had not considered the changing legal environment. This evidenced one of my personal values: Keep trying and keep asking—maybe the next attempt will be successful.

I was delighted to watch as my professional grit and tenacity would eventually facilitate law firm change and would also open doors to a remarkable platform of my own personal and professional growth. The grit won the respect and esteem of the senior partner who made the above remark, and he offered me a personal mentorship. This was no small offering. He was on the task force for the state supreme court. Here was an attorney assisting the state supreme court in drafting legal provisions and procedures for our firm's core area of law—and this attorney was now offering to mentor me.

Grit had paid off again and had given ME opportunities for astronomical growth: in networking, professional development, and legal skill. The mentorship was challenging. The senior partner took care in ensuring that I was up-to-date on the latest legal theories, pending legislative proposals, and current nationwide case law.

Soon I found myself at a dinner table with a vice president (VP) of one of the firm's largest clients. This was an important dinner for our firm. For the first time ever, and largely because of the mentorship with the partner, I was able to engage this VP throughout the dinner with the professional insights and current understanding of the business and legal environment that I had learned through discussions with my mentor. Both the VP and I were learning from each other and appreciating the differing perspectives on such critical issues. At the end of the dinner, the VP remarked how he had been impressed with our conversation and offered to meet with me further to discuss some lucrative additional referrals to our firm.

In facilitating grit, I am careful not to use limiting language. Often, I can feel that I "must" or "should" do something. Granted, there are times of deadlines and legal requirements, but outside of these structural limitations are many opportunities. If I get into a limiting mindset, then my focus can become too narrow—and I overlook and miss potential growth occasions.

In other words, grit is not about keeping my head down and just working super long hours. Grit is not about paper-pushing to keep all partners and clients happy. Instead, grit is being a team player, but also being tenacious about my own priorities and living consistent with my values. After all, the choices I make today can open doors, or close doors, of future opportunities.

Grit also involves the language of intention used in phrases such as "I will" or "I choose." During my graduate training at Oxford University and HEC Paris, I learned to watch for challenges that are meaningful to me and to consistently prioritize relationships over tasks. The tasks must still be accomplished but with a continual recognition of the importance of relationship. Above all, grit is about a choice—and with the choice, an open door into fabulous growth.

Stephanie Goble, Ph.D., is president and general counsel for Hope for the Heart in Dallas. www.hopefortheheart.org

Anna M. Lozoya

My first job as an attorney was with a workers' compensation defense law firm. I was hired on the spot because I am also a registered nurse. I was both excited and anxious to begin my legal career. The firm's partners were all men at the time. There were only two other women associates, and I was the only minority attorney at the firm. The firm was not the right fit, to be quite honest, and I was miserable.

This job seemed like a perfect fit. The problem was the firm exerted power through fear. All the associates, especially my female colleagues, feared the partners. The majority of my time was spent reviewing medical records. A task that would take a novice attorney three days would take me perhaps eight or ten hours at most. I would fly through the medical records.

At the outset, I arrived early, stayed late, and worked diligently. I continuously asked for new projects, new tasks, or to observe or sit in litigation. I was bored and wanted to learn more. I eventually became disenchanted with my work environment. A partner even told me my job was to "sit at the office and bill hours."

The straw that broke the camel's back was a nomination for a leadership opportunity. I was nominated to participate in the Hispanic National Bar Association's (HNBA) Inaugural Latina Leadership Academy. The managing partner gave me approval, but it was more of a threat than a blessing to attend the leadership academy. I attended the academy and the HNBA convention. Three weeks later, I was fired. I was extremely happy to say the least.

I only worked at the firm for about four months. I learned nothing, absolutely nothing. I wanted to augment my other skills. I previously worked as an auditor for a CPA firm, I possessed extensive sales experience, and I had over eight years of nursing in two states under my belt. Yet, I was expected to be confined to my beautiful office on the Chicago River for at least six months. Why? Because that was just "the way things are done around here."

I was fortunate that I could continue to work as a nurse on a part-time basis to make ends meet. Through networking I landed an in-house position for a real estate investment corporation. The owners were extremely excited that I was a woman and I had a sales background. The corporation needed a negotiator who had no interest in the deal and was not a man. Initially, I was overwhelmed because I knew nothing about a closing or real estate contracts, much less negotiating multi-million dollar deals, but the corporation took a chance.

Having a growth mindset has assisted me in excelling in various professions. My mantra, "the more you learn, the more you earn," has carried the day for me many times. I attended every real estate continuing legal education course I could get to. Some days I would sit in on eviction or foreclosure court calls. I would write down the case numbers and then go research the documents at the circuit court counter. There are only a handful of firms in the Chicago area that handle all aspects of real estate litigation and transactions. I began focusing on their cases and listening to their attorneys handle trials. I would Google relevant areas of law and read every blog that was pertinent to topics my bosses discussed at meetings. I even became a title agent with a couple of title companies to use as a resource for closings.

I can humbly admit that I am no expert in real estate transactions, but I can definitely hold my own. I have acquired a couple of mentors along the way, as well. On occasion, I have to litigate matters for the corporation, and I utilize my mentors to litigate or consult on the matter. A vast majority of my learning has come from my mentors. I was blessed that most of my mentors are women and two are Latinas.

Next on my "learn to earn more" task list is obtaining a real estate agent's license to thoroughly understand the dynamics of a real estate transaction. This will require more independent learning and future collaboration with real estate agents. I would never have imagined working the small niche of real estate transactions. However, my adjustment to this area of law has been more than a pleasant surprise.

Anna M. Lozoya is in-house counsel for Maida Vale LLC in Chicago, where she focuses on commercial and residential transactions, including drafting and negotiating contracts.
www.linkedin.com/in/anna-lozoya-jd-rn-179b873a/

Pamela Nelson

In many ways, I fell into the practice of law backward. Although I always intended to go to law school, I got married shortly after graduating from college and moved around for a few years in support of my husband's career. We were in small towns that did not have local law schools, so it became less and less of a priority. During that time, I started working as a paralegal, mostly as a contractor. I enjoyed the work, but I always knew I could do more. After the birth of my second child, I went through a difficult divorce and found myself without a career that fulfilled me and very aware that I would have to take financial responsibility for my children. My first few child support checks were delivered late, which gave me great concerns for the future. As a paralegal, I had worked for a family law attorney and had seen all too many times the desperation on women's faces when their child support was not timely paid. I knew I did not want that path for myself or for my children. It was very important to me that my daughters not see their mother as a victim, but instead as someone who was able to fight back when times were tough. I needed to make a change, so suddenly law school was back in the picture.

It was my mother who made me believe that law school was still an option, even at 30 years of age and while raising two small daughters on my own. My youngest one was 15 months old when I started law school. I worked part-time during the day, went to classes in the evenings, and, with significant support from my parents, I made it through. My grades were good, so I had plenty of offers from on-campus recruiting, but I was very aware that with my special circumstances, I had to take extra care in my choice of employers. I initially leaned toward the few in-house opportunities that were offered, but I then decided that I shouldn't limit myself—if I tried to work for a big firm and couldn't make it work, was that really the end of the world? I was able to find a firm that understood and welcomed my circumstances, so I decided to give it a shot.

Working as a first-year associate at a large law firm is difficult under even the best of circumstances, and my situation certainly did not make it any easier. Although I knew the importance of getting off to a strong start in my new career, I was always clear that my children were my priority. Fortunately, I've always gotten by on very little sleep, and that served me well during my early years of practice—and the years of juggling motherhood and law school were incredible training for my first years of practice. It required great flexibility on the part of myself, the partners and associates I worked with, my kids, and my parents, who were my back-up child care, but we made it work. I was able to meet my billable hours quota and still attend soccer games, piano recitals, and ballet recitals—although admittedly, taking the time out to attend those activities meant some very late hours catching up on work.

During those early years of practice, there were plenty of times when I thought about throwing in the towel. There are certainly easier ways to earn a living. But I knew I had to push through for my children, so that they could see the importance of setting and achieving a goal. I think this mindset has served me well throughout my career and has helped me achieve a level of professional success that I never would have expected. After a few moves, I have now been with Shell Oil Company for 10 years. I am currently the associate general counsel for contracting and procurement and IT. I lead a global team of 20 lawyers, and we are responsible for providing legal advice for all goods and services purchased by Shell and for its IT operations.

I think grit and growth mindset was thrust upon me, rather than me realizing that I had it within me all along. Having the responsibility for two young children was an excellent driver. To anyone who is struggling in pushing through a difficult situation, I would say that the best way to get through it is to picture those around you who will be most affected by your success—and do it for them. I can crumble on my own, but I know that my family, friends, team, and other co-workers are counting on me to help them push through the hard times. When I remember that I'm not in it alone, it gives me the strength that I need to continue.

One of my favorite parts about my current role is that I get to work with many lawyers who are early in their careers and are trying to balance career and family life. Although I am in a very different place in my life now—my daughters are both in college—I keep my early struggles top-of-mind, and I try to help the lawyers on my team recognize when they may need to re-focus their priorities. The legal profession attracts bright, driven people who tend to be very hard on themselves when things aren't going exactly right, so I try to share my experiences to let them know that even though things may feel out of sorts from time-to-time, we have to trust in the long run. One of my favorite sayings (and I don't know where it came from, but certainly not me) is that life is a marathon, not a sprint!

Pamela Nelson is associate general counsel—trading and supply at Shell Oil Company in Houston, where she focuses on transactional work supporting Shell companies' oil and oil products trading and supply businesses. www.shell.com

Evelyn Sullen Smith

Introduction

The concepts of grit and the growth mindset, as articulated by the ABA Commission on Women in the Profession's Grit Project, support a powerful premise that many women are living and breathing: We can achieve seemingly unreachable goals and can define success by our own terms. So, as we consider the external barriers that are placed before us, we know that incorporating grit and growth into our arsenal will enable us to better navigate them with determination and resolve to reach our goals.

I journeyed through 20 years of my practice and identified some defining moments that underscore the important work of the project. Some of these pivotal moments occurred before and during my childhood, while in law school, and throughout my career. I invite you to take a journey into the *Personal Grit Project of Evelyn Smith.*

My Origins of Grit and Growth

I could not adequately describe my grit and growth mindset without highlighting three important women who naturally infused these concepts into my fiber: my grandmother, Evelyn Lewis; my mother, Thoris Walton; and the Honorable Denise Page Hood.

My grandmother, in the early 1940s, like many African Americans in pursuit of a better life, traveled from Birmingham, Alabama to Detroit during the period known as the *Great Migration.* She achieved only a ninth grade education. Yet, she led a dignified and well-traveled life and encouraged her offspring to do the same. She retired as a seamstress at Ford Motor Company. Her good credit and financial acumen were a source of pride for her. In this way, she modeled fiscal responsibility, and I paid close attention. But it was her declaration to me when I was nine years old that I would one day become a lawyer that was a defining moment for me and a lofty goal, especially because I was painfully shy and barely audible when speaking. Thankfully, my grandmother lived long enough to see her words manifest into reality when I received my law degree in 1995.

In 1974, my mother displayed grit and growth when she, with five children in tow, left an abusive husband—my father. Through my mother's demonstration of fearlessness, I learned that all setbacks are finite, both in duration and scope. Because of my mother's brave act we were positioned to flourish. My mother's own educational and professional goals were met after obtaining two master's degrees, and in 2009 retiring as an educator from Detroit public schools.

Chief Judge Denise Page Hood of the U.S. District Court for the Eastern District of Michigan epitomizes the grit and growth mindset. I met Judge Hood as a teenager and admired her for her seemingly unflappable ability to manage her successful career, her role as a wife and mother of two sons, and her dedication to community service. Judge Hood expressed an unwavering belief in my ability to succeed and took a vested interest in my legal career and personal development. During my second year of law school, I successfully completed a judicial externship when she was a county circuit court judge. After her federal appointment, I became her judicial law clerk from 1997 to 1998 and saw firsthand her shining example of grace and leadership.

Law School Lessons

I received my public affairs management degree from Michigan State University in 1991, but no other profession intrigued me more than law. In 1992, I was accepted into Michigan State University's College of Law but quickly learned that I was unprepared for the undertaking. Perhaps it was blind courage that propelled me forward in the face of challenging obstacles. Nevertheless, I graduated law school with a newfound determination and a powerful lesson in hand along with my law degree: Be willing to make prompt and necessary adjustments when facing challenges.

Up until the point of graduation, I still wasn't ready for the monumental shift in thinking needed beyond law school. Skills that I regularly use today had not yet taken root: professional mentorship, strategic planning, and the art of mindfulness and eliminating "noise" to meet the challenges of the day. It was tough learning skills at the precise moment in which they are needed, but it activated my grittiness.

The Practice

Following my clerkship and work as a government attorney, my growth mindset was further refined when I joined a Detroit-based firm as an associate in 1998. The environment was extremely demanding, yet the experience allowed me to hone my grit and confidence.

During a risky display of grit, I challenged work undertaken by the firm from a client whose business model seemed to disproportionately impact the elderly. I presented this information to the firm's leadership. The firm reviewed my request to phase out the work being done, and the firm agreed and ended the client relationship. As I reflect on that experience, it is a reminder that others can be beneficiaries of one's grit and growth mindset.

I remain grateful to the firm for developing my legal and advocacy skills. The firm back then, however, was not without some of the challenges faced by many firms today: (1) lack of diversity, (2) conflicts between family life and professional ambitions, and (3) few client development opportunities. Since then, the firm and countless others are doing more to support its current and former women associates and partners. As evidence, I proudly maintain many mentor relationships with my former firm's partners.

In 2003, I transitioned to my first in-house role. During the years since then, I've worked within three multinational organizations. Each organization had its own unique culture, providing me direct access to top-notch business leaders who honed my legal and business acumen. Simply put, they wanted problems solved and results delivered. This methodology of law practice had its fair share of rewards both personally and professionally.

Later in my in-house career, however, I learned that the complexities of corporate culture and in-house legal departments by no means foster a perfect model for women or for attorneys of color.

Even in 2016, the ranks of general counsel are still not diverse. This is where grit and growth materialize as helpful tools for navigating the mercurial waters of corporations.

As of this writing, my grit and growth journey has propelled me forward to even greater opportunities, with a keen desire to hone my brand of authentic leadership. I recently shared my aspirations with a community leader, and I was introduced to Perez & Morris LLC, a 20-lawyer full-service firm based in Columbus, Ohio. With its demonstrated commitment to diversity and inclusion and work-life balance, I was intrigued. After years of in-house lawyering, I've return to private practice.

Final Thoughts

The women in my life made me malleable to grit and growth concepts. Although my beloved profession tends to lean toward a fixed mindset—where women are sometimes marginalized and misbranded in ways that may hinder their success—doing the work of the Grit Project allows us all to navigate efficaciously toward even greater achievements.

My husband, Jason, and I are blessed with two beautiful daughters, ages seven and nine, who are now witnessing my Grit Project. I pray that they will each take lessons from me and cultivate their own grit and growth to help them better navigate their personal and professional lives.

Evelyn Sullen Smith is an attorney at Perez & Morris LLC in Columbus, Ohio, where she focuses on transportation and logistics, business transactions, and state and federal regulatory matters. www.perez-morris.com

Sandra Zubik

As I grow older, I have the opportunity to reflect on my experiences of practicing law for almost 30 years. I have had the opportunity to work with, and to oppose, many lawyers, including many male lawyers. I wanted to take this opportunity to share some reflections on my career path and motivations in hopes that it inspires or educates younger lawyers in their journey.

I had a slightly different upbringing than most of my colleagues. I grew up on a family farm in the 1960s. The world of my childhood was far different than today, but it was also far different than my urban counterparts. I grew up in a world without central heat, with the telephone as a party line (in which multiple families shared the same telephone line and anyone could listen in on a call), and where things like indoor plumbing and electricity were not benefits shared by all the neighbors. We had both, I am happy to report. One thing that was shared by the neighbors was the idea that the sons inherit the farm, and the daughters get married. My mother had slim hopes of a scrawny daughter with thick glasses and a propensity to say what she thought. In fact, my mother used to tell me I was too dumb and ugly to get married, so I needed to make sure I got a job. She had hopes that I would learn to type well enough to become a secretary.

I had other hopes and good grades and managed to score in the 99 percent of my college board tests. Not bad for someone attending one of the smallest high schools in the state and who had 67 people in her graduating class. I attended the University of Michigan on a scholarship, mostly because a week after I applied some nice woman from the admissions office called me personally to let me know I got in. I thought that was nice. The idea that there were 40,000 people in the student body at that time didn't exactly register. I vividly recall walking into class the first day of school and marveling at the amount of people sitting in the room. There were probably 200 more people in that auditorium for that single class than there were in the entire student body of my high school.

To say the University of Michigan was tough, that it was an academic challenge and an emotional stretch, would be an understatement. And 35 years ago, there were no counseling programs, or tutoring programs, or acclimatizing programs for those with a different background to lean on. I showed up in August, having never been there before, and stayed until December 22, the day after my last exam. All in all, I left campus six times after I enrolled. I graduated in three years, with a GPA of 3.2. It was tough. I learned not just "book learning" but also about the cruelty and snobbery of people.

Why did I continue? As I look back, I attribute it to two reasons: (1) I didn't think I had any fallback options—my mother made it clear that the normal option of marriage wasn't open to me. I could not fail. I had no choice but to keep going. (2) I am pretty stubborn. I would not admit to the world that I could not cut it, that the city kids were smarter than I was. In fact, I was convinced that was not the case, and that I was brighter than them, harder working than them, and I would succeed.

In those days, there was an expectation that you went to school to earn a living, the more lucrative and prestigious the better. No one gave career advice about "doing what you love" or "making a difference."

Getting into law school wasn't the problem, but affording it was. I didn't have such good grades or good test scores to get that full tuition scholarship I had landed at the University of Michigan. Because I have a lot of stubbornness and perseverance, I decided that I would go to night school and find a job during the day. I had relatives in Chicago, and there were several law schools that had night programs. I was accepted to the John Marshall Law School and sent a resume to every law firm listed in the Sullivan's law directory with more than 30 lawyers. I landed a job as a paralegal and worked full time during the day. I graduated in three-and-a-half years, passed the bar, and started practicing law in 1987.

My experiences of working full time and attending law school in the evening with people generally much older than I was, would be a second, longer letter. Suffice it to say it required a great deal of perseverance to put in a full day at the office, trudge over to law school for three hours of classes, and then spend a harrowing hour or more commuting in the dark on public transportation, especially when my peers were all at the bar.

Because I wasn't graduating from a top-tier law school, I knew I needed to practice in a unique area of the law or develop some sort of expertise that would transcend my law school reputation. My first job out of law school was working for the Illinois attorney general, for which I took a pay cut from my job as a paralegal. It gave me an excellent opportunity to be exposed to employment law cases, which were very interesting to me. I seized on the area of traditional labor law and went to work for the National Labor Relations Board. While I only spent a few years there, it gave me an excellent grounding in traditional labor law, which is not a common area of practice. From there, I moved in-house, and I have been an in-house lawyer ever since.

As I reflect on this career and what advice to give a young lawyer, two areas of advice occur to me:

1. Don't be afraid to move jobs. The biggest regret of my career is that I spent 16 years at one job. That meant that I passed up earning opportunities I would have had if I had changed jobs, because yearly wage increases are small compared to the wage increase you get when moving to another company. That meant I missed learning opportunities in new areas of the law and developing my career in other ways. Finally, it meant promotion opportunities were limited, because the company had no need to promote someone who seemed content with the role; instead, they promoted and recognized people who were more of a flight risk.

2. Don't whine. I mean that in two ways. In one sense, attitude is everything. If you cannot find positive value in your work and in your contribution to the company, why would anyone seek you out for your counseling and your expertise? Suck it up.

In the other sense, your co-workers all have their own challenges and life experiences. Some of them are far more horrific
than yours, and even if they aren't, the person who is living those
experiences doesn't see it that way.

Good luck. The practice of law is stimulating and rewarding.

Sandra Zubik is senior counsel at Tyson Foods, Inc. in Chicago, where
she focuses on labor and employment law. www.tyson.com

5

Government and Nonprofit Lawyers

KEY FINDINGS

➤ Grit is a reliable indicator of how well a woman performs in a government or nonprofit role.

➤ Both grit and growth mindset are closely related to how far a woman has advanced within her organization.

➤ Ambition is closely tied to both the grit and growth mindset scores of women practicing in government and nonprofit organizations.

THE WOMEN WE SURVEYED

We heard from roughly 300 women who were currently working for the government or for nonprofit organizations. Within that group, a little more than half (about 56 percent) worked for the government and a little less than half (about 44 percent) worked for nonprofits. As was the case with the other groups of women we surveyed, we heard from women who represented a broad range of practice areas, years of experience, length of time with their current employers, and number of positions (both legal and

nonlegal) since law school graduation. The most commonly represented practice areas were criminal and labor and employment
for those working in government, and civil rights and children and
family for those working in the nonprofit world. In terms of longevity with current employers, there was an even mix among the
women in both groups, with no significant concentrations. Most
of the women in both groups had held at least two other legal
positions prior to joining their current employers, and the vast
majority had held at least one full-time, nonlegal position since
graduating from college. About two-thirds of the women in both
groups were planning to stay with their current employers for at
least the next three to five years; one-third of those in government
and one-quarter of those in the nonprofit sector planned to stay
with their current employers for the duration of their careers.

When we looked at family structure for the women in government, we learned that two-thirds of them were married or in
a domestic partnership, and half of them had children. Of those
who had children, most had one or two children, and about
80 percent of those who had children had them while they were
working as lawyers. Roughly 65 percent of the women working for
nonprofits were married or in a domestic partnership, and about
60 percent of those women had children. The average number of
children was two; 82 percent of those who had children had them
while practicing.

In terms of academic measures of success, the women in both
groups had performed quite well in law school, although there
was also a healthy mix across the board in terms of GPA, class
rank, and tier of law school.

MEASURING SUCCESS

We spent quite a bit of time trying to determine the appropriate
measures of success for women lawyers practicing in government
and nonprofit organizations. As was the case throughout this
study, this undertaking led to many interesting conversations with
women lawyers, all of whom provided us with valuable insights on
how they understood and defined success in their own practices

and how success was defined by their organizations. Of course, there were a plethora of ideas around what constituted success, but a few key themes emerged, and those themes informed our penultimate lists of success measures. The final list of success measures for women in government is as follows:

1. Which of the following best describes your current title? (various choices)
2. How long have you been in your current position? (various ranges)
3. To the best of your knowledge, are you part of a succession plan? (yes/no)
4. Do you currently supervise other lawyers? (yes/no)
5. How often do other lawyers seek out your advice/consult with you? (often, sometimes, rarely, or never)
6. Have often are you asked to participate in the training and/or development of more junior lawyers? (often, sometimes, rarely, or never)
7. Based on the most recent feedback you have received from your supervisor(s), either formal or informal, which of the following best describes your understanding of how you are performing in your current role? (my performance is outstanding, very good, average, below average, or poor)
8. How often do you get to work on the most high-profile, complex, and challenging cases/issues? (always, most of the time, sometimes, rarely, or never)
9. How much control do you have over the nature or genre of the cases that you work on? (none, very little, some, or a lot)

For most of the women in government that we heard from, formal performance reviews were uncommon. Unlike in law firms, where they seemed to be a standard and reliable yearly event, in government they seemed to be the exception rather than the rule. That said, most of the women still reported that they had some sense of how they were doing and that this often came in the form of informal feedback from supervisors. Some women were also told that they were part of a succession plan or made to feel as if they had promising futures and could expect an upward career trajectory based on their past performance, and this was another important measure of success.

In addition to informal performance feedback, many women also reported that a good indicator of how well someone was doing and how they were viewed within the hierarchy was the extent to which they were put in leadership positions, either by being given some kind of supervisory role or else by being sought out to train and develop more junior lawyers. Along those same lines, and similar to what we saw with the in-house lawyers, the extent to which a particular lawyer was sought out— either to provide advice and counsel to colleagues throughout the organization or to work on the organization's most complex and high-profile matters—was also reported as a way in which a woman could tell that she was performing well. Those who were frequently sought out tended to be the highest-performing lawyers, while those who were rarely consulted and felt that they were passed over for the important assignments were generally among the less well-regarded lawyers. Control over the nature of the work that a woman took on was also an important factor in evaluating success. To some extent, control seemed to go hand in hand with seniority—the more senior the lawyer, the more control she generally had—but seniority alone did not fully account for how much control someone had. Often there were lawyers who had very little control in spite of having been with the organization for many years (this was generally an indicator that the woman was not performing at the highest level), while others—even those who had been with the organization a relatively short period of time—had lots of control (and this was generally an indicator of strong performance).

Last, we looked at title vis-à-vis length of time in current position under the theory that those who had been in their current roles for very long periods of time without any upward movement or promotions would likely be less well-performing than those who were advancing within the organization at a more rapid pace. That said, we also recognized that the people with the most senior titles—those who had already reached the top of the organizational chart—had no room for advancement and that, therefore, length of time in those positions could be, in and of itself, an indicator of success.

Our conversations with lawyers in the nonprofit world suggested a number of parallels in the way in which lawyers measured success. Length of time in current position and history of promotion and advancement were equally relevant, with similar caveats. The extent to which lawyers were given supervisory roles and consulted by other lawyers was also an important factor, as was the role that individual lawyers played in the training and development of more junior lawyers. Feedback in the nonprofit world tended to be informal—perhaps even less formal than it was in government—and most women relied on the measures mentioned above when assessing the quality of their performance in their roles.

The main differences between the success measures for those in government and those in the nonprofit world were centered around decision-making and compensation. Many nonprofit lawyers worked in small organizations where they were required to wear multiple hats—sometimes serving as general counsel, chief financial officer, head of human resources, and, in one case, "chief coffee-maker" simultaneously. For this reason, many women considered it a red flag—suggestive of poor performance or inability to add value—if they were not brought in and consulted on important business decisions frequently and from the outset. In a smaller environment where everyone is expected to contribute, being left out of key conversations was a cause for concern. On the flip side, regular inclusion and requests for advice and consultation were clear markers of success.

Compensation was not a reliable indicator of success within government, as many government agencies paid lockstep salaries and/or were subject to compensation restrictions that had nothing to do with performance or perceived ability. Nonprofits' salaries were significantly lower than those of lawyers practicing in-house or in private practice, but nevertheless provide some measure of how well an individual was doing, even if on a smaller scale. The differences in performance measures are reflected below in the final measures of success for women in nonprofits:

1. Which of the following best describes your current title? (various choices)
2. How long have you been in your current position? (various ranges)
3. How long has it been since your most recent promotion? (various ranges)
4. Do you currently supervise other lawyers? (yes/no)
5. How often do other lawyers seek out your advice/consult with you? (often, sometimes, rarely, or never)
6. How often are you asked to participate in the training and/ or development of more junior lawyers? (often, sometimes, rarely, or never)
7. At what point in the process are you generally brought into discussions about important decisions? (the planning phase, the execution phase, when legal advice is needed, or not at all)
8. Based on the most recent feedback you have received from your supervisor(s), either formal or informal, which of the following best describes your understanding of how you are performing in your current role? (my performance is outstanding, very good, average, below average, or poor)
9. How often do you get to work on the most high-profile, complex, and/or challenging cases/issues within your organization? (often, sometimes, rarely, or never)
10. Are you the lead lawyer on most of your cases? (yes/no)
11. Relative to your peers (within your organization), your base salary is: (above average, average, or below average)
12. Relative to your peers (within your organization), your total compensation package is: (above average, average, or below average)

Key Finding #1

Grit is a reliable indicator of how well a woman performs in a government or nonprofit role.

Recognizing that many government and nonprofit organizations approached the formal evaluation process differently, and that many did not have formal evaluations as a matter of course, we nevertheless felt that in a research effort focused largely on the extent to which grit and growth mindset predict success, we needed some basic measure of how well a woman was performing. To that end, and in an attempt to make comparisons and gain an understanding—and be able to generalize—about the influence of grit on performance across organizations, we asked the following question of all participants (see questions #7—nonprofit measures and #8—government measures above): *Based on the most recent feedback you have received from your supervisor(s), either formal or informal, which of the following best describes your understanding of how you are performing in your current role?* We asked the same question of women from both groups and got amazingly consistent results. The way in which they responded was frankly unsurprising given the earlier research on grit, both in 2013[1] and in this study. We found for both groups that the higher the woman's grit score, the more likely she was to be a top performer in her organization (as demonstrated by receiving higher review ratings—on a consistent basis—than those with lower grit scores). Now that we have explored the nuances of the relationship between grit and performance in three other contexts (for solo practitioners, those in private practice, and in-house lawyers) and seen similarly strong connections between grit and performance, this finding may seem less than novel. That said, its importance really cannot be overstated. Any organization would do well to have the highest performing women lawyers, and any female lawyer should understand the importance (and potential rewards—financial and otherwise) associated with demonstrations of gritty behavior.

When we consider how this plays out in practice for the women in our study, we see similar patterns across the board. Sometimes it is the case that a woman struggles initially to perform at the highest levels and then employs grit and/or growth mindset strategies to improve her performance. Other times, the woman performs perfectly well at the outset but must use grit or growth mindset strategies to overcome obstacles or hurdles that may arise and be conquered before she can achieve her desired objectives. Here is a perfect example of the former situation that one lawyer shared with us:

> I didn't know I had grit until I found myself sitting across from one of my first-year law professors, about one month into my first semester of school. I received another "R" for "rewrite" on a legal writing and research assignment. In college, I had done well and I had never worked as hard as this. What was expected of me in my first year? I was out of my element, convinced I was just not smart enough to hang with the crowd I found myself surrounded by in law school . . . getting an "R" in his class was proof of what I already knew—I was not cut out for this.

After sharing her fears with her professor, this lawyer got some great advice that ultimately convinced her that "knowing the answer is less important than knowing how to find the answer." While this was initially a dark moment for her, she was able to turn it around and emerge on the other side, stronger for having overcome a serious case of self-doubt.

Another lawyer shared a story that illustrates another way in which grit can impact performance. She had just joined the State Department as the youngest deputy assistant secretary of state in its history. One of her first assignments was to be part of the U.S. negotiation team working with the Micronesian government to settle long-standing litigation. During the final 18 months of negotiations, they had to deal with the most difficult of the remaining issues, which were complex and challenging in all respects. As she describes it:

> This case, single-handedly, was the most complex, difficult negotiation of my career, involving seriously disadvantaged people experiencing critical issues impacting so many areas of their lives. My determination to move this case forward is one of the great examples of my use of grit and perseverance in my career.

As this example makes clear, the challenge in this case—resulting in a need for grit—was the complexity of the matter and the need to be able to weed her way through these challenging issues without giving up. These challenges may have led less-gritty individuals to throw in the towel, and had that been the case, they would not have achieved the tremendously important victory—in this case a historic $2.1 billion agreement—that was the ultimate measure of success.

A final example of grit and growth mindset leading to high performance in a government role is described below:

> One example that truly shows my perseverance and grit to get the job done occurred during my time as an Assistant U.S. Attorney handling civil cases. . . . In order to get the requested documents and other evidentiary materials in a timely fashion for court deadlines, on more than one occasion I showed up unannounced at these agency employees' offices and offered to help them gather the requested information then or talk to their supervisors while I was there. Instantly my requests became these agency employees' first priority. . . . None of my other colleagues had conducted those kinds of unannounced visits to agency clients until I started to do those to meet court deadlines.

Key Finding #2

Both grit and growth mindset are closely related to how far a woman has advanced within her organization.

We asked women in both nonprofit and government to share with us their titles and the length of time they had been in their current roles. We then looked at their individual grit and growth mindset scores in order to understand more about the nature of the relationship between grit and seniority and growth mindset and seniority. The data suggested that the more senior the role, the higher the grit scores were and the more likely the women were to be growth mindset oriented. There are several possibilities that might help to explain the nature of this relationship.

The first possibility is related to finding key finding #1 in this chapter, which is that grit is a reliable indicator of performance in the government and nonprofit world. Since we also know—from the literature as well as from our own common-sense observations of the world—that high performance is an excellent predictor of advancement within any organization, it logically follows that those who are gritty perform well, and those who perform well are given additional responsibilities and opportunities for advancement.

The second possibility is that grit is both an outcome of and a precursor to success. On the one hand, most women lawyers are gritty—at least more so than the average person—because the path to practice is a challenging one that requires hard work and long-term commitment (law school takes at least three years and is a very challenging undertaking). Therefore, many lawyers enter the practice of law having developed gritty tendencies, and as we have heard in previous chapters, they learned from their experiences in law school just how important and effective both grit and a growth mindset orientation can be. This suggests that grit is, at least in part, something that precedes a woman's entry into practice.

On the other hand, grit is also clearly something that is developed and enhanced while practicing. Especially for those rare few who did not find law school to be especially challenging, when they finally graduate with their degree and begin working as a lawyer, they are often shocked and overwhelmed by how difficult the practice of law can be. Working as a lawyer is challenging—mentally as well as physically—and often women further develop their grittiness out of necessity. In other words, grit can be a learned coping mechanism—an outlook that women would pick up over time in order to persevere in a high-stress environment. Along those lines, Duckworth and Eskreis-Winkler found that grit increases monotonically—which is to say that one's grit score consistently goes up over time rather than going down or otherwise bouncing around—throughout adulthood.[2] Duckworth and Eskreis-Winkler suggest that this may be because people tend to appreciate the value of effort more as they get older or because they may simply be more interested in specializing later in life.[3] Either way, the practice of law seems to be an ideal location for growing grit.

One lawyer shared her "precursor" story of using grit and a growth mindset when she was only five years old and "[she] had two choices: give up or persevere." Thankfully, she had strong paragons of grit in her family who had shown her that quitting was not an option. As she puts it:

> Wallowing in victimhood hurt only me. If I was silenced by others, they had won, and I had lost. If I didn't succeed, it would be only after I had tried my hardest, not because I allowed others to define me or my circumstances.

Another lawyer shares a powerful example of how grit and a growth mindset were developed and enhanced while she was practicing law. In her case, this was specifically related to a transition from private practice to the nonprofit world and her ability to call on these traits helped her to advance in her new role:

> To really dive into [my] new job and make an impact, I had no choice but to adopt a growth mindset—I needed to believe that, with sufficient effort, I was capable of learning what I needed to know in order to meaningfully and substantively contribute to the work. Also important and related to having a growth mindset was identifying and pursuing specific projects and work streams within my organization that (a) were the kind of thing where you could get better with practice and repetition and (b) would permit me to dive in deep and become an expert (either because I had a unique knowledge base or skillset or because it was novel and there was no existing institutional expertise). Simply put, without a growth mindset, I would never pursue these kinds of projects and work streams in the first place.

Key Finding #3

Ambition is closely tied to both the grit and growth mind-set scores of women practicing in government and nonprofit organizations.

The final finding of this chapter echoes the findings in earlier chapters about the relationship between the grit, growth mind-set, and ambition scores of women lawyers. The women in our government and nonprofit groups, like nearly all of the women we surveyed, were highly ambitious, and ambition was highly correlated with grit and growth mindset, which in turn was highly correlated with high performance and advancement. Why is ambition such a powerful predictor of grit and growth mindset and—by extension—performance? There are several possible explanations for this. First, it could be the case that the women in the study who most wanted to be successful in life were also predisposed to think of themselves as successful in their current positions—perhaps more so than those who had less of a vested interest in being seen this way. In other words, it is possible that lawyers who really want to be successful see themselves that way. Because the survey asked lawyers to describe the feedback that they had most recently received from their supervisors (a self-reported measure of success), it could be the case that the ambitious lawyers tended to give themselves higher ratings in this category. Alternatively—and I think this is the more likely of the two explanations—it could be the case that the ambitious lawyers want to succeed, are willing to do whatever it takes to make that happen, and so therefore they do. It could also be the case that the connection between grit, growth mindset, and ambition can be explained in much the same way as the connections we saw earlier between grit and quality of work: Ambitious individuals tend to be among the highest performers on the job, and, therefore, they tend to receive and request the best work and to develop at the most rapid pace. One lawyer who works in government provides a great example of how ambition drove her to excel academically:

Growing up in a male-dominated family with four brothers meant that I was the one least expected to excel. My family was happy but surprised when I graduated as my high school valedictorian, something my older brothers had not accomplished. I was not surprised; I had deliberately set out to surpass my brothers' achievements, as well as those of the men in my high school as the clear but unspoken message of my classmates was that women were not as smart as men.

I will conclude this chapter where we began many of the others—and that is with a look at whether women practicing in government and nonprofit organizations believe that grit and growth mindset have played an important role in their success. In so many ways, this is the heart of what we have been trying to understand through this effort—do these traits really matter and, if so, how? As to the first part of the question, the fact that 99 percent of women working in government said that they do matter and have been an influential factor in achieving career success speaks for itself. As to the second part, I will let these impressive, gritty, and growth mindset–oriented women explain it to you themselves.

Notes:

1. Hogan, M.L. 2013. Non-cognitive traits that impact female success in BigLaw. Diss. University of Pennsylvania.
2. Duckworth, A.L. and Eskreis-Winkler, L. 2013. "True grit." *The Observer* 26.4:1-3.
3. *Id.*

Kathryn Pirrotta Caballero

I was once stranded at the top of an entry staircase to the New York subway while seven months pregnant and with two small children in tow. In the absence of an escalator or elevator, I was sure that I would fall down the icy stairs if I tried to balance the two-year-old in the stroller on my hip while holding my four-year-old daughter's hand. No one stopped to help—I was invisible in a sea of people as I returned home from child care after my New York University Law afternoon classes. Approaching this as an engineering problem, I walked the four-year-old to the bottom of the stairs, told her to hold on to the stair railing, and, keeping my eye on both children, walked back up to collect the two-year-old and the now folded-up stroller. Before I could start the second descent, an elderly man took the stroller and my daughter's hand, and we together worked our way to the bottom. This situation exemplifies my experience as a lawyer and engineer—challenging problems, "laugh or cry" situations, and gratefully accepting the help of others.

Women entering the field of law might think that it is impossible to have multiple children and achieve stability and success as a parent and lawyer. Last week, a recently married young lawyer told me that she never expected to marry, much less have future children. She asked me if it was possible to do both or if it was too stressful. I assured her that one could certainly do both well, and we are meeting for lunch next week to discuss a plan for success.

I am a senior enforcement attorney in the Environmental Protection Agency's (EPA) Office of Civil Enforcement and have four children ranging in age from 14 to 21 years. I have been focused on the protection of human health and the environment since I was a Princeton chemical engineering graduate student creating biological polymers (plastics) that would biodegrade, something that has since become commonplace. Later, as a new EPA chemical engineer, I quickly realized that the lawyers often had a more powerful opportunity to protect the environment than the technical staff. I thought that the work ethic and intense focus needed to survive the lengthy problem sets and research experiments in chemical engineering would be helpful in under-standing and resolving complex legal concepts. However, I would need to juggle a legal education with family responsibilities, as my husband and I had already started our family. I had been fortunate in finding a partner who fully supported my aspirations and loved children, and my past had prepared me for challenges.

Growing up in a male-dominated family with four brothers meant that I was the one least expected to excel. My family was happy but surprised when I graduated as my high school valedic-torian, something my older brothers had not accomplished. I was not surprised; I had deliberately set out to surpass my brothers' achievements, as well as those of the men in my high school, as the clear but unspoken message of my classmates was that women were not as smart as men. As an undergraduate chemical engi-neer at Notre Dame, I was known by my professors for constantly asking questions. Rather than having both my male and female classmates exchange confused glances when complicated mate-rial was introduced, I would plunge in with questions until we all understood the concept. While my chemical engineering major was intense and time-consuming, the women engineers banded together to become the top students. There was a similar pattern in the graduate chemical engineering program at Princeton. The women supported each other in a male-dominated field without a single woman department professor. When Mattel released a Barbie that said "math is hard," the long-corded phone line was passed from research lab to research lab, from graduate student to graduate student, until all the women had conveyed to Mattel cus-tomer service what they thought of this toy for young girls.

As a first year at NYU, I found a few other parents and started a group that shared toys and commiserated about the challenging curriculum. I have vivid memories of pushing a stroller through a foot of snow en route to a rescheduled civil procedure exam review. By the next semester, I was ready to stand up for myself and others and request rejection of the student proposal for reschedul-ing a civil procedure review outside of child care hours; the origi-nal schedule had conflicted with a keg softball party. Fortunately, unlike graduate school in chemical engineering, the law school had women professors and mothers who modeled excellence and professionalism. I followed their example.

After an EPA hiring freeze prevented me from joining the agency, I joined the private sector. As a new associate at a BigLaw firm, I sought others who had a similar focus on family and tried to avoid the "mommy wars" over flexible schedules and child care arrangements. We sacrificed lunches with colleagues to read books to our children at the on-site child care facility, a firm benefit for which I am still thoroughly grateful. There was overt sexism from some sharp-elbowed associates. I will never forget the male associate who stopped by my office to ask me why I "even thought" I was valuable to the firm given my reduced schedule of 35 hours a week. Ironically, I was reviewing thousands of chemical plant blueprints for a difficult environmental liability analysis, a review that would have been extremely challenging without my engineering degrees. He has since left law to become a life coach. I angered the senior male partners by delaying an off-site business dinner when I provided a statement to the police at the site of a car accident after the client in the car ahead of us had inadvertently hit a teenager. This was after the female in-house counsel and I had both run to help the teenager, with the other attorney placing her beautiful white coat over the bleeding boy.

When I finally obtained a highly sought-after EPA enforcement attorney position, I felt that I was prepared because of my experience, much of which required me to perform multiple, complex tasks. I had developed a grit and growth mindset that allowed me to concurrently work with an expert witness, proof a brief, gather evidence for a deposition, coordinate with regional counterparts, and visit a site. My mindset helped me to obtain injunctive relief and penalties to both eliminate and mitigate emissions of hazardous chemicals. As EPA headquarter attorneys, we often battle the best lawyers and law firms in the country. I rely on my technical and legal expertise, my colleagues, and our savvy management to craft the best outcome for environmental protection.

Asking multiple questions. Working in harmony with a team. Absorbing the wisdom and lessons of those women who have come before you. Finding a way to laugh in those frequent "laugh or cry" moments. In mentoring more than 25 law clerks and law-yers, primarily young women, I try to provide this advice and teach them that they each bring something to the table. Through hard work, perseverance, and flexibility, they can be both successful parents and attorneys, regardless of the perception of others.

Kathryn Pirrotta Caballero is a senior attorney in the Office of Civil Enforcement at the U.S. Environmental Protection Agency in Washington, D.C., where she currently focuses on enforcement of Titles I and II of the Clean Air Act and previously has practiced in hazardous waste enforcement pursuant to the Resource Conservation and Recovery Act (RCRA). www.epa.gov

Juanita C. Hernández

As I focused on the topic of grit and a growth mindset, I realized that my family, especially my mother, taught me the fundamentals of grit and growth at home. As the third of four daughters, I was raised in an immigrant household of two loving Mexican parents to be independent and have a strong work ethic. To this day, one of my mother's favorite mantras as we faced adversities in life was to always have *"valor y fe"* (courage and faith) to help us work through the obstacle and never give up. My father had a military background and training that instilled discipline and perseverance in our family.

Having a strong value system along with a loving family and community support, I was able to succeed against great odds to leave south central Texas where I grew up and attend Harvard University and continue on through Harvard Law School. I had read and dreamed about attending an Ivy League school to become an attorney, although I had never met anyone who attended an Ivy League school or even met a Latina lawyer. I worked steadily toward my goals.

After I was admitted to Harvard College, my mother was torn to let me go so far from home on my own without knowing anyone there or having any family in the area. My father was more practical and worried we could not afford such an elite school. My toughest audience was these two. If I could convince them, the rest would be manageable. For mom, I reminded her that both she and dad had left their families and came to this country with a vision of unlimited opportunities with the right work ethic to improve their lives and those of the next generation. I was determined to do the same via my educational achievements and continuing their journey.

For dad, I quickly got well versed in student financial aid forms and policies and formulated a budget and business plan. I gave him all the completed paperwork and asked him to sign the forms. To both of them, I pointed out that previously children of immigrants had attended Harvard and had succeeded in achieving the American dream of success. In particular, I noted that many of the

Kennedy family members and their kids went there. I knew my folks were big fans of President Kennedy, who was Catholic and the son of Irish immigrants. Working with his wife Jackie, who was Spanish fluent, Kennedy was the first candidate who had reached out in his presidential election to the Hispanic community for their votes. My plan worked, and my parents gave me their blessings and support for my educational quest. Then came the hard work.

By using the strong values of determination, discipline, and perseverance, I could achieve my goals of educational achievement and career success. I yearned to be a courtroom advocate to make a positive difference to my community and in time to my profession. I also figured out later that working in public service meshed with my own values.

After law school, I clerked for the Honorable William Wayne Justice, a federal trial judge who was considered one of the foremost brave southern jurists who helped uphold civil rights cases in Texas. The judge was my hero before I worked for him and was even more so after my clerkship because of how he ran his court and the values he instilled in his mentees—all his law clerks. He reminded us to treat all persons with equal respect who appeared before the court or with whom we interacted, such as clerical or janitorial staff workers. The judge also strongly encouraged his clerks to give back to our communities and the legal profession by getting involved in civic and volunteer groups and, in particular, bar associations.

When I later worked at the large law firm in San Antonio after clerking, the secretaries, legal assistants, and support staff were amazed that I treated them well and valued their assistance. They always went out of their way to help me. They also confirmed I was the first Latina attorney who had been hired as an associate by any firm in the city that had a Latino majority population. Regularly, others mistakenly thought I was the court reporter or legal assistant when I appeared at depositions or hearings. I used these assumptions to my advantage, because you should never underestimate an opposing counsel. I was always prepared for my cases and had studied my legal opponents and judge, not just my case.

Although I did well at the law firm, it was not personally fulfilling. I had taken a law firm job to pay law school loans but planned on moving on once I paid those down. To help with my career satisfaction and development, I also got involved in bar association activities and civic and political volunteer work, where I took leadership roles. The firm was very supportive even when I became the national chair of the Hispanic National Bar Association's national conference in my home town. I was also elected nationally as a director for my alumni association.

In time, I left private practice and my hometown to work in the public sector, first at the state capitol level in Austin for the Texas attorney general. After that I served as a political appointee in Washington for the Clinton administration as counsel to the head of the Civil Rights Division of the Department of Justice, Honorable Deval Patrick. He became another good friend and mentor. I then became a civil assistant U.S. attorney in Texas, where I loved working and serving as counsel to various federal agencies.

One example that truly shows my perseverance and grit to get the job done occurred during my time as an assistant U.S. attorney handling civil cases. I normally dealt with law enforcement agencies as my clients. Their employees were typically my witnesses or client representatives in my cases who had busy work schedules. These agencies were understaffed and overworked and rarely met my deadlines for requests for information. The agency offices were located far away from my downtown office and not conveniently located. In order to get the requested documents and other evidentiary materials in a timely fashion for court deadlines, on more than one occasion I showed up unannounced at these agency employees' offices and offered to help them gather the requested information then or talk to their supervisors while I was there. Instantly my requests became these agency employees' first priority, and I obtained the requested information and conducted witness interviews or gathered responsive documents during those surprise visits. None of my other colleagues had conducted those kinds of unannounced visits to agency clients until I started to do those to meet court deadlines.

I left the public sector for some time and returned to another large firm in San Antonio to help my family and moved closer to them. By that time, I realized that career satisfaction alone did not make a person happy. Personal fulfillment and family were more important to me; I wanted to be in a position to help my family as my father retired and dealt with health problems. I still continued my outside volunteer activities where I also mentored younger attorneys and pre-laws, especially women and minorities.

Although I have returned to Washington and work at another federal agency, the values of grit and growth have served me well throughout my career and in my personal life. I cannot forget the values and wisdom my family instilled in me when encountering challenging times. One must always have courage, faith, determination, and perseverance. It is these same values that I now share with my mentees and the next generation in my family. Thank you for allowing me to share my thoughts on this subject.

Juanita C. Hernández is an attorney at a federal government agency in Washington, D.C., where she focuses on general civil litigation matters and investigations including federal securities law, employment law, FOIA, and administrative law issues.

Noorain F. Khan

I've had countless moments in my professional career when I know that grit (defined by psychologist Angela Duckworth as "the perseverance and passion for my long-term goals") and having a growth mindset (my belief in the power of effort) were game-changing, but one stands out among others: my transition from BigLaw to a nonlegal job in the nonprofit world. Although making that move was something I'd wanted to do for a long time, there were several nonobvious factors that complicated the transition.

For some context, after two-and-a-half years of practicing transactional law, during which I focused primarily on mergers and acquisitions deals and corporate governance, I moved into a nonlegal management role at a global education nonprofit as a chief of staff. I was thrilled to move to a more public-minded space and eager to engage. Although some of the same organizational and management skills were required for both roles, I'd had virtually no professional experience in the realm of education, and I privately worried about that.

To really dive into the new job and make an impact, I had no choice but to adopt a growth mindset—I needed to believe that with sufficient effort, I was capable of learning what I needed to know to meaningfully and substantively contribute to the work. Also important and related to having a growth mindset was identifying and pursuing specific projects and work streams within my organization that (a) were the kind of thing where you could get better with practice and repetition, and (b) would permit me to dive in deep and become an expert (either because I had a unique knowledge base or skillset or because it was novel and there was no existing institutional expertise). Simply put, without a growth mindset, I would never pursue these kinds of projects and work streams in the first place.

In my whole portfolio of work, I found it comforting to be able to focus on something and become good at it. You can't be great at everything at once. By narrowing the scope and focusing on some specific things, I was allowed to see myself at my best in my new environment. And I could share it with others. It turns out there are lots of things you can't control at work, but how hard I work is truly in my control, and seeing that and doing something about it were crucial for me. For me, the space that I truly owned was nonprofit board governance. It was a place where knowing the rules and applying them actually got easier with practice. It was also a space where there wasn't a lot of organizational knowledge and there was room for me to own the work and become an internal expert.

Grit was the key to thriving in other ways. My job as an attorney was the first job I'd ever had, not counting internships and other shorter term professional experiences. Until I left the law, I didn't fully appreciate the clarity and purpose that the structure and hierarchy of a law firm brought to the work of an associate: You know what a first-year is supposed to do, you know what it takes to advance, you know to whom you are accountable, and you know the division of labor for a matter. I found that moving to a nonlegal job introduced new ambiguity to these fundamental questions, especially because I moved to a leanly staffed organization into a role with a broad scope and general mandate. Another dynamic was at play, too: As with many transitions across professions, some seniority is lost in transition in the sense that, in a new space, you might have to work your way up a bit to regain seniority or expertise that isn't valued, understood, or recognized in a new profession. These factors made grit even more crucial in helping me thrive and navigate the ambiguity. Perseverance and the passion I carried for my long-term goals helped me see the bigger picture and orient me toward the longer term. I thought of my end game—what did I want to get out of being at the organization? Identifying that helped me move from simply working hard to working hard in a more purposeful and sustained way that really transcended all of the ambiguity.

Lots of people make the transition out of working in BigLaw, and many of these people leave law altogether. I still feel very rooted in the legal profession, and I feel like there have been so many points where grit and having a growth mindset helped me navigate otherwise complex situations, structures, relationships, and experiences. It feels especially rewarding to know that opportunities to leverage these qualities will come up again and again, and I really do have the tools needed to make good on my aspirations.

Noorain F. Khan is a program officer at the Ford Foundation in New York, New York, where she is responsible for the grant-making portfolio of the foundation's president. www.fordfoundation.org

Alice Shih LaCour

I was so excited to start school. I was 5 years old and had watched my brother go to school for years, counting down the days until I too could go. When the day finally arrived, I meticulously picked out my outfit, packed my favorite books into my new backpack, and reached the bus stop 30 minutes early.

When I made it to school, I confidently strode over to the closet to hang up my backpack. I found a seat at a round table, folded my arms, and excitedly waited for class to begin. Suddenly I felt a sharp pain as my ponytail was jerked downward. Shocked, I turned around to see a boy with strands of my black hair in his still-clenched fist. "Hey ching ching chong, go back to China." I was confused. I opened my mouth to ask him what he had said, but the words that came out of my mouth only drew thunderous laughter from the rest of the class. I was dumbfounded.

What I didn't know was that I spoke Mandarin while everyone else spoke English.

For 5 years, I had spoken only Mandarin to my family and friends. I didn't know that outside of that community, others couldn't understand me. The jeering continued. Another girl grabbed my chair out from under me, causing me to tumble to the floor, resulting in even more laughter. I blinked hard through tears. For the first time, I realized that I was the only nonwhite person in the room. My confidence and chatty demeanor disappeared overnight. Speaking outside of the home became too difficult. I had lost my voice.

I had two choices: give up or persevere. Thankfully, I had the example of my grandfather to show me that giving up was simply not an option.

It was 1949. My grandfather was a high-ranking officer in the Qing nian dang party in China when Mao Zedong declared that the Communist Party was the new government in China. One of my grandfather's friends, a Communist Party member, warned my grandfather that his life was in danger. So, in the middle of the night, he fled the country with my grandmother. They left behind my then one-year-old aunt, as the road was too dangerous for an infant, and they did not think that they would be gone long. But we know how history unfolded. My grandparents never laid eyes on their homeland or their daughter again. When they arrived as refugees in Taiwan, they had nothing. The gold they had sewn into their clothes had been stolen during their escape. My grandfather found himself in a new land with no friends, no family, and no job. He may have wanted to retreat into silence—after all, look where speaking up had led him. But he knew that others depended on his voice. He spent the rest of his life working tirelessly for the rule of law in Taiwan.

My grandfather's dedication to the rule of law certainly inspired me to become a lawyer, but the life he lived impacted much more than my career choice. It affected my approach to the hills and valleys throughout life. My experience at five years old was not the last time I would face unfair judgment or hostility for my sex or the color of my skin. However, my grandfather's life taught me that, although my obstacles and struggles may be unique to me, it is not unique for each person to face challenges throughout his or her life. From my grandfather's example, I learned that, although I could not control my circumstances, I could control how I responded to those situations. Wallowing in victimhood hurt only me. If I was silenced by others, they had won, and I had lost. If I didn't succeed, it would be only after I had tried my hardest, not because I had allowed others to define me or my circumstances.

This lesson of having grit, in controlling my response to unfair situations, has come in handy many times in my legal career. One standout example: As a trial attorney for the federal government, I have the privilege of being given much responsibility despite being only a few years removed from law school. As a result, I am often litigating against seasoned partners from the nation's largest law firms. During one particularly contentious dispute with opposing counsel, the attorney, who was many years my senior, spat a nasty, personal insult my way, demeaning me as inexperienced and incapable. I was shaken as this attorney voiced my biggest fears about myself. Though I could feel confidence drain from my body and anger boil up, I bit my tongue. Rather than sinking to his level by returning an insult, I calmly ended the conversation. I knew that the legal position the attorney had staked out on this particular dispute was untenable. And if I had chosen to react to his low blow, I would have lost my credibility. Thus, I let the law speak for itself. I presented my legal argument in writing to the attorney and included the dozen other attorneys on his team who had not been a part of our conversation. Once reduced to writing, the opposing attorney's position looked absurd. Within minutes of sending the email, I received a call from another attorney on the case who agreed fully with my position. He even apologized for his colleague's baseless position (though he did not know about the personal insults that his co-counsel dealt). This concession was a big win for my client. Had I let this attorney control my emotions or silence me, I would not have had such a clean victory. Instead, I kept my cool, found my voice, and obtained a win for me and my client.

Being creative with problem-solving that's specific to the situation has been critical to my success. While I did not know then that this was considered grit, I know now that this trait will serve me well throughout my career.

Alice Shih LaCour is a trial attorney for the federal government, where she focuses on constitutional, statutory, and regulatory litigation at the district court level.

Ginger Ehn Lew

A lot has been written about grit and how it is an important characteristic of successful people. As fashionable as the term may be, when I was growing up, we called it determination and perseverance.

I personally believe grit is an acquired skill—taught and re-enforced by your parents, your teachers, your coaches, your peers, your bosses, your work colleagues, and your significant partners. It can be inspired by pure survival. It can be inspired by both positive and negative examples. It is a skill that is learned and internalized and becomes a core characteristic that is lived and amplified in your daily life. How did I learn grit?

I was born in the San Francisco Bay Area—the only girl, the youngest of immigrant parents with three older brothers. My grand-father lived with us, which was a fairly traditional practice among immigrant families—having multigenerations living under one roof. Around the age of five years, I remember hearing murmurs that his immigration status was "fuzzy." My parents were afraid my grandfather would be found and deported. My brothers and I were told to be quiet, to not speak up, and to not draw attention to ourselves. We were taught to make ourselves invisible as much as possible. As a result, we lived in the shadows until he passed away.

Then there was my mother. I grew up speaking Chinese as my pri-mary language; there was no English as a second language in school. I learned English by watching TV. My mother spoke only Chinese, and because of my mother's poor health, I became her translator around the age of 12. I became her voice—her communication channel with all her doctors and nurses. In my teens, I learned that it was crucial to ask a lot of questions, challenge proposed medical treatments, to question and sometimes challenge authority figures. If I didn't push, she did not get proper medical care.

On top of multiple illnesses, she had a brain aneurysm, which caused her to lose her short-term memory. And yet, she desper-ately wanted to become a U.S. citizen. Despite being a full-time mother, and working at the family business, she persisted and went to evening English and citizenship classes. After years of extraordinary determination and perseverance—made all the more difficult because of her medical condition—she was able to obtain her citizenship.

My parents and grandfather's lives were powerful examples of perseverance and focused determination against enormous odds—a skill that became a core part of their personas. By living the example, they taught us the power of grit and how it can transform one's own life.

How does grit square with my own story? I learned how fearful and constrained it can be to live in the shadows. I learned I had to fight for whatever I wanted—to constantly push myself if our family was going to have a better life. Since I did not have past expectations to which I had to conform, I had the freedom to pursue paths that were unexpected of me. My parents had a very traditional life laid out for me: get married, raise a family, and possibly have an "at home" job to bring in extra income. But I chose my own path, sometimes to the dismay of my parents, who believed that the law was not an honorable profession. I've been blessed and had an extraordinary career as a lawyer, as an entrepreneur, and as a public policy advisor.

To be honest, when I first ventured out, I wasn't quite sure what I wanted to do. I did not have role models to guide me, but my high school and college guidance counselors told me I had potential. Potential to do what, was unclear. Despite the fact I did not have a specific goal in mind, I was open and I was willing to push the boundaries. I chose the law because I knew it would give me the fundamental tools to do what I wanted to do and what I needed to do, and I was confident I would know what "it" was when I got there. How I envied my fellow colleagues who knew exactly what they wanted to do with their professional careers or studies.

In some respects, I have been an accidental traveler along a somewhat unexpected personal and professional journey. But I knew I wanted to be involved with and contribute to something that made an outsized and positive difference, a contribution to my community and to society—and in doing so, I also thought I'd break through some glass ceilings.

Some suggest that grit may be an indicator of professional success. But to be wholly successful, the lessons of grit must be combined with lessons about heart and honor. Grit can be used for dark purposes. Many horrific instances in humankind have occurred because someone was determined to achieve some unspeakable goal. But is this the type of grit I want my grandchildren to have? No.

While I learned the power, indeed the necessity, of determination and perseverance from my family, more importantly, they taught me lessons about having both heart and honor.

Having heart and honor—what are these? My personal definition of heart includes words such as compassion, empathy, caring, and love—both self-love and love for others. Can you learn heart? Yes, but you have to live it as well.

And what is honor? In the movie *The Blind Side* I recall a particularly moving moment when a young high school football player muses about courage and honor:

"Courage is a hard thing to figure. . . . But honor, that's the real reason you either do something or you don't. It's who you want to be. . . . [Y]ou should try for courage and hope for honor."

In 1980 I joined the State Department as the youngest deputy assistant secretary of state in its history. I worked with then Assistant Secretary Richard Holbrooke on East Asia and Pacific Island matters. One of my first assignments was to be part of the U.S. negotiation team (consisting of more than 10 agencies) working with the Micronesian governments (at that time U.S. territories) to settle long-standing litigation. In the 1950s, the United States had detonated more than 50 nuclear devices in the atmosphere. Prior to the testing, the islanders were removed from their homes and told they could return in a few years. After their return, monitoring showed an 11-fold increase in various types of cancer. Subsequent testing showed that the effects of radiation made their land uninhabitable for the next 25,000 years. The lawsuits about their resettlement and compensation dragged on for years. During the final 18 months of negotiations, we had to deal with the most difficult remaining issues, such as continued comprehensive health care and environmental monitoring (for how many future generations); long-term U.S. access to certain military facilities; the political relationship of the governments with the United States moving from their territorial status to a new status called "freely associated"; the use of certain services, such as U.S. currency and the postal service; and immigration rights. The negotiations were complex, not only because of the number of agencies involved but the emotional undercurrent of the islanders' sense of loss and displacement compounded by serious illnesses. We worked continuously, determined to conclude these negotiations with both honor and heart. In late 1981, we concluded the historic $2.1 billion agreement that enabled the islanders to move on with their lives with dignity and some certainty.

This case, single-handedly, was the most complex, difficult negotiation of my career, involving seriously disadvantaged people experiencing critical issues impacting so many areas of their lives. My determination to move this case forward is one of the great examples of my use of grit and perseverance in my career.

One can only hope that you live your life with honor and heart, and try to teach others these core values. If you can live your life with grit, heart, and honor—and if you can teach your children, your co-workers, and your community the skills and values of grit, heart, and honor—then in my humble opinion, you have achieved success.

Ginger Ehn Lew is the managing director and general counsel of Cube Hydro Partners, LLC in Bethesda, Maryland. www.cubehydro.com

Conclusion

At the end of the day, then, are grit and growth mindset two secrets to success for female lawyers? The results of this study suggest that they are indeed and offer an important path to help reduce the gender gap at the leadership level. Fortunately, these traits can be learned. As detailed in appendix B and on the Commission's website at www.ambar.org/grit, the Commission offers the Grit Project Toolkit and other resources that enable women lawyer committees, bar associations, law schools, and employers to present training programs to educate women concerning the importance of grit and a growth mindset and how to improve these traits. Appendix A contains suggestions for how employers can utilize grit and growth mindset to recruit, evaluate, and advance women lawyers in their work environments.

As you have read in this book, grit and a growth mindset are linked to several important measures of success for women lawyers. This is true across all work environments, practice areas, or stages of career. The contributors of these 47 letters confirm that grit and growth mindset have been and continue to be critical to their success.

The study of grit and growth mindset remains a relatively nascent field, and there is need for further exploration of these important traits and how they can best be leveraged to help women achieve success within the practice of law. The good news is that this research provides us with a deeper understanding of how the women lawyers who succeed are able to do so, and it brings us one step closer to being able to solve the gender gap at the leadership level. Ultimately, we hope you find the results of this research to be as inspiring and valuable as we do and, further, that you will share these critical findings with others who may benefit from them on their paths to success in the law.

Appendix A

What Employers Can Do

Given that grit is linked to workplace success, employers can take action to recruit the kinds of women who are likely to withstand the challenges that they may encounter along the path to leadership. Furthermore, legal employers can nurture grit in their high-potential women and, thus, provide them with a useful tool that would be likely to assist at least some of them in achieving success at the highest levels.

HOW CAN WE NURTURE GRIT?

Let's start with a few suggestions for ways that employers can seek to reward and encourage grit in their employees. One way to do this is by transparently measuring—and rewarding—grit in their performance evaluation processes. Simply inserting a question that seeks to acknowledge demonstrations of gritty behavior (e.g., to what extent did this lawyer demonstrate sustained effort and enthusiasm while seeking to achieve the best possible outcome for the client?) can have a significant impact on behavior. As Harvard Law School professor Scott Westfahl has noted elsewhere, "You get what you measure."[1]

Another way to do this is by hosting educational programming that teaches lawyers about the demonstrated value of grit and the impact of a growth mindset. Just a basic introduction of these concepts, even in a short, 45-minute session, has been shown to have a surprisingly powerful impact on performance.[2] Employers can learn more about how to host a grit program—and how to take advantage of the many, off-the-shelf, online materials and resources in appendix B. While further research is needed to identify the best ways of nurturing such traits in a legal environment, there is sufficient reason to believe that employers can accomplish this relatively easily (this topic is discussed more fully in appendix C).

HOW CAN WE EVALUATE GRIT?

In addition, recruiting for grit represents an appealing possibility for employers who are committed to finding a strategy to change the current landscape and increase the pipeline of female leaders who are likely to stay the course. As food for thought, we will leave you with some preliminary information about how law firms and other legal employers might begin to evaluate grit and growth mindset at the hiring stage. Perhaps the simplest and most obvious way to measure these traits is to administer the grit test and mindset quiz during the candidate assessment phase before an offer of employment is made. Although most law firms do not—at present—seek to categorically measure the personality traits of their prospective employees, consulting firms and corporations have been doing this for quite some time. Indeed, a number of organizations have come to rely more heavily in recent years on personality traits when assessing whether a candidate will be the right fit for the company. Some organizations also use such assessment measures when determining not only whether someone is the right fit for the organization at large but also for which team within the organization they are best suited. In general, law firms tend to be more cautious in their approach to hiring and to rely on more traditional, intelligence-based predictors of success, such as impressive academic credentials from competitive and rigorous academic institutions. Although it is clearly the case that intelligence is an important contributor to success, it is not the only predictor nor a sufficient condition for success in the practice of law.

    In addition to administering the grit test or the mindset quiz, law firms and legal employers who wish to evaluate for these traits might also consider looking for signs of them on resumes or in formal interviews. Duckworth has done some initial research that suggests it is possible to identify evidence of perseverance and passion on a resume.[3] Typically this is done by giving careful consideration to the applicant's past work experiences and extracurricular activities. For example, an applicant who has managed to achieve mastery in any domain, including those outside the scope of the position they are currently applying for, is likely to be a gritty applicant. Evidence of mastery might include high-level achievements in competitive sports, music, or some other comparable activity. Similarly, employers might ask a series of behavioral interview questions designed to ascertain how applicants might behave in certain circumstances. For example, an interviewer might ask an applicant to tell her how she responded to a recent setback and what steps she took to get back on track. The answer to this question can potentially provide significant insight into whether an individual is gritty and has a growth mindset orientation. Understanding how someone behaves in a challenging situation and how they think about—and approach—adversity can be very telling and will provide useful information to employers about potential hires (even over and above what it suggests about grit and/or a growth mindset). Of course, recruiting employees with high grit scores and a growth mindset orientation by no means guarantees future success, but having such employees seems very likely to serve any organization well.

Legal employers might also consider evaluating grit and growth mindset among their current employees. They might administer the grit test and the mindset quiz as an initial matter with recruits, but they might also choose to administer these tests to current employees (or to the same employees at various points in time) to see how their lawyers fare and what conclusions, if any, can be drawn about the importance of these traits within their own specific environments. It could be the case, for example, that grit matters more or less within certain practice groups or at certain key points in time. Understanding these nuances is an important first step for employers who are committed to incorporating them in the most effective way.

WHY EMPLOYERS SHOULD CARE ABOUT GRIT AND GROWTH MINDSET

If the findings in this book have not convinced you that grit and growth mindset are important contributors to the success of female lawyers in all areas of practice, you can take comfort in the fact that it has been argued elsewhere that having women in leadership positions is not only a cultural imperative[4] but also directly impacts the bottom line.[5] Thus, there are both social and financial reasons to motivate legal employers to reduce the gender gap, even in those organizations that are not already committed to achieving more equality at the highest levels of leadership. Giving some thought to understanding the importance of grit and growth mindset in this context may well provide a viable first step toward advancing such a strategy.

Notes:

1. Westfahl, S. 2008. *You Get What You Measure: Lawyer Development Frameworks & Effective Performance Evaluation.* National Association for Law Placement.
2. Dweck, C.S. 2008. *Mindset: The new psychology of success.* Random House Digital, Inc.
3. Duckworth, A. 2016. *Grit: The power of passion and perseverance.* Simon and Schuster.
4. Rhode, D.L. 2016. *Women and Leadership*, at 112–117. Oxford University Press.
5. Cohen, R., and Kornfeld, L. 2006. "Women leaders and the bottom line." *Bloomberg Corporate Law Journal* 1.1:1–8.

Appendix B

ABA Commission on Women in the Profession Grit Project

The Grit Project educates about the science behind grit and growth mindset and, through its online toolkit, provides women attorneys, bar associations, law firms, and corporate legal departments the resources to assess, teach, and learn these traits. By providing women lawyers with the tools to assess and learn these traits, and apply the grit approach to their careers, the Grit Project enhances the effectiveness, as well as the retention and promotion, of women lawyers.

Toolkit materials include:

1. Program Agenda—Format, sequence of presentations, and various segment options
2. PowerPoint Slides—A customizable PowerPoint slide deck to use as part of an opening presentation, with notes for the presenter(s) and details on key points
3. Program Materials—PDFs of recommended articles to use as background information for speakers and as handouts in the program, as well as the grit and mindset tests
4. Library of Scenarios—Includes digital video of several scenarios, as well as a library of written scenarios
5. Discussion Guide—A how-to guide for presenters to lead small or large group discussions of the scenarios
6. Speakers Bureau—Potential speakers and panelists
7. Marketing the Program—Text that can be used to create a marketing flyer

8. Bibliography—Extensive list of articles that can be referenced for a more in-depth understanding of the issues, to be distributed to speakers in advance of the presentation and to attendees as appropriate

With the Toolkit, you can:

➤ Tailor the program to any audience.

➤ Present tools women lawyers can use to measure their grit and growth mindset.

➤ Instruct women attorneys on how to apply the grit approach to their law careers.

➤ Facilitate discussion of how to handle challenging situations in the legal profession using grit and a growth mindset.

➤ Customize the program to the format and time allotted.

➤ Offer future reading and learning opportunities.

For more information, visit www.ambar.org/grit.

Appendix C

Summary of the Research on Grit, Growth Mindset, and Women Lawyers

This appendix provides an overview of some of the preexisting research on grit and growth mindset, as well as some of the key research on success for professional women—and in some cases men—both within and outside of the practice of law. As a reminder, the definition of grit relied on for this research effort is Duckworth's definition: "perseverance and passion for long-term goals."[1] In order to fully comprehend the nature of grit, it is important to understand how grit differs, in some cases quite subtly, from other, similar character traits, including achievement orientation, dependability, the need for achievement, and self-discipline. In the following pages, all four of these character traits will be compared and contrasted with grit, and the differences will be examined in further detail.

ACHIEVEMENT ORIENTATION

The "Big Five" is a popular, five-factor model of personality that categorizes virtually all personality measures into one of five dimensions: neuroticism, extraversion, openness to experience, agreeableness, and conscientiousness.[2] Of those five, conscientiousness is the single Big Five construct most closely related to performance across jobs, and achievement orientation is one of three related facets of conscientiousness (the other two are dependability and orderliness, and we'll discuss dependability further in a moment).[3] Although there is some overlap between grit and achievement orientation, ultimately the two concepts diverge. An achievement-oriented individual is one who works hard, tries to do a good job, and completes the task at hand.[4] Thus, achievement-oriented individuals are both persistent and hard-working.[5] Although this definition appears to be very similar to the definition of grit, and measurements of achievement orientation have been found to predict both job proficiency and educational success, grit differs from achievement orientation "in its emphasis on long-term stamina rather than short-term intensity."[6] A gritty individual not only will complete immediate tasks but also will pursue goals over extended periods of time. In many cases, a gritty individual will devote several years to the completion of a single task, such as mastering the case law concerning certain antitrust matters, whereas an achievement-oriented individual might well lose interest in the task at a far earlier stage of the process.

DEPENDABILITY

Grit also differs from the dependability facet of conscientious-ness. A dependable individual, who is characterized as being both responsible and careful, may be very good at demonstrating self-control but may not share the gritty individual's consistent dedication to her goals and interests. As Duckworth and Peterson point out, a highly dependable individual "may resist the urge to surf the Internet at work yet switch careers annually."[7] She may show up for work on time, every day, even when a loved one is ill or there is an unexpected emergency at home, but she may only practice law for a few years before opting out to do something else entirely. As is the case with achievement orientation, the difference between dependability and grit underscores the fact that long-term commitment—decades rather than weeks, months, or even years—is imperative to the construct of grit. A gritty individual doesn't just show up, she shows up with enthusiasm and passion and she does so day after day, year after year, and decade after decade. As mentioned earlier in the book, this is not to say that passion always precedes grit—sometimes persistence leads and passion follows.[8] That said, the two must ultimately go hand-in-hand for grit to exist in its purest form.

NEED FOR ACHIEVEMENT

Additionally, grit differs from the need for achievement. McClelland defined the need for achievement as a drive to complete manageable goals that will result in immediate feedback on performance.[9] Individuals who have a need to achieve tend to pursue goals that are neither too hard nor too easy—for these individuals the emphasis is on getting regular, real-time feedback as often as possible. It is the need for feedback and validation that drives them forward and motivates them. In contrast, gritty individuals will set long-term goals for themselves and will persistently pursue those goals, regardless of whether there is regular feedback and positive reinforcement.[10] McClelland, Koestner, and Weinberger also point out that because the need for achievement is a nonconscious drive for implicitly rewarding activities, it is impossible to measure using self-report methods.[11] In other words, if you are doing something unconsciously you will be unable to describe or report on how, when, and why you are doing it because you may not even be aware that you are doing it in the first place.

As discussed earlier in the book (and in further detail below), grit can entail dedication to implicitly or explicitly rewarding goals and can be measured using a self-report questionnaire—the Grit Scale—as gritty individuals tend to be motivated by a conscious drive.[12] Thus, the difference between grit and the need for achievement has to do with both the need for feedback and the individual's conscious awareness of this need. This is particularly important when it comes to the practice of law because constant feedback (and particularly positive feedback) is something that many lawyers suggest is severely lacking, especially in law firms but also throughout the industry. As a profession that is still, at its core, very much an apprenticeship profession, women who rely too heavily on positive bursts of feedback as a source of motivation may find themselves in trouble.

SELF-DISCIPLINE

Finally, grit differs from self-discipline. Self-discipline is defined as the ability to suppress compelling and sometimes dominant responses in the service of a higher goal—a choice that is not automatic but rather requires conscious effort.[13] Examples of self-discipline include paying attention to your boss rather than daydreaming, saving money so that it can accumulate interest in the bank rather than spending it on something you would like to have right away, and persisting on long-term assignments despite boredom and frustration. While self-discipline is very similar to grit, and gritty people tend to be self-disciplined,[14] there are important distinctions between the two concepts. First of all, self-discipline implies the ability to refrain from doing something—to stop eating desserts or stop staying up so late.[15] In contrast, grit requires the ability to keep doing something, such as engaging in deliberate practice over a significant period of time, in spite of obstacles or challenging setbacks along the way. Second, self-discipline does not require the ambition, gusto, fire-in-the-belly needed to undertake a challenging task or pursue a long-term goal.[16] In other words, although one must be at least somewhat self-disciplined in order to be truly gritty, there are self-disciplined individuals who are not necessarily gritty. As Duckworth points out, "self-discipline is probably necessary for grit but it's not sufficient."[17]

GRIT AND SUCCESS

In spite of the surprising lack of attention paid to the importance of noncognitive skills in the academic literature, there have been some attempts to identify universal traits that are essential to success in all domains.[18] Howe studied the biographies of many prominent, reputable thought leaders, including Darwin, Einstein, and Newton, and found that "perseverance is at least as crucial as intelligence" to lasting success.[19] The Newton story in particular provides a great example of the disconnect between the notion that great ideas come to us as sudden epiphanies and the reality of how major discoveries are most often made. In what has been referred to as the single most famous story of scientific discovery, Newton was walking in his garden when an apple suddenly fell from a tree, prompting him to devise the concept of universal gravitation. While this story has a certain romantic appeal to it, as it implies that genius can strike at any moment, it nevertheless ignores the fact that while Newton was unquestionably brilliant, he also had "an astonishing ability to persist in the face of obstacles [and] to stick with the same stubborn mystery until he found the answer."[20] Howe's study, and similar work by Simonton, highlights the fact that many well-known geniuses were relatively ordinary children who happened to be extremely passionate about pursuing certain goals—even to the point of obsession—and who ended up making enormous contributions mostly as a result of their passion, persistence, and grit.[21] These findings are supported by a growing body of evidence that suggests that an individual's grit may be a good predictor of her ultimate success. The most explicit evidence that an individual's grit can be linked to success comes from the research of Duckworth.

The Grit Scale

In building the case for grit as a legitimate construct worthy of further exploration and study, Duckworth and colleagues developed the self-report questionnaire referred to as the Grit Scale. We have already provided an overview of the Grit Scale in chapter 1, but we will discuss it in more depth below. The Grit Scale was designed to be a stand-alone measure of grit. When Duckworth first introduced the construct in 2006, she argued that "grit differs from existing constructs in its emphasis on both sustained effort and focused interest over time."[22] Once they had developed and validated the Grit Scale, Duckworth and her colleagues used it in a series of studies designed to test the hypothesis that grit may be as essential to high achievement as IQ and furthermore that it might be more important than similar traits, like self-control and conscientiousness—both discussed earlier in this appendix—in setting exceptional individuals apart from their less-exceptional peers.[23] The results of these studies suggest that the presence of grit does indeed predict a variety of success measurements over and beyond IQ and other cognitive traits and measures of pure intelligence. Duckworth and Peterson argue that "collectively, these findings suggest that the achievement of difficult goals entails not only talent but also the sustained and focused application of talent over time."[24] This view is shared by others and has been the focus of several recent studies.

The first of these studies collected data on more than 1,500 adult participants aged 25 years or older. Participants were asked to indicate both how old they were and what level of education they had achieved: some high school, high school graduate, some college, associate's degree, bachelor's degree, or post-graduate degree.[25] These data points were then compared to participants' individual grit scores, and, as predicted, the more highly educated adults were grittier than their less-educated but same-age peers. In this study, success was defined as the level of education that individuals were able to complete. It is important to note, however, that although high levels of education are often associated with a general, broad definition of success, there are other, more specific measures of success, such as salary or position in the workplace hierarchy—the measures that we looked to in trying to understand more about how grit affected success for women in the law—that are not necessarily linked to the level of education that one obtains. Thus, while it may be the case that highly educated individuals are more successful than their less-educated peers, it is by no means a certainty. Most lawyers in the United States have earned a J.D. or a J.D.-equivalent, such as an LL.M. or an LL.B., and yet not all lawyers go on to be successful practitioners, and even for those who do, the level of success can and does vary tremendously. Nevertheless, this study does provide evidence that gritty individuals tend to achieve more in the academic domain than those who are not gritty, and, as will be discussed in greater detail later, achievement in the academic domain is often an important factor when it comes to a woman's ability to secure a legal position.

Along those same lines, a second study considered the association between grit and cumulative GPA while controlling for general mental ability or intelligence—as measured by SAT scores—at an elite undergraduate university. The results of this study demonstrated that gritty students outperformed their less-gritty peers.[26] In this study, success was defined as cumulative GPA, which is a clear measure of success in the academic domain—that may or may not translate to success in the workplace—but does seem to be generally predictive of workplace success or, at the very least, of securing a spot in a highly ranked law school.

It is not surprising given the results of these two studies that many institutions of higher education are beginning to rely more heavily on noncognitive measures when making admissions decisions.[27] Sedlacek points out that this is partly a recognition that assessments, such as the LSAT, provide only limited measurements of intelligence and partly a recognition that we need a fresh approach that reflects the fact that our student bodies are quite diverse and include women, gays, people of color, and international students, to name just a few of the groups that are now more heavily represented in academic institutions. Sedlacek argues that in order to accurately determine the true potential of students from such diverse backgrounds, particularly nontraditional students (i.e., nonwhite males), admissions officers should incorporate new, noncognitive measurements, such as demonstrations of determination, when evaluating and selecting desirable applicants. Similarly, organizations like the Educational Testing Service (ETS), which is known for creating tests like the SAT and the GRE, among others, are beginning to explore the case for noncognitive assessments, such as dependability and persistence (and even, potentially, grit), because of their apparent importance to employers.[28] Thus, there is growing interest, if not yet a full-blown trend, toward using noncognitive skills as predictors of success in the academic domain. Although the link between grit and GPA is a key finding, not all of the women achieved success in law school (or at least were not able to do so initially), as you heard from some of the women who contributed to this study. Some of them relied on grit to help them persevere when the academic hurdles were overwhelmingly challenging, and some of them didn't discover how to use grit effectively until later on in their careers. In any case, it seems clear that when applied in an academic setting, grit can be a powerfully effective tool when it comes to earning a high GPA.

A third study (which, again, was previously discussed) expanded the scope beyond pure academic achievement by considering whether grit was predictive of cadet retention and GPA at West Point, the U.S. Military Academy. More than 1,200 freshman cadets completed the Grit Scale upon arrival at West Point in 2004.[29] This data was compared to other data maintained by West Point, such as Whole Candidate Score—a weighted average of SAT scores, class rank, demonstrated leadership ability, and physical aptitude—that is used in their rigorous admissions process.[30] The results of the study revealed that grit predicted whether a candidate would survive his or her first summer as a cadet better than any other known predictor. Additionally, grit was predictive of both a cadet's first-year GPA and his or her Military Performance Score, a combined measure of performance ratings and grades.[31] Importantly, the results of this study demonstrate that grit is predictive not only of success in a traditional academic environment but also of success in a challenging environment in which success is defined not only in terms of pure academic performance but also in terms of physical ability, endurance, and leadership—all of which are critically important to success in the practice of law.

A fourth study looked at success outside of the academic environment by looking at grit as a predictor of success at the Scripps National Spelling Bee.[32] In this study, success was defined as the number of rounds each competitor was able to complete in the competition. The higher the number of rounds, the more success the competitor achieved. The results demonstrated that grittier spellers were more likely to engage in deliberate practice prior to the competition, which in turn made them more likely to get further along in the competition.[33] The results of this study have significant implications for workplace success, as it has been shown—and was discussed in chapter 1—that deliberate practice often leads to expert performance and that expert performance is difficult to accomplish without deliberate practice to pave the way.[34] Thus, if grit can predict, even to some extent, an individual's willingness to engage in deliberate practice, it seems likely that it can also predict those who are likely to excel in other domains, including the legal workplace.

These four studies demonstrate the predictive nature of grit, and although there are other studies that we will not cover here that offer further evidence of the importance of grit, there are still relatively few studies of this kind. Although increasing attention is being paid to the effects of noncognitive skills like grit on earnings and schooling outcomes, the importance of such skills in predicting workplace success remains largely unexplored, and this was one of the reasons we wanted to learn more through the present research.

MINDSET AND SUCCESS

Like the literature on grit, most of the literature that addresses mindset is primarily concerned with its potential contributions to an individual's success. A large subset of this literature focuses on students' academic achievements. Dweck and others argue that students' beliefs about their own abilities can and do significantly impact their academic achievement.[35] Specifically, these researchers argue that students with a fixed mindset respond much differently to failure than those who have a growth mindset. Those who have a growth mindset tend to be less afraid of—and therefore less deterred by—failure because they recognize that failure presents an opportunity for learning and improvement. Students with a growth mindset believe that intelligence is "malleable," and, thus, they view setbacks and failures as an inevitable result of learning new things rather than an indication that they may be personally deficient.[36] In this way, students with a growth mindset are resilient and tend to rebound from failure relatively quickly.

In contrast, students with a fixed mindset often believe that failure reflects negatively on them and on their personal abilities and capacity to be successful. Those students with a fixed mindset place great emphasis on performance metrics (e.g., test results), which establish and document their intelligence and abilities in a measurable way. These individuals view these performance metrics as proof of their intelligence and value them immensely because they provide some measure of validation—e.g., I must be smart because I did well on this test. These students tend to be less interested in setting learning goals and extremely concerned with setting performance goals. For example, a student with a growth mindset might set a goal to master the Pythagorean theorem, whereas a student with a fixed mindset would set a goal to get a 95 on an upcoming math quiz.

Mangels, Dweck, and others found that there is a significant difference in the way that fixed and growth mindset students respond to performance feedback. Specifically, they found that following the delivery of negative feedback, students with a fixed mindset demonstrated less-sustained memory-related activity to corrective information, which suggests reduced effort in conceptual encoding of the material. They also appeared less likely to engage in sustained semantic processing of learning-relevant feedback.[37] In other words, those with a fixed mindset may have heard the feedback, but they reacted to it differently than those with a growth mindset—essentially processing it to a lesser degree. Due to the importance of proper processing of feedback to successful encoding of information for later recall and recognition tests, the differences in the level of sustained semantic processing of learning-relevant information between those with a fixed mindset and those with a growth mindset may help to explain why those with a growth mindset are better able to rebound after suffering academic failures.[38] Those with a growth mindset did not get the results that they wanted, but they processed the negative feedback in the right ways and then went on to learn from their mistakes in the best possible way, and this led to better performances at the next opportunity. Harkening back to our earlier discussion of the practice of law as an apprenticeship profession, the ability to rebound from failures, whether academic or professional or both, is essential to long-term success in the profession, as you hear directly from many women who contributed to this research. This is a very important finding because it supports the idea that those who have a growth mindset are more likely to continue to put forth effort and work hard despite setbacks, and it underscores the link between mindset and grit.

Dweck also found important differences in how the attribution of success ultimately affects behavior.[39] Students who attributed their success to their own innate talents and abilities—those with a fixed mindset—tended to exhibit what Dweck refers to as the "low effort syndrome" when faced with a challenge that threatened their identities as the "smart" students. Rather than confront the fact that they might not be good at something, these students would stop putting forth effort, largely as a protective measure.[40] In other words, they wanted to avoid the experience of legitimately trying hard and failing at something, because they were afraid of how it would reflect on them or others' perceptions of them (e.g., does this failure mean that I am not smart?). Conversely, students with a growth mindset, who attributed their success to hard work and persistence rather than innate ability, were far more likely to embrace challenging tasks that require effort and progressive skill acquisition.[41] In other words, students with a growth mindset will try much harder because they believe in the direct link between effort and success and are less afraid to confront what failure says about them.[42]

There is additional research on mindset that we will not have time to address in this appendix, but to summarize the major findings: those with a growth mindset have been shown to focus on learning goals rather than performance goals,[43] believe in the effectiveness of effort and persistence,[44] and generally demonstrate behavior that is likely to lead to increased learning and advanced mastery of skills. All else being equal, the research suggests that students with growth mindsets are more likely to outperform those with fixed mindsets.

Changing Your Mindset

Dweck argues that an individual's mindset can be influenced in a number of ways, including through environmental cues, such as receiving certain kinds of directed praise from her parents.[45] For example, children who are praised for their hard work are far more likely to develop a growth mindset than those who are praised for their intelligence. Thus, it is possible to encourage students to persist in the face of failure by encouraging them to think about learning in a certain way.[46] These findings are supported by Blackwell, et al., who suggest that a student's mindset can be changed relatively easily if she is presented with alternative ways of thinking about intelligence, such as likening the brain to a muscle and explaining that the more you exercise this muscle the more powerful it becomes.[47] This finding represents encouraging news for other noncognitive traits that contribute to an individual's success, including grit, since grit can also be taught and used to improve not only an individual's academic performance, but also her likelihood of having a successful and rewarding life.

WOMEN, GRIT, AND MINDSET

As we've learned, grit and growth mindset are powerful traits that have been shown to have important implications for individuals of both genders. While the universal importance of these traits to career success is certainly worth exploring further, we are focusing on the implications for women lawyers, in particular, and have suggested that demonstrations of grit and a growth mindset may ultimately be more important for the career success of women lawyers than it is for their male counterparts. Because there has been very little scientific work done to date that focuses exclusively on lawyers and their paths to success (which is, again, one of the reasons we undertook the present analysis), I will rely on several studies that explore the career dynamics of highly successful women—in comparably challenging professions—in order to explore this issue further. In particular, we will consider how these two traits relate to and impact other factors known to contribute to a woman's career success—namely career commitment, power, core competencies, performance evaluations, and law school performance.

Career Commitment

White argues that a true understanding of the career psychology of women requires an acknowledgment that women encounter fundamentally different issues than men do along the path to powerful leadership positions.[48] To that end, she derives a stage model of career development over a typical woman's life span. White studies women managers and entrepreneurs in commerce and industry and senior members of high status professions—such as law and accountancy—who have already achieved career success. Success, in White's study, is peer defined and thus determined by the woman's peers in her national business networks.[49] The results of her study suggest that regardless of the nature of their occupation, most successful women have passed through four broad life stages: early career development, early thirties transition, settling down—late thirties transition, and finally achievement and maintenance. It can generally be said that the successful women in the study experienced periods of career satisfaction and commitment followed by periods of instability and questioning of career and family choices—which often led to significant change (either with respect to the woman's employer or her personal life).[50]

One of White's key findings was that successful women tend to be firmly committed to their careers. Indeed, the women in the study can aptly be described as gritty.[51] In order to investigate the dynamics of their grit and career commitment—explicitly defined as the motivation to work in a career role instead of a series of unrelated jobs—White draws on the work of Farmer.[52] Farmer suggests that career commitment and the motivation to achieve career success can be explained by relying on three components: (1) mastery, (2) aspirations, and (3) career centrality. Mastery is defined as the "tendency to choose difficult tasks and to persevere in the face of problems," aspirations as the level of education or the position to which an individual ultimately aspires, and career centrality as the extent to which an individual sees involvement in her career as central to her life.[53] The sum of these three components closely approximates the definition of grit and seems to lend support to Duckworth and Peterson's idea that "the achievement of difficult goals entails not only talent but also the sustained and focused application of talent over time."[54] Thus, in order to be successful, a woman must also be committed, and this kind of sustained commitment is second nature to gritty individuals who have incremental theories of intelligence (growth mindsets).

Power

Impatient with the speed at which women are reaching the highest levels of management, many companies have invested in strategies designed to ensure that high-potential women are sponsored for the most-senior positions. One such strategy, Ibarra, Carter, and Silva suggest, is that women learn to exercise their power.[55] For many women, this is a daunting prospect, as "the behavioral styles that are most valued in traditionally masculine cultures—and most used as indicators of 'potential'—are often unappealing or unnatural for high-potential women, whose sense of authenticity can feel violated by the tacit leadership requirements."[56] For women who are uncomfortable with demonstrations of power, the exercise of power may also require the ability to make peace with power, if for no other reason than the fact that power has been shown to be a very effective management tool. Indeed, empirical research indicates that seeking power pays off.[57]

Ibarra, Carter, and Silva developed a list of things that powerful people do to advance their agendas in the workplace. Among the items on this list, which is designed to provide women with the leverage they need in order to advance to high-level positions, are the ability to advance on multiple fronts, co-opt antagonists, remove rivals (nicely if possible), and, as is most relevant to the current analysis, persist in the face of adversity.[58] Importantly, Ibarra, Carter, and Silva see persistence—or grit—as a key factor in women's ability to exercise power in the workplace, citing numerous powerful women who attribute their success to dogged persistence over time (this "dogged persistence" is a recurring theme in the letters from the women who participated in this study). Ultimately, they suggest that persistence is a useful tool because it wears the opposition down.[59] Thus, gritty women who have the ability to persist over time are more likely to outlast their competition—indeed, some of the women in the study describe outlasting a particularly difficult or prickly partner or supervisor along the road to success. Similarly, women must also believe in their own ability to exercise power in appropriate and effective ways, even if this is not something that comes naturally to them, and in this respect a growth mindset also contributes significantly to a woman's capacity to demonstrate power in the workplace.

Along those same lines, Chanow and Rikleen argue that women must get, use, and maintain power in order to accelerate their advancement in the legal profession.[60] In order to accomplish this, women lawyers must master both the language and the dynamics of power. Chanow and Rikleen offer seven strategies for accomplishing this, including "don't give up or surrender or cede the field to others," which is essentially an argument for demonstrating grit.[61] Similarly, Pfeffer argues that persistence and resilience are the most important qualities for getting and keeping power.[62] As Pfeffer points out, "[t]he way you become masterful at something is that you persist, you do not give up. You don't die in the face of failure."[63] Both Pfeffer and Chanow and Rikleen highlight the importance of power to success in the practice of law, and their work suggests that grit and a growth mindset can help women lawyers both demonstrate and sustain it.

Core Competencies

In a study for the Center for Creative Leadership (CCL), Leslie attempts to identify the leadership competencies that are needed to address what she refers to as the leadership gap.[64] The leadership gap is defined as the gap between the crucial leadership skills needed by organizations and the leadership skills their high-potential employees currently possess. Leslie surveyed executive leaders at 15 companies and asked them to identify the competencies most critical for success. This exercise produced a list of seven competencies: leading people, strategic planning, managing change, inspiring commitment, resourcefulness, being a quick learner, and doing whatever it takes. The final competency—doing whatever it takes—is defined as "persevering under adverse conditions."[65] The results of Leslie's study lend further support to the notion that perseverance, or grit, is an important contributor to success in the workplace. Many of the women we heard from use that phrase exactly—doing whatever it takes—when describing what it took to succeed in the practice of law.

Leslie went on to explore the projected importance of these seven competencies to career success over the course of the next five years. The results of this subset of the study reveal that grit, or doing whatever it takes, had a relative importance of 64 percent in 2009 but is projected to have a relative importance of 77 percent in five years.[66] This is a significant finding as it seems to suggest that grit will be an increasingly vital and necessary tool in a female lawyer's arsenal. Leaders who are already effective in this area, then, have a strength that is needed and will continue to be needed in law. Conversely, leaders who are not gritty will have much learning to do to remain as relevant and effective as their peers.[67]

The relative future importance of grit, or of any competency, is at best difficult to predict as it depends, in part, upon a number of variables, including an uncertain political and economic landscape. Nevertheless, Leslie suggests that even if the current working environment were to remain unchanged, today's leaders are not as skilled as they need to be to effectively manage the current challenges. For example, when it comes to traits like grit, she finds a current skill level of only 28 percent while a skill level of 54 percent is needed.[68] Leslie's findings not only underscore the fact that grit will be an increasingly vital tool for women lawyers, but grit may also help to explain why women who do not have the requisite level of grittiness are not advancing to the highest levels of leadership.

Performance Evaluations

Biernat, Tocci, and Williams analyzed the performance evaluations of male and female junior attorneys in a large law firm. They found that male supervisors judged male attorneys more favorably than female attorneys on numerical ratings but provided narrative comments that showed either no gender preference or greater favorability toward women.[69] In addition, the performance evaluations of the male attorneys were more consistent than they were for female attorneys. Finally, narrative ratings of technical competence mattered more for men than women, and narrative ratings of interpersonal warmth mattered more for women than men.[70] Importantly, open-ended use of positive performance words did not necessarily translate into positive numerical ratings for women. In other words, a woman might receive a review with a glowing narrative, peppered throughout with lovely adjectives, and yet still receive numeric ratings below those of her male counterparts, even if their narratives were far less enthusiastic. The data from Biernat, Tocci, and Williams suggests subtle patterns of gender bias, in which "women were harmed by not meeting gendered expectations of interpersonal warmth but were less benefited than men by meeting masculine standards of high technical competence."[71] This conundrum has been referred to elsewhere as "tightrope syndrome."[72] Because job performance evaluations play such a prominent role in determining employees' advancement prospects, and many advancement decisions are made as a direct result of an employee's perceived abilities and efforts, any bias in the performance appraisal process will inevitably lead to bias in promotion decisions over time.[73]

The presence of evaluation bias in the performance review process suggests that women are more likely to need to rely on traits like grit and a growth mindset to provide them with the determination, perseverance, and belief required to overcome such biases. A woman who lacks grit, or believes that whatever talents she possesses are fixed and immutable, may be more likely to become frustrated and to disengage when faced with biased reviews. If she does disengage, she will be less likely to ascend the corporate ladder and reach the partnership or leadership ranks. Conversely, a man who lacks grit will generally have less of a problem since the performance evaluation bias tends to work in his favor—at least on paper, he will have the higher ratings. These findings highlight, at a minimum, the fact that the female career path tends to be more treacherous than the typical male career path, thereby making grit and a growth mindset more critical tools for women than for men.

Law School Performance

In general, girls tend to outperform boys when it comes to grades. Duckworth and Seligman argue that this is the case because girls are both more self-disciplined than boys and better at delaying gratification.[74] These characteristics manifest themselves in the amount of time that girls typically devote to homework (almost twice as much time as boys) and help girls to earn better grades, resulting in higher GPAs.[75] Interestingly, although a young woman's ability to exercise self-discipline and log in hours of hard work often enables her to outperform young men on the GPA scale at both the secondary and undergraduate levels, this does not seem to translate into better grades in law school. Indeed, several studies have shown that although women may enter law school with higher GPAs than their male counterparts, they are more likely to underperform in this environment.[76] A study at the University of Pennsylvania Law School found that men were three times more likely than women to fall in the top 10 percent of the class as measured by their overall GPAs.[77] Similarly, a longitudinal study at the University of Texas Law School found that female students' grades were lower than male students', particularly in the first year of law school, which had a strong effect on the female students' ability to secure a law review membership, a prestigious BigLaw job, and/or a judicial clerkship after graduation.[78] Furthermore, in a statistical analysis of all ABA-accredited law schools, Neumann found the same pattern of higher undergraduate grades for women followed by lower law school grades.[79] Recent evidence is somewhat more optimistic.[80]

The fact that women tend to receive lower grades at most law schools has far-reaching implications for the BigLaw hiring process. On the one hand, because law review membership is determined, at least in part, by grades at most elite law schools, this tends to result in fewer female students on law review. For example, in the early 1990s, female students at the University of Pennsylvania represented 43 percent of the student body eligible for law review membership but occupied only 30 percent of the law review editor positions.[81] Similarly, at the University of Texas, the percentage of female law review members was only 71 percent of what their overall numbers in the general student body would predict.[82] These data points were echoed in a larger analysis of more than 50 law schools over a period of 10 years in which it was found that the average female student population was 47 percent of the student body but only made up 39 to 43 percent of law review members.[83]

The disparity in law school performance (both in grades and in law review representation) is a key finding, because within the legal profession, and particularly within BigLaw, a critical criterion in the hiring process is where one went to law school and how well one performed relative to her peers.[84] Indeed, the profession's devotion to elite educational credentials has been a cornerstone of the hiring process for attorneys entering BigLaw since the early days of the profession. Henderson and others have even referred to this tendency to place extreme weight on such academic credentials as "the pedigree problem."[85] Given the heavy reliance of the legal profession on grades—and the fact that, in many cases, men tend to outperform women in this area—it is clear that men may be better positioned, at least at the outset, for a successful legal career.

Importantly, the disparity in law school performance is not the only thing that negatively impacts women's experience in the law school environment. As Purvis points out, women also experience higher levels of stress and depression in law school.[86] Indeed, at one Ivy League university, women were significantly more likely to report eating disorders, sleeping difficulties, frequent crying, and symptoms of anxiety.[87] The emotional state of female students is a critical factor in their ability to succeed in law school. As Iijima points out, there "is an intimate relationship between students' psychological state and academic performance. . . . [H]igh levels of hope, optimism, perseverance, and motivation may be stronger predictors of academic achievement than SAT scores or previous grades."[88] Thus, it may be the case that having grit and a growth mindset may well be among the keys to success for women in law school. Those women who lack these traits, and the dispositions associated with them, may find themselves overwhelmed by the pressures of law school and at an early disadvantage when beginning their careers in law.

Like Iijima, Purvis argues that there is reason to believe that having a positive outlook (and generally displaying qualities associated with grit and a growth mindset) may help to explain the differences between the women who excel in law school and those who struggle. To explore this issue further, Purvis looks at the small subset of women who manage to thrive in the law school environment—despite the somewhat bleak state of affairs for women in law school, there is "a distinct cohort of successful female students" who manage to stand out.[89] Although their numbers are small, the success of this subset is impressive—not only do they earn higher grades in law school than their male counterparts, but they also hold prestigious roles on the law review, including, a recent study at Yale Law School found, the same number of editor-in-chief positions as their male counterparts.[90]

What do these exceptional women have in common? For one thing, they do not have a tendency to give themselves poor self-assessments or judge themselves unfavorably, which is something that many female law school students do with alarming frequency. For example, Neufeld found that 33 percent of male students believed themselves to be in the top 20 percent of their class in terms of their legal reasoning skills, compared to only 15 percent of women.[91] Similarly, 40 percent of men believed themselves to be in the top 20 percent in terms of their quantitative skills, compared to only 11 percent of women.[92] Such discrepancies were still present when controlling for grades, meaning that female students who were actually performing at the same level as their male counterparts still gave themselves lower self-assessments.[93]

In contrast to the majority of female law school students, the highly successful female students tended to view themselves as intelligent and capable. Indeed, they had full confidence in their own abilities to achieve long-term success, both in law school and in the legal profession. In essence, they were demonstrating a growth mindset and a commitment and passion that can aptly be described as gritty. Rather than let challenging experiences lead to feelings of frustration and low self-esteem, these women channeled their energy into pursuing opportunities that advanced their academic and professional success. Conversely, the less-successful women tended to self-select out of such opportunities, including applying for clerkships, resubmitting notes for publication in law reviews following a "revise and resubmit" letter, and signing up for classes known to be taught by well-known professors whose mentorship, support, and letters of recommendation would benefit them greatly down the line.[94]

Purvis suggests that those women who demonstrated what is known in positive psychology as optimistic attribution, or a positive way of explaining and understanding things about the world, not only had more faith in their capabilities but also were more likely to be happier.[95] As Dweck suggests, pessimistic statements that demonstrate seemingly permanent, personal deficiencies suggest a fixed mindset, whereas an individual with an optimistic attribution style, or a growth mindset, will frame negative experiences as temporary and specific to the situation rather than indicative of larger shortcomings.[96] As a result, the latter group will be more likely to overcome temporary setbacks and to excel in law school.

GRIT, MINDSET, AND THE GLASS CEILING

It would be difficult to fully consider the career trajectory of women in law without addressing the current state of thinking about the glass ceiling. While many have suggested that the glass ceiling no longer exists, there is still sufficient evidence to suggest that men and women continue to progress along different career trajectories. Simpson and Altman have demonstrated that younger women seem to have a significant advantage over their male counterparts as 48 percent of those they studied occupied senior roles compared to only 25 percent of men in comparable positions.[97] Interestingly, while the survey data suggests that women have been promoted into more senior roles at an earlier age, the number of women over age 35 who hold senior management positions does not increase much and rather seems to hover around 50 percent.[98] Thus, while women under 35 are making remarkable career advancements, this does not appear to be the case for older women.[99] These findings echo recent findings of the National Association of Women Lawyers (NAWL)[100] and underscore the fact that there has been a steady decline in the number of women occupying advanced positions of authority and leadership in many areas of law. This troubling trend suggests that demonstrations of grit and an incremental theory of intelligence may ultimately be more important to the career success of women since the path to leadership for women is more fraught. For example, Scharf and Liebenberg found an "uneven level of participation by men and women in civil and criminal litigation." Their research provides benchmark data to "make the case and offer strategies for increasing the number of women as lead trial counsel."[101] Importantly, Scharf and Liebenberg believe that the data are typical of courts across the United States.[102] It should also be noted that men still do not seem to experience the same drop-out levels or noticeable decreases in promotions at the leadership level.[103]

Along those same lines, Simpson and Altman found that although men tend to be promoted within their existing organizations, women are much more likely to make lateral moves and accept positions outside of their organizations.[104] In other words, they are often so committed to the advancement of their careers that they are willing to make a life-altering change, even if that change may have significant and far-reaching implications. In effect, these kinds of sacrifices are measures of an individual's grit.

Nevertheless, while young women are able to override "lesser barriers" further down the hierarchy, by the time they reach the upper levels of senior management and beyond, they encounter more "intractable barriers."[105] Simpson and Altman argue that there is a need for a new way of conceptualizing the career trajectories and experiences of women, and, to that end, they offer three alternative ways of thinking about this progression. The first alternative assumes that the "glass ceiling" has been demolished and that the rapid career progression of young women provides evidence to support this. The second alternative suggests that the glass ceiling is generally intact but has been "punctured" such that some women—particularly young women who are seen as having high potential and grit—are able to pass through. According to the latter view, the glass ceiling is likely to acutely affect older women. The third and final alternative is that the glass ceiling has been shifted upward and deferred in time so that the barriers intensify as women move up the hierarchy.[106] Ultimately, Simpson and Altman conclude that the glass ceiling is time-bounded, which is to say that it occurs at a later stage of a woman's career, closer to the time when she approaches the top levels of management, and that this final alternative provides the best explanation for understanding female managers' career progress over time.[107]

Importantly, Simpson and Altman examine the careers of successful women as opposed to studying the careers of women who enjoy only average success. Thus, there is an implicit focus on the strategies and experiences that have led to significant career achievements. It is clear that grit and a growth mindset may help to demystify why some women hold senior leadership positions within today's organizations while others never progress beyond the middle management level.

We've now made the case that grit may ultimately be more important for the career success of women in law than it is for their male counterparts, but there is a need for more research in this area. The body of research on grit and growth mindset is still relatively new by scientific standards and is ripe for further exploration. Although this study has brought us closer to a more comprehensive understanding of grit, mindset, and success for women in the law, we hope further work will be done to expand upon this emergent and exciting body of research.

Notes:

1. Duckworth, A.L., et al. 2007. "Grit: perseverance and passion for long-term goals." *Journal of Personality and Social Psychology* 92.6:1087.
2. Judge, T.A., et al. 1999. "The big five personality traits, general mental ability, and career success across the life span." *Personnel Psychology* 52.3:621–652.
3. *Id.*
4. Hough, L.M. 1992. "The 'Big Five' personality variables—construct confusion: Description versus prediction." *Human Performance* 5.1-2:139–155.
5. Judge, T.A., et al. 1999. "The big five personality traits, general mental ability, and career success across the life span." *Personnel Psychology* 52.3:621–652.
6. Duckworth, A.L., et al. 2007. "Grit: perseverance and passion for long-term goals." *Journal of Personality and Social Psychology* 92.6:1087.

7. *Id.*

8. Duckworth, A. 2016. *Grit: The power of passion and perseverance.* Simon and Schuster.

9. McClelland, D.C. 1961. *The Achievement Society.* Princeton, NJ: Von Nostrand.

10. Duckworth, A.L., et al. 2007. "Grit: perseverance and passion for long-term goals." *Journal of Personality and Social Psychology* 92.6:1087.

11. McClelland, D.C., Koestner, R., and Weinberger, J. 1989. "How do self-attributed and implicit motives differ?" *Psychological Review* 96.4:690.

12. Duckworth, A.L., and Quinn, P.D. 2009. "Development and validation of the Short Grit Scale (GRIT–S)." *Journal of Personality Assessment* 91.2:166–174.

13. Duckworth, A.L., and Seligman, M.E.P. 2006. "Self-discipline gives girls the edge: Gender in self-discipline, grades, and achievement test scores." *Journal of Educational Psychology* 98.1:198.

14. Duckworth, A. 2016. *Grit: The power of passion and perseverance.* Simon and Schuster.

15. Doskoch, P. 2005. "The winning edge." *Psychology Today* 38.6:42–52.

16. *Id.*

17. Duckworth, A. 2016. *Grit: The power of passion and perseverance.* Simon and Schuster.

18. Duckworth, A.L., and Seligman, M.E.P. 2006. "Self-discipline gives girls the edge: Gender in self-discipline, grades, and achievement test scores." *Journal of Educational Psychology* 98.1:198; Heckman, J.J., and Rubinstein, Y. 2001. "The importance of noncognitive skills: Lessons from the GED testing program." *The American Economic Review* 91.2:145–149.

19. Howe, M.J.A. 1999. *The psychology of high abilities.* New York University Press.

20. *Id.*

21. Simonton, D.K. 1999. *Origins of genius: Darwinian perspectives on creativity.* Oxford University Press; Simonton, D.K. 1999. "Talent and its development: An emergenic and epigenetic model." *Psychological Review* 106.3:435; Dweck, C.S. 2002. "The development of ability conceptions." *Development of Achievement Motivation* 17:57–88.

22. Duckworth, A.L., and Seligman, M.E.P. 2006. "Self-discipline gives girls the edge: Gender in self-discipline, grades, and achievement test scores." *Journal of Educational Psychology* 98.1:198.

23. Duckworth, A.L., et al. 2007. "Grit: perseverance and passion for long-term goals." *Journal of Personality and Social Psychology* 92.6:1087.

24. *Id.*

25. *Id.*

26. *Id.*

27. Sedlacek, W.E. 2010. "Noncognitive measures for higher education admissions." *International Encyclopedia of Education,* Third Edition: 845–849.

28. Kyllonen, P., Walters, A.M., and Kaufman, J.C. 2005. "Noncognitive constructs and their assessment in graduate education: A review." *Educational Assessment* 10.3:153–184.

29. Duckworth, A.L., et al. 2007. "Grit: perseverance and passion for long-term goals." *Journal of Personality and Social Psychology* 92.6:1087.

30. *Id.*

31. *Id.*

32. Duckworth, A.L., et al. 2011. "Deliberate practice spells success why grittier competitors triumph at the national spelling bee." *Social Psychological and Personality Science* 2.2:174–181.

33. *Id.*

34. Ericsson, K.A. 2006. "The influence of experience and deliberate practice on the development of superior expert performance." *The Cambridge Handbook of Expertise and Expert Performance* 38:685–705.

35. Ahmavaara, A., and Houston, D.M. 2007. "The effects of selective schooling and selfconcept on adolescents' academic aspiration: An examination of Dweck's self-theory." *British Journal of Educational Psychology* 77.3:613–632; Mangels, J.A., et al. 2006. "Why do beliefs about intelligence influence learning success? A social cognitive neuroscience model." *Social Cognitive and Affective Neuroscience* 1.2:75–86; Murayama, K., and Elliot, A.J. 2009. "The joint influence of personal achievement goals and classroom goal structures on achievement-relevant outcomes." *Journal of Educational Psychology* 101.2:432; Pekrun, R., Elliot, A.J., and Maier, M.A. 2009. "Achievement goals and achievement emotions: Testing a model of their joint relations with academic performance." *Journal of Educational Psychology* 101.1:115.

36. Mangels, J.A., et al. 2006. "Why do beliefs about intelligence influence learning success? A social cognitive neuroscience model." *Social Cognitive and Affective Neuroscience* 1.2:75–86.

37. Butterfield, B., and Mangels, J.A. 2003. "Neural correlates of error detection and correction in a semantic retrieval task." *Cognitive Brain Research* 17.3:793–817; Mangels, J.A., Picton, T.W., and Craik, F.I.M. 2001. "Attention and successful episodic encoding: an event-related potential study." *Cognitive Brain Research* 11.1:77–95; Nessler, D., et al. 2006. "On why the elderly have normal semantic retrieval but deficient episodic encoding: A study of left inferior frontal ERP activity." *Neuroimage* 30.1:299–312.

38. Craik, F.I.M., et al. 1996. "The effects of divided attention on encoding and retrieval processes in human memory." *Journal of Experimental Psychology: General* 125.2:159.

39. Dweck, C.S. 2007. "The perils and promises of praise." *ASCD* 65.2:34–39; Mangels, J.A., et al. "Why do beliefs about intelligence influence learning success? A social cognitive neuroscience model." *Social Cognitive and Affective Neuroscience* 1.2:75–86.

40. Dweck, C.S., and Leggett, E.L. 1988. "A social-cognitive approach to motivation and personality." *Psychological Review* 95.2:256.

41. *Id.*

42. Dweck, C.S. 2008. *Mindset: The new psychology of success.* Random House Digital, Inc.

43. Dweck, C.S., and Leggett, E.L. 1988. "A social-cognitive approach to motivation and personality." *Psychological Review* 95.2:256.

44. Hong, Y-Y., et al. 1999. "Implicit theories, attributions, and coping: A meaning system approach." *Journal of Personality and Social Psychology* 77.3:588.

45. Dweck, C.S. 2007. "The perils and promises of praise." *ASCD* 65.2:34–39.

46. *Id.*

47. Blackwell, L.S., Trzesniewski, K.H., and Dweck, C.S. 2007. "Implicit theories of intelligence predict achievement across an adolescent transition: A longitudinal study and an intervention." *Child Development* 78.1:246–263.

48. White, B. 1995. "The career development of successful women." *Women in Management Review* 10.3:4–15.

49. *Id.*

50. *Id.*

51. *Id.*

52. Farmer, H.S. 1985. "Model of career and achievement motivation for women and men." *Journal of Counseling Psychology* 32.3:363.

53. *Id.*, pg.6.
54. Duckworth, A.L., et al. 2007. "Grit: perseverance and passion for long-term goals." *Journal of Personality and Social Psychology* 92.6:1087.
55. Ibarra, H., Carter, N.M., and Silva, C. 2010. "Why men still get more promotions than women." *Harvard Business Review* 88.9:80–85.
56. *Id.*, pg. 84.
57. *Id.*
58. *Id.*
59. *Id.*
60. Chanow, L.B., and Rikleen, L.S. 2012. *Power in law: Lessons from the 2011 Women's Power Summit on Law and Leadership.* Center for Women in Law, University of Texas School of Law.
61. *Id.*, pg. 12
62. Pfeffer, J. 2010. "Power play." *Harvard Business Review* 88.7/8:84–92.
63. Id., pg. 21
64. Leslie, J. 2009. *The Leadership Gap.* Center for Creative Leadership, 1–14.
65. *Id.*, pg. 4
66. *Id.*
67. *Id.*
68. *Id.*
69. Biernat, M., Tocci, M.J., and Williams, J.C. 2012. "The language of performance evaluations gender-based shifts in content and consistency of judgment." *Social Psychological and Personality Science* 3.2:186–192.
70. *Id.*
71. *Id.*, pg. 186
72. http://mesvicissitudes.com/the-tightrope-syndrome/
73. Igbaria, M., and Shayo, C. 1997. "The impact of race and gender differences on job performance evaluations and career success." *Equal Opportunities International* 16.8:12–23. See also Fair Measure: Toward Effective Attorney Evaluations, Second Edition (ABA Commission on Women in the Profession 2008).
74. Duckworth, A.L., and Seligman, M.E.P. 2006. "Self-discipline gives girls the edge: Gender in self-discipline, grades, and achievement test scores." *Journal of Educational Psychology* 98.1:198.
75. *Id.*
76. Bowers, A.L. 1999. "Women at the University of Texas School of Law: A call for action." *Tex. J. Women & L.* 9:117.

77. Guinier, L., et al. "Becoming gentlemen: Women's experiences at one Ivy League law school." *University of Pennsylvania Law Review* 143.1:1–110.

78. Bowers, A.L. 1999. "Women at the University of Texas School of Law: A call for action." *Tex. J. Women & L.* 9:117.

79. Neumann, R.K. 2000. "Women in legal education: What the statistics show." *Journal of Legal Education* 50.3:313–357.

80. Bartlett, K.T., Rhode, D.L., and Grossman, J. 2017. *Gender and law: Theory, doctrine, commentary.* Wolters Kluwer: New York, 546–547. See also Rhode, D.L. 2003. "Midcourse corrections: Women in legal education." *J. Legal Educ.* 53:475.

81. Guinier, L., et al. 1994. "Becoming gentlemen: Women's experiences at one Ivy League law school." *University of Pennsylvania Law Review* 143.1:1–110.

82. Bowers, A.L. "Women at the University of Texas School of Law: A call for action." *Tex. J. Women & L.* 9:117.

83. Neumann, R.K. 2000. "Women in legal education: What the statistics show." *Journal of Legal Education* 50.3:313–357.

84. Henderson, W.D., and Zahorsky, R.M. 2012. "The pedigree problem: Are law school ties choking the profession." *ABAJ* 98:36.

85. *Id.*

86. Purvis, D.E. 2012. "Female law students, gendered self-evaluation, and the promise of positive psychology." *Mich. St. L. Rev.* 143 (2012): 1693.

87. Guinier, L., et al. 1994. "Becoming gentlemen: Women's experiences at one Ivy League law school." *University of Pennsylvania Law Review* 143.1:1–110.

88. Iijima, A. 1998. "Lessons learned: Legal education and law student dysfunction." *Journal of Legal Education* 48:524–526

89. Purvis, D.E. 2012. "Female law students, gendered self-evaluation, and the promise of positive psychology." *Mich. St. L. Rev.* 143 (2012):1693.

90. *Id.*; Bashi, S., and Iskander, M. 2006. "Why legal education is failing women." *Yale JL & Feminism* 18:389.

91. Neufeld, A. 2005. "Costs of an outdated pedagogy-study on gender at Harvard Law School." *Am. UJ Gender Soc. Pol'y & L.* 13:511.

92. *Id.*

93. *Id.*

94. Purvis, D.E. 2012. "Female law students, gendered self-evaluation, and the promise of positive psychology." *Mich. St. L. Rev.* 143 (2012):1693.

95. *Id.*
96. Dweck, C.S. 2008. *Mindset: The new psychology of success.* Random House Digital, Inc.
97. Simpson, R., and Altman, Y. 2000. "The time bounded glass ceiling and young women managers: Career progress and career success–evidence from the UK." *Journal of European Industrial Training* 24.2/3/4:190–198.
98. *Id.*
99. *Id.*
100. http://www.nawl.org/p/cm/ld/fid=82#surveys
101. Scharf, S.A., and Liebenberg, R.D. 2015. "First chairs at Trial: More women need seats at the table." *American Bar Foundation and ABA Commission on Women in the Profession.* American Bar Foundation Retrieved from http://www.americanbar.org/content/dam/aba/marketing/women/first_chairs2015.pdf
102. *Id.*
103. Catalyst Statistical Overview of Women in the Workplace. 2010. Retrieved from http://www.catalyst.org/publication/219/statistical-overview-of-women-in-the-workplace.
104. Simpson, R., and Altman, Y. 2000. "The time bounded glass ceiling and young women managers: Career progress and career success–evidence from the UK." *Journal of European Industrial Training* 24.2/3/4:190–198.
105. *Id.*, pg. 195
106. *Id.*
107. *Id.*

About the Author

Milana L. Hogan is the chief legal recruiting and professional development officer at Sullivan & Cromwell LLP. In this role, Dr. Hogan runs the firm's professional development and legal recruiting functions. She has responsibility for the firm's formal assignment systems, partner-led associate mentoring programs, upward and downward lawyer performance evaluations, and formal training and CLE programs. In addition, she works with firm leadership to oversee the firm's  worldwide recruiting efforts across 13 offices around the globe. Dr. Hogan is an active member of the National Association for Law Placement and is the vice chair of the Professional Development Consortium. She also serves as a liaison to the American Bar Association Commission on Women in the Profession and is the co-chair of the Commission's Grit Project.

Dr. Hogan received her B.A. in political science from Brown University, and she holds a doctor of education (Ed.D.) from the University of Pennsylvania. While at the University of Pennsylvania, Dr. Hogan had the good fortune to learn about grit from Dr. Angela Duckworth. She then learned of Dr. Carol Dweck and her exciting work on growth mindset. Dr. Hogan eventually went on to write her dissertation on the ways in which these two traits impact female success in the nation's largest law firms, and it was this "first round" of research that ultimately inspired the present research effort.

Dr. Hogan lives in New Canaan, Connecticut, with her husband, Phil, and their four young children (ages six and under). She remains committed to using a gritty, growth mindset–oriented approach to find practical, solution-driven ways to advance women in the practice of law. She is thrilled to share these findings with others in the legal profession.

About the ABA Commission on Women in the Profession

As a national voice for women lawyers, the ABA Commission on Women in the Profession forges a new and better profession that ensures that women have equal opportunities for professional growth and advancement commensurate with their male counterparts. It was created in 1987 to assess the status of women in the legal profession and to identify barriers to their advancement. Hillary Rodham Clinton, the first chair of the Commission, issued a groundbreaking report in 1988 showing that women lawyers were not advancing at a satisfactory rate.

Now entering its fourth decade, the Commission not only reports the challenges that women lawyers face, but it also brings about positive change in the legal workplace through such efforts as its Grit Project, Women of Color Research Initiative, Bias Interrupters Project, and the Margaret Brent Women Lawyers of Achievement Awards. Drawing upon the expertise and diverse backgrounds of its 12 members, who are appointed by the ABA president, the Commission develops programs, policies, and publications to advance and assist women lawyers in public and private practice, the judiciary, and academia.

For more information, visit www.americanbar.org/women.

Author Index